Curriculum, Religion, and Public Education

CONVERSATIONS FOR AN ENLARGING PUBLIC SQUARE

D1103461

Curriculum, Religion, and Public Education

CONVERSATIONS FOR AN ENLARGING PUBLIC SQUARE

EDITED BY
James T. Sears with James C. Carper

Teachers College
Columbia University
New York and London

TEACHERS
COLLEGE
PRESS

Published by Teachers College Press, 1234 Amsterdam Avenue, New York, NY 10027

Library of Congress Cataloging-in-Publication Data

Curriculum, religion, and public education : conversations for an
  enlarging public square / edited by James T. Sears with James C.
  Carper.
      p.   cm.
    Includes bibliographical references and index.
    ISBN 0-8077-3707-0 (alk. paper). — ISBN 0-8077-3706-2 (pbk. :
  alk. paper)
    1. Religion in the public schools—United States.   2. Education—
  United States—Curricula.   I. Sears, James T. (James Thomas),
  1951–   . II. Carper, James C.
  LC111.C844   1998
  379.2'8'0973—dc21   97-39386

ISBN 0-8077-3706-2 (paper)
ISBN 0-8077-3707-0 (cloth)

Printed on acid-free paper

Manufactured in the United States of America

05 04 03 02 01 00 99 98   8 7 6 5 4 3 2 1

Contents

PART V: OUTCOME-BASED EDUCATION: WHO SHOULD SET THE STANDARDS?

PART VI: SCIENCE: WHO AND WHAT ARE WE?

Curriculum, Religion, and Public Education

CONVERSATIONS FOR AN ENLARGING PUBLIC SQUARE

Introduction

James T. Sears

As we attempt to come to terms with who we are and what we should become as a nation, public school educators are on the front lines of the much-
ballyhooed culture wars. The skirmishes over sex education or condom distribution, a science textbook or an English series, Halloween pageants or
counseling programs, reveal deep national fissures along the fault lines of
religion and culture. These local battles have become arenas for competing
factions, each with self-righteous certainty, brandishing particular versions
of "the truth": Citizens for Excellence in Education and the People for the
American Way; the NRA and the NEA; the Christian Coalition and the B'nai
Brith; the Concerned Women of America and the National Organization of
Women.

Many teachers and administrators have experienced tensions, bitter-
ness, and acrimony as their school becomes yet another battleground for
cultural warriors. Relatively few public school educators, however, have
engaged in sustained dialogue toward understanding the meaning of the free-
exercise and establishment clauses of the Constitution as they apply to public
education. Seldom have schools, colleges, and departments of education
offered extended courses or workshops that provide the historical, legal,
philosophical, and cultural foundation to understand the complex relationships between public education and religion vis-à-vis curricular issues. Further, few school districts encourage substantive discussion of such issues
among educators or parents. Although public educators may profess an
interest in better understanding this diverse constituency of fundamentalist
and evangelical Christians and while several organizations have published
useful guides for educators (e.g., Haynes, 1994; National Issues Forum,
1995), the fear of controversy or the absence of commitment have resulted
in meager dialogue within schools and communities.

As skirmishes escalate into battles, opportunities to cross borders and
engage in conversation with "the other" dwindle. Caught up in a whirlwind
of cultural differences, many public school educators and community leaders are unable or unwilling to contribute to civil dialogue and civic under-

standing. There is an absence of the communication skills and community trust necessary for thoughtful discussion and resolution of differences relating to public education.

As citizens, we enter the public square from separate communities, speaking in diverse tongues, worshiping in churches, synagogues, temples, mosques, and ashrams or in realms of our own creation. As Americans, for too long we have had no need to communicate across the racial, class, gender, religious, or sexual borders and so we did not—and *now*, it seems, we cannot. Demagoguery has foreclosed dialogue as obfuscation has triumphed over understanding. The result is polarization, simplification, and recrimination.

In this book I have sought to bring together thoughtful persons for a sustained dialogue on educational issues. The result, hopefully, is a common primer for people holding differing views to think, participate, decide, and act.

I acknowledge my debt to other scholars who have examined the role of religion in public education or who have sought innovative formats fostering dialogue and understanding. Dialogue across ideological lines, for example, was a cornerstone of *Democracy and the Renewal of Public Education* (Neuhaus, 1987). Under the leadership of Father Richard Neuhaus, the conservative-oriented Institute on Religion and Public Life in New York City sponsored an "encounter series," publishing papers by scholars in religious studies and philosophy. Several writers in that volume, including Neuhaus, share their insights here.

More recently, Warren Nord's *Religion and American Education* (1995) provides synoptic summaries and analyses of a range of educational issues relating to religion. Nord was the first to extend analyses beyond the positions articulated by progressive secularists and conservative theists (e.g., Hunter, 1991; National Issues Forum, 1995; Provenzo, 1990; Wuthnow, 1989), acknowledging other positions such as those held by postmodernists and orthodox culturalists. Thus, this volume fully integrates these voices into the dialogue, creating interesting and, at times, unexpected juxtapositions of agreement among participants.

Curriculum, Religion, and Public Education: Conversations for an Enlarging Public Square also builds upon the conceptual framework of Nel Noddings. In *Educating for Intelligent Belief or Unbelief* (1993), Noddings lays out a compelling argument for the inclusion of controversial issues in the school curriculum—one which, as editor, I fully embraced in structuring this volume.

Finally, given the relative absence of communication across borders, this volume would not have materialized without James Carper, whose scholarship and activism is deservedly recognized within the conservative scholarly and Christian communities. As the framework for this book emerged,

Jim indulged me with long conversations while also serving as an "honest broker" on those occasions where editorial conflicts arose across religious or scholarly borders.

CONTEMPORARY CURRICULAR DEBATES

Thirty years ago school prayer was the educational intersection for dissonance between secular progressives and theistic conservatives, as evidenced in Sizer's classic, *Religion and Public Education* (1967). Court rulings and a changing society have created new and more congested intersections. At these crossroads we find persons today differing on long-debated as well as recently emerging curriculum issues.

This book revisits old controversies such as the teaching of creation science and sex education. Seventy years ago the Scopes Trial placed the teaching of evolution on the defensive; today those who believe in divine intervention for human origins have transformed their political marginalization into electoral mobilization. Similarly, although sex education dominated community headlines a generation ago, contemporary issues of AIDS, cultural diversity, and homosexuality add qualitatively different dimensions to this longstanding controversy.

This volume incorporates newer controversies as well, such as the implementation of outcome-based education, raising issues regarding the role of the state in setting effective performance criteria. It also is published in an era marked by the growing political influence of conservative Christians of various stripes and the new ecumenical coalitions among religious groups, such as evangelical Christians, traditional Catholics, and orthodox Jews, who lack a common theology but share an ideology evidenced in their support of pro-life legislation and abstinence-based sex education.

While you will find a broad range of voices here, this text focuses on curriculum areas frequently criticized by the secular conservatives and evangelical Christians. Nearly two dozen distinguished and diverse scholars and practitioners address five issues that have become critical arenas for disputation on the meaning and application of the First Amendment as it applies to public education: science and human evolution, textbook selection, sexuality instruction, character development, and outcome-based education.

While other educational and public policy issues, such as academic freedom and school vouchers, arise from these five curricular controversies, these issues in and of themselves directly relate neither to the content teachers must teach nor to the expectations students must meet. Choosing character development programs such as the Heartwood Curriculum or Pumsy, including subjects such as psychology and personal awareness in the social studies curriculum, teaching the science of human origins from a naturalistic or theistic perspective are the day-to-day classroom matters that have become catalysts for parental concern and community discord.

BOOK ORGANIZATION

Curriculum, Religion, and Public Education has three main parts. The first provides a working foundation for readers unfamiliar with the underlying issues and history that preceded these contemporary curricular debates. In Chapter 1 James Carper, former educational advisor to the governor of South Carolina and an authority on religion and education, examines historical contours of the debate since the 17th century. Following his essay, Chapter 2 includes brief "encounters" with several leading scholars in the fields of education, history, religious studies, and law.

In Chapter 3 I begin by discussing the genesis of the controversy that erupted in my summer graduate seminar on the Christian Right and the most important lessons learned from that experience which served as the basis for this book. I then discuss four traditions of thought that underlie various religious and ideological positions, resulting in differing assessments of public education represented in this volume: evangelical conservatism, orthodox culturalism, secular progressivism, and critical postmodernism. Following this discussion are brief encounters with several persons who articulate one of these four traditions.

In Chapter 4 Kenneth Strike details the creation of dialogue and the assumptions underlying it. Perhaps most critical is Strike's elaboration of the importance of searching for "overlapping consensus." This he defines as "claims that can be accepted by all reasonable people regardless of differing religious or philosophical perspectives." It is this search that those participating in this volume were asked to pursue and that you embark upon as a reader.

The second section of this volume, Parts II through VI, focuses on five curriculum arenas that have been "ground zero" for community debate. The essayists in each curriculum arena reflect two of the four traditions of thought. For example, in the science section, Phillip Johnson, an orthodox culturalist, writes opposite Nancy Brickhouse, a postmodern feminist, and William Letts IV, a doctoral student in science education. This section is guided by Theodore Brameld's (1956) principles of "defensible partiality" and "social consensus." As in a reconstructionist school, within this volume are faculty with viewpoints at variance with one another. Representing conflicting positions in a community, these essayists write frankly from their convictions using supportive data and logical arguments that best support their position. These convictions—what Brameld terms "reasoned-out, evidentially grounded beliefs" (p. 351)—are then submitted to the process of social consensus. Here the conversationalists, like students in a reconstructionist school, are called upon to weight the conflicting testimony and to engage in dialogue. Brameld writes:

> The reconstructionist teacher, like the reconstructionist citizen, has convictions about his cultural goals. Sometimes these goals are expressed as values, sometimes as politics, sometimes as institutional designs. He is frank in his commitment to these at any given time, but he is willing to change or modify them if criticism warrants. . . . Unlike . . . religious authoritarianism, these goals are to be accepted or not accepted as the majority agrees after considering and communicating testimony for or against them. The school is considered a chief agency of the community through which such consensus may occur. (p. 358)

It is at this point that social consensus—based on evidence and communication—may be tested:

> Maximum communication, nonverbal as well as verbal, maximum evidence of every relevant sort, and maximum testing of every agreement—all this is integral and necessary to social consensus. . . . The truths and values arrived at by social consensus aren't necessarily established forever, however complete an agreement may be. . . . This leaves plenty of room for possible correction in the light of still further evidence, still further communication, still further agreements and testings. (p. 350)

Following each set of twin essays is a dialogic encounter among educational practitioners and community leaders representative of these four traditions of thought: Dr. Carolyn Murphy, a middle school teacher of earth science and a practitioner of the Baha'i faith; the Reverend Bob Shearer, a charismatic Christian pastor who holds a law degree; the Reverend Gary Burgess, an African-American public middle school principal who is also an ordained minister and pastor of the Universal Body of Christ Non-Denominational Church; Ms. Pamela Pritchett, special assistant in the division of curriculum to the superintendent of public education for South Carolina; Dr. James Carper, an associate professor of educational foundations who was on leave to serve as special educational assistant for the governor of South Carolina; Dr. Aretha Pigford, an African-American professor of educational administration and formerly assistant superintendent of an urban school district; and Mrs. Elaine Lindsey, academic director of a private Christian school.

Engaged in a year-long series of dialogues, these seven individuals explored areas of difference and agreement while examining the day-to-day considerations arising from the essayists' advocacy. As facilitator, I encouraged the group to approach each set of essays as a starting point for the exploration of differences, expansion of understanding, and examination of educational implications. Following each section, there is a short list of suggested readings that reflect the diversity of ideas articulated in this area.

The final part of *Curriculum, Religion, and Public Education* is an encounter with several leading educational scholars and educators who, like you, have read these essays and community dialogues. Articulating one of the four traditions of thought, these participants address several broad questions: Is there evidence of common ground among persons with differing religious and ideological positions? Is the search for overlapping or social consensus a realistic goal within our communities? Can educators facilitate these dialogic encounters? This dialogue is notable not only for its occasional pungency but for unexpected areas of agreement.

A CHANGE OF THINKING

I conceptualized and constructed this book in collaboration with James C. Carper with the belief that educators and parents, civil and religious leaders, undergraduate and graduate students are willing and able to cross boundaries and, in the process, transform ourselves and our nation.

In the movie *Groundhog Day*, Bill Murray plays an egocentric and cynical television news reporter. On February 1, he makes his yearly trip to document whether groundhog Punxsutawney Phil sees his shadow. Arriving at the town that evening, Murray's character makes his routine catty remarks about the townspeople and the event to his camera crew and then heads off to bed. The next day he gets up and, in a sarcastic and demeaning manner, covers the sacred event. As the news crew returns to Philadelphia, an approaching snowstorm forces it to return to Punxsutawney, where Murray is forced to spend another dreadful night. The following morning, a strange event occurs— there is no following morning. Instead, he reawakes to another Groundhog Day hearing the identical song on the radio to begin his morning, running into the same old high school classmate, enduring the same groundhog shadow sighting, and again failing miserably with a romantic pass at his co-worker. February 2 follows February 2 as Murray's character struggles with himself until one day he realizes that the key to having a future is self-understanding.

Until we experience a change of thinking, a change of heart, we, like this movie character, are condemned to repeat an endless set of tomorrows today with the dreary sameness of yesterday. Only by confronting "the other" in ourselves and by crossing the other's border will such transformation occur. Others are bridges to Self. In order to transcend ourselves we must not separate from the other but confront it within ourselves in the stillness of solitude. Our challenge is to become dead to what we have become in order to be resurrected into what we have the potential of being.

Curriculum, Religion, and Public Education affords an opportunity to see ourselves through the eyes of those who are different and to peer into those parts of ourselves that we prefer not to see. In so doing we embark on a journey of the self, crossing borders to explore our fears, to voice our doubts, to challenge our assumptions, to strengthen our faith, and to celebrate our differences. I dedicate this book to that personal and cultural transformation.

James T. Sears
Hilton Head Island, SC
February 1997

REFERENCES

Brameld, T. (1956). *Toward a reconstructed philosophy of education.* New York: Dryden.

Haynes, C. (Ed.). (1994). *Finding common ground: The First Amendment guide to religion and public education.* Nashville, TN: Freedom Forum First Amendment Center.

Hunter, J. (1991). *Culture war.* New York: Basic Books.

National Issues Forum. (1995). *Contested values: Tug-of-war in the school yard.* New York: McGraw-Hill.

Neuhaus, J. (Ed.). (1987). *Democracy and the renewal of public education.* Grand Rapids, MI: Eerdmans.

Noddings, N. (1993). *Educating for intelligent belief or unbelief.* New York: Teachers College Press.

Nord, W. (1995). *Religion and American education.* Chapel Hill: University of North Carolina Press.

Provenzo, E. (1990). *Religious fundamentalism and American education.* Albany: State University of New York Press.

Sizer, T. (1967). *Religion and public education.* Boston: Houghton Mifflin.

Wuthnow, R. (1989). *The struggle for America's soul: Evangelicals, liberals, and secularism.* Grand Rapids, MI: Eerdmans.

PART I

Foundations for Conversations

CHAPTER 1

History, Religion, and Schooling: A Context for Conversation

James C. Carper

In the wake of the controversial U.S. Supreme Court decisions that declared unconstitutional state-composed or -selected prayer and Bible reading in the public schools (*Engel v. Vitale*, 1962; *Abington Township v. Schempp*, 1963; *Murray v. Curlett*, 1963), Robert Michaelsen (1966) contributed a seminal essay to the already voluminous literature on religion and education. He drew a distinction between "America's two religions"—he called them "A" and "B"—and their relationship to the public schools. In brief, Michaelsen described the former as church or denominational religion and the latter as the "common faith"—those beliefs, assumptions, and myths that provide the "glue" for a society. Other scholars have used the terms *civil religion* or *public theology* to refer to this "faith" in the United States, which, according to political scientist James Skillen (1994), is rooted in two sources that are fundamentally at odds with one another—biblical Christianity with its emphasis on revelation and transcendent authority and the Enlightenment tradition with its emphasis on rationalism and human experience (Johnson, 1995; Linder, 1975; Neuhaus, 1984; Reichley, 1985).

Both religions have been inextricably intertwined with the American educational enterprise from colonial times to the present. Since both involve basic assumptions about the nature of the cosmos, moral authority, humankind, truth, and society, it is not surprising that considerable debate has surrounded the role of each in the schooling of children. This has certainly been the case in public schools. Since the mid-1800s, they have been expected to transmit the "common faith" to future generations. In this respect public education has functioned as our "established church." As Sidney Mead (1963) once pointed out: "The public schools in the United States took over one of the basic responsibilities that traditionally was always assumed by an established church. In this sense the public school system in the United States is its established church" (p. 68). Not surprisingly, our "established church" has been frequently rocked by debates over the content of the supposedly common faith and the rights of dissenters to be free of control of the "church" and to obtain a share of the taxes levied for its support (Arons, 1983; Hunter, 1994; Jorgenson, 1987). This chapter provides a historical context for the present conversation regarding the role of religion in American public education.

PROTESTANT PLURALISM AND SCHOOLING IN EARLY AMERICA

Prior to the advent of mandatory, state-supported and -controlled common schooling in the middle decades of the 19th century, the rich religious diversity that characterized overwhelmingly Protestant colonial and early national America was manifested in an equally rich diversity of educational arrangements. With few exceptions—namely, cases in which parents were unwilling or unable to manage their children's education—families fashioned an education for their children that was consonant with their religious beliefs (Cremin, 1970; Noll, 1992).

For the better part of the colonial period the family was the primary unit of social organization and the most important educational agency. As historian Steven Mintz and anthropologist Susan Kellogg (1988) assert:

> Three centuries ago the American family was the fundamental economic, educational, political, social and religious unit of society. The family, not the isolated individual, was the unit of which church and state were made. The household was not only the locus of production, it was also the institution primarily responsible for the education of children, the transfer of craft skills, and the care of the elderly and infirm. (p. xiv)

In general, then, during the colonial period parents bore the primary responsibility for the education of their children—and frequently those who had been "fostered out" from other families. Although most 17th- and 18th-century white parents sent their children to school for short periods of time—and with increasing frequency in the 1700s—much education took place in the church and the household.

In contrast to late-20th-century schooling arrangements, the colonial mode of schooling was unsystematic, unregulated, and discontinuous. The initiative for schooling resided with parents, not the state. As William J. Reese (1983) points out:

> Early school laws of Massachusetts, which called for the creation of various levels of schools in response to population growth, were widely ignored and unenforceable. Whether in New England, the Middle Colonies, or the South—and regional differences would long prevail in schooling—schools were an irregular, incidental, and unsystematic part of a child's life. (p. 3)

Although schooling in colonial America was unsystematic and primarily the product of local community or church efforts and parental initiative, it was not neglected. According to Lawrence Cremin (1970), school opportunities increased more rapidly than the increase in the population during the 1700s, even though the "increase was neither linear over time nor uniform from region to region" (p. 500). By the eve of the American Revolution, most white children attended school at some point in their lives. Schooling was not, however, controversial. In great measure, this was because most schools mirrored the religious beliefs of their patrons.

The diversity of educational institutions and the blurred line between "public" and "private" schools were probably the most salient features of colonial schooling. The colonial education landscape was dotted with an incredible variety of institutions: from the town schools, dame schools (in which women taught reading skills in their homes for a small fee), and private-venture schools of New England; to the various denominational (e.g., Lutheran, Quaker, Presbyterian, and Reformed), charity, and pay schools in the Middle Colonies; to the old-field schools and Society for the Propagation of the Gospel in Foreign Parts (SPG) missionary efforts in the South; to academies that appeared throughout the provinces after 1750 (Cremin, 1977; Kaestle, 1983). Classifying these schools as purely "public" or "private" is problematic. As Bernard Bailyn (1960) has argued: "The modern conception of public education, the very idea of a clean line of separation between 'private' and 'public,' was unknown before the end of the eighteenth century" (p. 11). To most colonials, a school was "public" if it served a public purpose, such as promoting civic responsibility. Public education did not require public support and control. In his examination of schooling in New York City between 1750 and 1850, Carl Kaestle (1973) elaborates on the colonial concept of "public education":

> Long before the New Yorkers dreamed of public schools in the modern sense, they had a distinct concept of the relation of education to the public interest.

There was a dichotomy between public and private education in late colonial New York, but it does not correspond directly to later episodes under that heading. The term "public" education underwent a change in connotation in the nineteenth century which has somewhat obscured the importance of the word in the English-colonial context. The word had two related meanings, both inherited from Renaissance England. Education could be public in setting, meaning simply in a classroom as opposed to individual lessons, and it could be public in intent, directed toward the public good, as contrasted to selfish pleasure or gain. (pp. 16–18)

The colonial mode of schooling characterized by a diversity suited to the Protestant pluralism of the period persisted without major modification throughout the early national period (ca. 1776 to 1820). This is not to say that the late 18th century was devoid of proposals for educational change. Concerned about social fragmentation and desirous of a properly disciplined republican citizenry, Thomas Jefferson, Benjamin Rush, and a host of other educational theorists touted unprecedented plans for state systems of free common schooling, such as Jefferson's "Bill for the More General Diffusion of Knowledge," which failed in the Virginia legislature in 1779, and again in the 1790s and in 1817. Such was also the fate of other ambitious proposals. Most citizens did not share the belief that a uniform elementary school system was essential to the creation of a common citizenship and culture (Tyack, 1966). Neither were they enthusiastic about new taxes or increased government authority in education. Existing educational arrangements comprised of diverse private and quasi-public schools were satisfactory and were not tainted with British influence. Thus, unlike most other revolutions, America's war of independence had scant impact on the shape of the educational landscape (Kaestle, 1983).

Throughout the early national period states encouraged educational diversity in a variety of ways. As had been the case during the colonial era, the line between public and private schooling remained fuzzy. This was evident in some of the constitutions of the original 13 states. As Tyack, James, and Benavot (1987) have noted, these constitutions suggested that "the common good might be realized through a combination of diverse educational institutions. . . . Through such institutions American might realize both private and public aims" (pp. 26–27).

In addition to aiding the rapidly growing number of "district schools" in the rural North, which depended on property taxes, tuition charges, fuel contributions, and state appropriations, state governments aided a variety of privately controlled educational institutions for the purpose of promoting Protestant civility, piety, and learning. In his massive history of public funding of private and church schools, Richard J. Gabel (1937) documents the widespread nature of this practice between the Revolutionary Era and the 1820s. During that period, almost every state at one time or another provided land grants and/or financial aid to academies, which were usually governed by self-perpetuating boards of trustees, often pervasively religious, and enrolled students from broadly middle-class backgrounds.

Primary religious and private schools also received public aid in many states. In Connecticut, New York, Pennsylvania, Virginia, South Carolina, Maryland, Delaware, Georgia, Tennessee, Ohio, Indiana, and Illinois, such schools received state and local appropriations. Usually public support was conditioned upon providing charity education for the poor (Gabel, 1937).

During the late 1700s and early 1800s, public funds also flowed to Protestant voluntary associations, such as the much studied Free School Society (FSS) founded in 1805 in New York City, that built charity schools in numerous cities. These schools were intended to reach the growing number of children of the unchurched poor, who were perceived to be potential threats to the social and economic order, as well as persons in need. As organizations such as the FSS, in 1825 renamed the Public School Society, gained a near-monopoly on public funds and opened their schools to all children, they laid the foundations of urban public school systems. Even privately organized Sabbath schools, which like weekday charity schools attempted to inculcate in children of the poor and profaners of the Lord's Day basic literacy skills and Christian morality, received public funds from at least three states—Delaware, Virginia, and Maryland (Gabel, 1937; Swift, 1911).

By 1830, private and quasi-public schooling was widely available to white Americans in most settled parts of the United States, excepting the South. These educational opportunities were due primarily to the efforts of parents, churches, voluntary associations, entrepreneurs, and communities, not state mandates. In some areas, school attendance was nearly universal. Despite some references to common pay schools as "private" and charity school systems as "public," these terms still lacked their modern connotations. Public funding of privately controlled institutions was a widespread practice. With the exception of charity schooling, with its acculturative mission, most schools embodied the belief systems of their clientele. In sum, the structure of schooling reflected the "confessional pluralism" of the time and public policy generally recognized and even encouraged diversity.

EVANGELICALS AND THE ESTABLISHMENT OF "COMMON" SCHOOLS

The middle decades of the 19th century marked a period of intense educational debate and reform that led to major changes in educational beliefs and practices in the United States; namely, the gradual emergence of the modern concept and practice of public schooling. Distressed by the social and cultural tensions wrought by mid-19th-century urbanization, industrialization, and immigration (which included a large number of Roman Catholics) and energized by what one scholar has called the values and beliefs of republicanism, Protestantism, and capitalism, educational reformers touted the messianic power of tax-supported, universal common schooling. Common schools, they believed, would create a moral, disciplined, and unified population prepared to participate in American political, social, and economic life. "Private" schools, which reformers believed would sabotage the goals of common schooling, were cast as divisive, undemocratic, and inimical to the public interest (Glenn, 1988; Kaestle, 1983; Randall, 1994).

As Alexis de Tocqueville recognized in the 1830s, and several generations of historians have confirmed, public schooling was nurtured by a robust evangelical Protestant culture that emerged from the Great Awakening of the 1730s and 1740s and was nourished by the Second Great Awakening—a series of religious revivals stretching from 1795 through the Civil War. With few exceptions, notably several Lutheran and Reformed bodies, which opted for schools designed to preserve cultural and/or confessional purity, Protestants were generally supportive of common schooling. Indeed, many were in the vanguard of the reform movement. They approved of early public schooling because it reflected Protestant beliefs and was viewed as an integral part of a crusade to fashion a Christian—which, to the dismay of Roman Catholics, meant Protestant—America (Kaestle, 1983; Neuhaus, 1984; Noll, 1992; Smith, 1967; Tocqueville, 1835/1966). According to church historian Robert T. Handy (1971), elementary schools hardly had to be under the control of particular denominations because "their role was to prepare young Americans for participating in the broadly Christian civilization toward which all evangelicals were working" (p. 102).

Rather than countenance sharing public funds with Roman Catholic schools, such as requested by Bishop John Hughes in the early 1840s in the face of Protestant practices of the New York Public School Society (such as using the King James version of the Bible) or schools associated with Protestant groups, most Protestants united behind the "nonsectarian" (in reality pan-Protestant) common school as the sole recipient of public monies for education. Catholic schools and those of other dissenters from the common school movement were therefore denied not only legitimacy but tax dollars as well. To a significant degree, then, latent anti-Catholicism (rekindled by the immigration of the 1840s and 1850s, bishops' assertions of missionary intent in the United States, and provocative statements of Pope Pius IX [1846–1878]—such as the Syllabus of Errors [1864], an anthology of earlier condemnations of, *inter alia*, freedom of religion and separation of church and state—that were looked upon unfavorably in the United States) prematurely closed the debate on whether the education of the public could be accomplished by a variety of schools reflecting diverse moral/religious viewpoints funded by tax dollars or required the establishment of a government school system, embodying a supposedly common belief system, with a virtual monopoly on the public treasury—in other words, an educational counterpart to the traditional established church (Carper & Weston, 1990; Curran, 1954; Glenn, 1988; Hicks, 1990; Hunt & Carper, 1993).

While the common school, by means of Bible reading, prayers, teacher example, and the ubiquitous McGuffey Readers, taught the beliefs of non-denominational evangelical Protestantism, the public theology of 19th-century America (religion "B"), the Sunday School stressed the particular tenets of the various denominations (religion "A"). This educational arrangement of "parallel institutions" was satisfactory to most Protestants. As William B. Kennedy (1966), an authority on Protestant education, maintains:

> By 1860 there had emerged a general consensus in American Protestantism that the combination of public and Sunday school teaching would largely take care of the needed religious teaching of the young. In that pattern the public school was primary; the Sunday school was adjunct to it, providing specific religious training it could not include. (p. 27)

In sum, the public school became the vehicle for transmitting the common faith—evangelical Christianity—while the Sunday Schools taught "sectarian" specifics.

DEALING WITH DISSENTERS

By the turn of the century, almost 90% of elementary and secondary students in the United States were enrolled in public schools. Of the remaining 10%, approximately 65% (about 854,000 students in 1900) were in Roman Catholic schools—whose growth was being spurred by the forces of ethnicity, alienation from American culture and public education, a cheap labor force drawn largely from religious orders, and failed compromises with the public schools, such as the Faribault–Stillwater plan in Minnesota that would have allowed, among other things, some public control of and funding for Roman Catholic schools. The line between public and private institutions had been clearly drawn and widely accepted as a matter of public policy. Furthermore, most states had effectively forbidden tax support to nonpublic schools (Carper, 1991; Cross, 1965).

As noted earlier, most Protestants viewed public education as a means to Christian civilization, and, as historian Mark Noll (1992) points out, "they

⁄lmost universally suspected Roman Catholics of undermining Christian as well as American values" (p. 300). Protestant suspicions of Catholics were exacerbated by the latter's complaints about Bible reading in the public schools and the growing number of Catholic schools.[1] Hostility toward these schools and those of other dissenters from public education was particularly evident during the last decade of the 19th and the first quarter of the 20th century, when states attempted to either regulate private schools into conformity with the public school pattern or simply abolish them. In the late 1800s, Wisconsin and Illinois, for example, passed the so-called Bennett and Edwards Laws. The former required that the local public school board supervise enforcement of compulsory attendance at either a public or private school and that English be used in the teaching of reading, arithmetic, writing, and American history. The latter stipulated that *all* children between the ages of 7 and 14 attend the local public school for at least sixteen weeks (eight of which were to be consecutive) a year. Given typical school attendance patterns in the late 1800s, this law severely penalized parents desirous of nonpublic schooling for their children. Similar bills were introduced in Minnesota and South Dakota. In the early 1890s, these laws were repealed after Catholics and Lutherans, whose schools were the target of these statutes, joined forces to wrest control of both legislatures from the Republican party, which had supported the laws (Hunt, 1981; Jorgenson, 1987; Randall, 1994).

While restrictions on foreign-language instruction were the most common form of state regulation of nonpublic schools in the early 20th century, some states went much further. In 1922, Oregon required that, with few exceptions, all children between the ages of 8 and 16 attend public schools. Drawing upon *Meyer v. Nebraska* (1923), which overturned restrictions on foreign-language instruction, the U.S. Supreme Court in *Pierce v. Society of Sisters* (1925) declared Oregon's law unconstitutional. Here the Court asserted the right of private schools to exist and affirmed the right of parents to direct the education and upbringing of their children.

FROM ESTABLISHMENTARIANS TO DISSENTERS

The late 1800s and early 1900s also witnessed the gradual decline of evangelical Protestantism as the dominant force in America's public religion and the growing influence of the secular Enlightenment worldview. Pointing out the disruptive effect on American Protestantism of, among other things, Darwinism, higher criticism of the Bible, the fundamentalist–modernist controversy, growing cultural and religious diversity, and the failure of Prohibition, sociologist James Davison Hunter (1983) argues, with only slight exaggeration, that

> in the course of roughly thirty-five years (ca. 1895–1930), Protestantism had been moved from cultural domination to cognitive marginality and political impotence. The worldview of modernity [often termed secular humanism or civil humanism] had gained ascendancy in American culture. (p. 37)

Echoing Hunter's assessment, A. James Reichley (1985) maintains that since the 1950s this value–belief system—which posits an evolutionary view of the cosmos, touts science and reason as the keys to human progress, denies the relevance of the deity to human affairs, and claims that moral values derive from human experience—has been dominant within the intellectual community. This worldview, he asserts, has also exerted considerable influence on the entertainment industry, the news media, government, and certain parts of the educational enterprise (Carter, 1993; Noll, 1992; Reichley, 1985; Skillen, 1994).

Public education was affected, albeit gradually, by this shift in America's public theology. For example, prior to the Supreme Court's ruling on Bible reading in *Abington Township v. Schempp* (1963), 11 states forbade it on the grounds that it was a "sectarian" practice (religion "A"). Furthermore, Bible reading in some form was practiced in less than half of the nation's public school districts (Dierenfeld, 1962; Stokes & Pfeffer, 1964). Christianity also became less visible in the public curriculum after the turn of the century. For example, in his analysis of the religious content of American history textbooks, Charles Shannon (1995) documents a gradual shift from a Christian or theistic worldview to a more secular, "democratic" orientation between 1865 and 1935.

Although the Supreme Court's decisions on prayer and Bible reading (*Engel v. Vitale*, 1962; *Abington Township v. Schempp*, 1963; *Murray v. Curlett*, 1963) merely marked the culmination of better than a half-century-long process of "de-Protestantization" of public education (Nord, 1995), many conservative Protestants have interpreted the official removal of these symbols of the evangelical strain of the American civic faith as "yanking" God out of the public schools. Rather than making the schools "neutral" on matters related to religion, they have concluded that these decisions contributed to the establishment of secular humanism as the official creed of American public education.[2] This belief has, in turn, led them to scrutinize public education to a greater extent than ever before. Once crusaders for the establishment of public education, conservative Protestants are now, ironically, among the most vociferous critics of public schooling (Carper, 1984).

Since the mid-1960s these dissenters have responded to the "established church" in a variety of ways. Many conservative Protestants have sought to incorporate theistic symbols and perspectives in the public schools through, for example, discussing intelligent design in science classes, Ten Commandments displays, voluntary religious activities on high school campuses, and history texts that recognize the culture-shaping role of Christianity in America. Others have protested the use of curricular materials that they believe advance secularism, as in the widely reported Kanawha County, West Virginia, and Mobile, Alabama, textbook controversies, or sought to exempt their children from exposure to the offending materials, as in the deeply troubling Hawkins County, Tennessee case so richly recounted by Stephen Bates in *Battleground* (1993). Still other conservative Protestants have forsaken their historic commitment to public schools and founded dissenting Christian academies, which, like earlier Roman Catholic schools, have occasionally faced instrusive state regulation (Carper & Layman, 1995; Carper & Weston, 1990; Randall, 1994).

While evangelicals and fundamentalists have certainly been highly visible in the educational theater of the current culture war, they have not been alone in this conflict, which, according to James Davison Hunter (1991), is "political and social hostility rooted in different systems of moral understanding" (p. 42). He labels these systems "orthodox" and "progressive"—heirs of the two religious foundations of American culture, Protestant Christianity and the Enlightenment. In brief, partisans of the former are committed to external, definable, and transcendent authority. They are predominantly lower-middle-class and middle-class, culturally conservative Protestants, Roman Catholics, and Jews. For liberal, upper-middle-class Protestants, Catholics, Jews, and secularists, progressive moral authority is shaped by relativism, rationalism, and subjectivism. These competing bases of moral authority and derivative worldviews cut across old lines of conflict—cooperation between Pat Robertson's Christian Coalition and Cardinal O'Connor in the 1993 New York City school board election is a case in point—and create deep cleavages between adversaries in the current struggle for cultural dominion (Hunter, 1991).

As an evangelical Christian, university faculty member, and former education policy advisor to the governor of South Carolina, I have more than an academic familiarity with the culture war in education. While I am certainly aware of the diversity within each of the aforementioned traditions—for instance, Enlightenment naturalism and Enlightenment subjectivism in progressivism—and aware that a majority of Americans do not fit squarely within either orthodoxy or progressivism, my experience confirms that in debates regarding educational issues that have broad cultural implications—for example, moral education, creation/evolution, human sexuality, and humanities and history textbook content—the fissure line usually runs between those who believe in a transcendent source of moral authority—God, the Word—and those who are "this-worldly" in orientation (Hunter, 1991; Johnson, 1995; Plantinga, 1990).

Given that education is a value-laden enterprise, it is not surprising that it is contested territory in the conflict over how we will order our collective lives together, what is socially acceptable, and how we understand our past, present, and future. While serving as an advisor to Governor David Beasley, almost every week I spoke with or heard from someone who labeled those on the "other side" evil, crypto-fascists, divisive, extremists, threats to the public schools, and so on. Orthodox and progressive representatives frequently attempt to marginalize one another by equating competing agendas with, among other things, the politics of hate, imposition of alien beliefs, or a departure from the "American way." Emotive language and ad hominem attacks do nothing to advance public discourse regarding the issues at hand. Such rhetoric merely accentuates what passes for public debate and reduces the likelihood that we will be able to discuss rationally, let alone answer, a question that is at least as old as the Republic, namely, what kind of educational structure is best suited to our oft-denied yet persistent "confessional pluralism." Can our "established church" openly and honestly accommodate this pluralism? Or would it be preferable to follow the "lively experiment" of American denominationalism by separating school and state, and enabling parents to choose the kind of education they deem appropriate for their children without financial penalty?

Let the conversation begin.

NOTES

1. Most Protestants believed that the Roman Catholic Church was particularly hostile to the Bible—the most pervasive symbol of 19th-century "Christian America" (Hicks, 1990; Noll, 1992).

2. Clouser (1991), Johnson (1995, 1997), Neuhaus (1993), and Nord (1995) provide trenchant critiques of the concept of neutrality in science, religion, and education.

REFERENCES

Abington Township v. Schempp, 374 U.S. 203 (1963).

Arons, S. (1983). *Compelling belief: The culture of American schooling.* New York: McGraw-Hill.

Bailyn, B. (1960). *Education in the forming of American society.* New York: Norton.

Bates, S. (1993). *Battleground: One mother's crusade, the religious Right, and the struggle for control of our classrooms.* New York: Poseidon.

Carper, J. C. (1984). The Christian day school. In J. C. Carper & T. C. Hunt (Eds.), *Religious schooling in America* (pp. 110–129). Birmingham, AL: Religious Education Press.

Carper, J. C. (1991, May). *An historical view of private schooling in the United States.* Paper presented at conference on the Dollars and Cents of Private Schools, Washington, DC.

Carper, J. C., & Layman, J. (1995). Independent Christian day schools: Past, present and prognosis. *Journal of Research on Christian Education, 4,* 7–19.

Carper, J. C., & Weston, W. J. (1990). Conservative Protestants in the new school wars. *History of Education Quarterly, 30,* 79–87.

Carter, S. L. (1993). *The culture of disbelief: How American law and politics trivialize religious devotion.* New York: Basic Books.

Clouser, R. A. (1991). *The myth of religious neutrality.* Notre Dame, IN: University of Notre Dame Press.

Cremin, L. A. (1970). *American education: The colonial experience, 1607–1783.* New York: Harper & Row.

Cremin, L. A. (1977). *Traditions of American education.* New York: Basic Books.

Cross, R. D. (1965). Origins of the Catholic parochial school system in America. *American Benedictine Review, 26,* 194–209.

Curran, F. X. (1954). *The churches and the schools: American Protestantism and popular elementary education.* Chicago: Loyola University Press.

Dierenfeld, R. B. (1962). *Religion in American public schools.* Washington, DC: Public Affairs Press.

Engel v. Vitale, 370 U.S. 421 (1962).

Gabel, R. J. (1937). *Public funds for church and private schools.* Unpublished doctoral dissertation, The Catholic University of America.

Glenn, C. L. (1988). *The myth of the common school.* Amherst: University of Massachusetts Press.

Handy, R. T. (1971). *A Christian America: Protestant hopes and historical realities.* New York: Oxford University Press.

Hicks, L. E. (1990). Republican religion and republican institutions: Alexander Campbell and the anti-Catholic movement. *Fides et Historia, 22*(3), 42–52.

Hunt, T. C. (1981). The Bennett law of 1890: Focus of conflict between church and state in education. *Journal of Church and State, 23,* 69–93.

Hunt, T. C., & Carper, J. C. (Eds.). (1993). *Religious schools in the United States, K–12: A source book.* New York: Garland.

Hunter, J. D. (1983). *American evangelicalism: Conservative religion and the quandry of modernity.* New Brunswick, NJ: Rutgers University Press.

Hunter, J. D. (1991). *Culture wars: The struggle to define America.* New York: Basic Books.

Hunter, J. D. (1994). *Before the shooting begins: Searching for democracy in America's culture war.* New York: Free Press.

Johnson, P. E. (1995). *Reason in the balance: The case against naturalism in science, law, & education.* Downers Grove, IL: InterVarsity.

Johnson, P. E. (1997). *Defeating Darwinism by opening minds.* Downers Grove, IL: InterVarsity.

Jorgenson, L. P. (1987). *The state and the non-public school, 1825–1925.* Columbia: University of Missouri Press.

Kaestle, C. F. (1973). *The evolution of an urban school system: New York City, 1750–1850.* Cambridge, MA: Harvard University Press.

Kaestle, C. F. (1983). *Pillars of the republic: Common schools and American society, 1780–1860.* New York: Hill & Wang.

Kennedy, W. B. (1966). *The shaping of Protestant education.* New York: Association Press.

Linder, R. D. (1975). Civil religion in historical perspective: The reality that underlies the concept. *Journal of Church and State, 17,* 399–421.

Mead, S. E. (1963). *The lively experiment: The shaping of Christianity in America.* New York: Harper & Row.

Meyer v. Nebraska, 262 U.S. 390 (1923).

Michaelsen, R. (1966). The public schools and "America's two religions." *Journal of Church and State, 8,* 380–400.

Mintz, S., & Kellogg, S. (1988). *Domestic revolutions: A social history of family life in America.* New York: Free Press.

Murray v. Curlett, 374 U.S. 203 (1963).

Neuhaus, R. J. (1984). *The naked public square: Religion and democracy in America.* Grand Rapids, MI: Eerdmans.

Neuhaus, R. J. (1993). The couture of the public square. *First Things, 38,* 66–68.

Noll, M. A. (1992). *A history of Christianity in the United States and Canada.* Grand Rapids, MI: Eerdmans.

Nord, W. A. (1995). *Religion and American education: Rethinking a national dilemma.* Chapel Hill: University of North Carolina Press.

Pierce v. Society of Sisters, 268 U.S. 510 (1925).

Plantinga, A. (1990). *The twin pillars of Christian scholarship.* Grand Rapids, MI: Calvin College & Seminary.

Randall, E. V. (1994). *Private schools and public power.* New York: Teachers College Press.

Reese, W. J. (1983, October). *Changing conceptions of public and private in American educational history.* Paper presented at the meeting of the History of Education Society, Vancouver, BC, Canada.

Reichley, A. J. (1985). *Religion in American public life.* Washington, DC: Brookings Institution.

Shannon, C. K. (1995). *The religious content of secondary school American history textbooks.* Unpublished doctoral dissertation, Pennsylvania State University.

Skillen, J. W. (1994). *Recharging the American experiment.* Grand Rapids, MI: Baker Books.

Smith, T. L. (1967). Protestant schooling and American nationality, 1800–1850. *Journal of American History, 53,* 679–695.

Stokes, A. P., & Pfeffer, L. (1964). *Church and state in the United States* (3rd ed.). New York: Harper & Row.

Swift, F. H. (1911). *A history of public permanent common school funds in the United States, 1795–1905.* New York: Henry Holt.

Tocqueville, A. de. (1966). *Democracy in America* (G. Lawrence, Trans.). New York: Harper & Row. (Original work published 1835)

Tyack, D. (1966). Forming the national character. *Harvard Educational Review, 36,* 29–41.

Tyack, D., James, T., & Benavot, A. (1987). *Law and the shaping of public education, 1785–1954.* Madison: University of Wisconsin Press.

CHAPTER 2

Encounters in Law, Philosophy, Religion, and Education

In order to further set the foundation for this volume, several noted authorities have provided brief commentaries. These essays provide insight into various disciplinary perspectives relating to public schools and conservative Christians.

COMMENTARY BY *RICHARD JOHN NEUHAUS*

Most people who are opinion makers have extremely little contact with any living representative of the phenomenon that is so much discussed: the conservative right in public life. Particularly within educational establishments, there is a belief in the 18th-century Enlightenment doctrine that religion, with increasing education, will gradually wither away or be confined to the private sphere of life. This has become the conventional wisdom that has created this enormous cognitive disjunction between the societal elite and the great majority of the American people. It is that dissonance that is exploited by people on all sides of the culture wars.

The most feverish single issue that divides the sides in the culture war is abortion and related life questions such as euthanasia. It is a strange thing in our culture that politically we still have people on all parts of the political spectrum who view the "social issues"—abortion, school prayer, homosexuality—as some kind of alien invasion into the political project. That is, they see politics as primarily economics—"it's the economy, stupid." It seems to me that if we understand what politics is about, in the classic sense, it is most essentially about the social issues. Aristotle says in his *Politics* that politics is simply an extension of ethics and that the chief political question is how ought we to order our life together—which is clearly a moral question. I think the confusions, agitations, and conflicts that we are presently undergoing and that are so embroiled in our politics have at least the possibility, over time, of forcing us back to a more classic, more vibrantly democratic understanding of politics that just might lead to a great democratic renewal.

The concept of culture war also suggests a mindset that suspends all of the rules of civility. That is a real danger, especially if one ups the ante and declares that we are engaged in a religious war in this society. Now, there is an element of truth in that, but it is extremely troubling because it invokes the memory of the 16th- and 17th-century upheavals that destroyed the civil fabric of Europe. I do not choose to use the term *culture wars*; the choice of that term was made by others who display the mindset that attends it. The war was declared—although some people may not have meant what they said—in and has raged since the 1960s in American life and education. Sundry libertarianist and self-declared revolutionary movements became alien forces in American life. So, if we are worried about the term *culture wars*, we must ask who declared the war. The overwhelming majority of conservative Christians understand themselves as the ones being attacked.

The myth of the little red schoolhouse and American democracy was by no means entirely a myth. It was seen by many astute social observers as being one of the most important institutions in the American "melting pot." I think, however, for better and for worse, we are far beyond that today. When the common school movement was started by Horace Mann and others in the 19th century, there was no question whatsoever that it was a movement to acculturate a large number of immigrants and to Americanize aliens. Its purpose was explicitly moral and religious in nature, representing a kind of watered-down Protestantism. This, of course, explains why in the late 19th century Catholics moved to their own schools. When the public school was a socializing American institution—up until about 1962—under the banner of liberal Protestantism, it worked for everyone except orthodox Jews, Catholics, and conservative Christians. But once the hegemony of liberal Protestantism and its definition of the public school project was demolished, the public school could no longer play a socializing role and, unfortunately and perhaps inevitably, the law—the Supreme Court's reading of what is presumably constitutional—has made the public school classroom a naked square. It has removed from that forum the possibility of engaging the great questions around which the culture war turns.

The public school has become the cockpit for the playing out of the culture wars. The election of Christian Coalition–supported candidates to local school boards and the implementation of the Rainbow Curriculum in New York City suggest that these types of battles are going to continue and intensify. They cannot be accommodated in the public school context because of Supreme Court rulings that questions about the basic philosophies of life that are grounded in religion have to be excluded. So, what do we have to look forward to? Years and years of bitter battles over *Huckleberry Finn* or between radical feminists and fundamentalists.

Everyone is focusing in on the public schools, which are already, in many parts of the country, failing to educate our children. Schools are already distracted from this goal and will be even more distracted by all these great societal battles that people will try to fight out on the public school turf. We have to look for an alternative approach to education that is as diverse as the diversity of the American people themselves but that will, through other public forums, keep our disagreements within the bounds of civility.

COMMENTARY BY *MARTIN E. MARTY*

In the past, fundamentalists in America were not, by and large, involved in political and cultural scraps. They stood on the sidelines and complained about the world around them; their main goal was to get people out of it. The great pioneer fundamentalist and evangelical Dwight Moody once said, "I see the world as a flood. God gave me a life boat and said, 'Moody, save all you can.'" If they reached beyond this, they said, "We'll be good citizens."

When American Protestant fundamentalism was born in the early part of this century, biblical criticism (which simply meant treating the Bible like other ancient texts) and teaching evolution in the schools were the issues. This was also a time of great cultural change. Most Christians said, "Well, we'll take it or leave it; we'll nibble here and be nibbled at there. We will make our compromises and take our stand." Fundamentalists, though, said: "This is a total assault. If we give up one little thing, we lose it all."

Fundamentalists, then, are conservatives who see modernity, pluralism, relativism, and immorality as coming at them. So fundamentalists fight back—they are reactive. Some of them, such as those at Bob Jones University, fight back defensively. That is, "We will make rules for our campus. We will build little shells around ourselves. We will be separatists." But that is really a small minority in today's fundamentalism. Most fundamentalists are now saying: "Radio, television, cinema, abortion clinics, legislatures, Republican precincts are all places where we have to fight the battle."

For most people, when you say "politics" it means tariffs, taxes, trade agreements. Fundamentalists, though, are interested in your gender or sexuality, the family, and schools. In other words, fundamentalists are interested in those issues that are closest to them and over which they used to have most control. Like the Japanese martial artist, the fundamentalist takes the force of modernity and throws it back on itself. For example, what is more modern than the mass media? What better represents erosive and corrosive forces of the world than the mass media? Yet who is better at using it than fundamentalists? Fundamentalists care about creation research. Most Jews and Christians say there's something to the Creation story, but it is not literal. But fundamentalists say, "No; you have to have scientific creationism." They use very rationalistic arguments.

Starting in the mid-1970s, after the school prayer decisions of 1962 and 1963, many fundamentalists began to say, "We used to run the schools and now the godless do." Or, after the *Roe v. Wade* decision on abortion in 1973, "We used to set the standards for fetal life and now the courts do." The fundamentalists wanted to win the White House, the courts, and the Congress. They hoped to gain influence with Jimmy Carter, but it didn't work. The high years of their first strategy were 1980 to 1988. Early efforts to get President Reagan to make good on his promises to fundamentalists, evangelicals, and Pentecostals, who had helped put him in office, resulted in their getting almost nothing from him. They didn't win much by winning much.

The second stage of strategy was to say, "This battle is going to be won in 10,000 local communities." I call it "board fundamentalism." The battle has moved to the school board, the library board, the textbook board, the town meeting board, the zoning board, the hospital board—all those places where a few hundred people, usually indifferent and apathetic, set policy. It doesn't take a lot to move in and take over. While you won't win a lot and the Supreme Court will take away some things you do win—at least temporarily—you do make a lot of local gains.

With this second-stage strategy of what some people call "stealth candidacies," it is much more difficult to make people aware of these fundamentalist activities. It is hard to get national news coverage of a battle in the Minnesota Republican party, or in an Idaho school board, or in an Indiana textbook board, or in a clinic in Milwaukee. We haven't satisfied the fundamentalists, many of whom would like the public schools to be like their Sunday Schools, but they've prodded a lot of liberal and secular people to get involved in local issues.

I am very much in the spirit of James Madison, who acknowledged the many factions, interests, and sects and recognized that the strength of our Republic is our diversity and the liveliness of our arguments. If some of them organize for something you don't like, then counter with organized opposition. It's a free contest.

COMMENTARY BY *MAXINE GREENE*

The face of American democracy has changed profoundly over the past half-century. Our society, from its beginnings, has been pluralist; but the emphasis, especially in schools, has been on initiating diverse persons into what was viewed as a homogeneous community. Today, the invisibility imposed on newcomers and immigrants, on women and ethnic minorities, has to an extent been reduced; and we have begun to think of our communities in the making as marvelously heterogeneous. Even as we work to bring people together by means of communication and shared undertakings, we are more aware of and respectful of difference than ever before in the history of education. We celebrate difference today as we try to work for connections and as we probe the meanings of reciprocity and responsibility. Many of us who are teachers are eager to provoke questioning from young people who traditionally would have been silenced in the classroom, as they were taught to internalize the values and the icons of the dominant culture. We hope to release more and more students for a pursuit of meanings, constructed meanings, that will deepen and diversify what we conceive to be American.

In my writings, I have been obsessive about the role of imagination and the arts in freeing people to think beyond the taken-for-granted, the conventional frames of ordinary life. This can only take place in situations opened to dialogue and critical questioning. Most of us know how much depends upon the consciousness of aware, participant membership is some mode of community. Art experiences are likely to feed back into the lived lives of those related to others, involved in transactions with others, often persons who look through markedly different perspectives on the common world. Young people, like their elders, yearn to be members of the weddings taking place in the culture. They want, on some level, to play a part in bringing values into being—values that are cherished by those around.

The paradox is that the very openness now required, the regard for the integrity of the Other, and the recognition of that Other as a being-in-progress are precisely what open the doors to fundamentalists. If we did not recognize different people for what they are and what they might be, we would not allow fundamentalists into our secular schools. We would refuse to pay heed to their voices. The problem is that we cannot keep insisting on our beliefs in pluralism and refuse entry to "different" people outside the door. We cannot silence them as we silenced so many marginal people in the past. We know that they belong in the world. I think it necessary to make clear that democratic values and commitments are such that persons with beliefs that seem hostile to democracy (and sometimes an apparent danger to democracy) have the right to enter the conversation. We talk about opening spaces for freedom, about overcoming thoughtlessness. Our confidence must be placed in the power of dialogue, in possibilities of empathy, in a mutuality of human concern.

Pondering the appeal of fundamentalist ideas in so many places, I think of John Dewey's *The Quest for Certainty* (1929) and the desperate desire of so many people to have someone tell them what is true and what is right. We have to take seriously the spread of *anomie*, the sense of pointedness, and the fear that seems to dog so many people and send them on quests of certainty. I think about the connection between poverty or deprivation and that human longing. It is very difficult to develop a consciousness of meanings or a sense of clear direction if you do not have money enough to go to the movies, if your black and white television (your main source of information) blinks out, if you know no one who enjoys the splendid lives obviously lived by those who conduct the talk shows and those who act in the soap operas—which so often appear to be windows on the existing world.

Of course there are no certainties in the existential philosophies which captivate me in so many ways. There is only a reaching toward what is not yet an ongoing search for ways of making our own what we have been conditioned to be. Values are always being redefined, as new deficiencies appear in the social world. Prescriptions and formulas are nowhere to be found by existential thinkers in the literature they prize. Human existence is openended; we are forever in the making. No, that does not leave me asking for a world without standards or a nihilistic world. I believe in a community in which individuals involve themselves in deciding together what ought to be and how they choose to live together. That, for me, is the source of significant norms, of standards. The point is to create situations in which people will understand what it is like to incarnate those norms, to live by principle and, at once, to care for those around them.

Whatever changes we make can only be made in small spaces, I think: in classrooms, in playgrounds, in neighborhoods. That is where the conversations may occur, conversations about countering what is thought to be nihilism, cheapness, sensationalism, amorality. We have to find ways to help children internalize a sense of obligatoriness when it comes to shared and open questions with respect to what is good and right. Caring, connection, attentiveness: we have to make these visible, these to be chosen as fundamental to freely chosen ways of life. At once, we have to recognize that the sense of agency necessary for choosing cannot exist unless fundamental needs are met.

As we set up communities in schools, distancing and indifference must be counteracted somehow, very possibly by people working together for, at least in their town or village, a better social order. That means school lunches for many, Head Start programs, Habitat undertakings, immunization campaigns, the opening of gardens and playgrounds—the kinds of shared undertakings that respond to shared needs. Oftentimes (as we can tell from children's journals) this leads to classrooms that are restless, exciting, classrooms that make it possible to shape a social vision that allows for differences but engages people in shaping something new that can be communal, that can be shared.

How can we help people create and choose their lives as meaningful? How can we move them to come together and create projects in which they can invest themselves? How can we move them to use their imaginations so that they discover what empathy signifies and connect with the heart of the stranger? How can we get them to see that it is worth living in a world of change? How can we convince them that transformations are possible if people can come together in the name of justice and freedom? As educators, we need to communicate a sense of passion, commitment, and desire, so they can expand their own searches, find something more redeeming than certainty.

We do not have to agree on everything; but we do have to live together. I have to allow fundamentalists space to talk, read, and demonstrate; but I will insist on their giving me space, so that we can listen to each others stories and discover what we have in common, what—looking at the children—we can share.

Reference

Dewey, J. (1929). *The quest for certainty*. New York: Minton, Balch & Co.

COMMENTARY BY *GEORGE MARSDEN*

William Allen White once remarked that William Jennings Bryan was always correct in diagnosis but always wrong in prescription. The same might be said regarding fundamentalism and public education.

Fundamentalists are correct in that public school claims to neutrality are not accurate; these schools really represent a broad moral perspective that emphasizes on tolerance. Because of the complex nature of society, tolerance is about the only concept that a wide variety of people are likely to agree on. But this begs the question, "What is it that one should tolerate?" Public schools' concept of tolerance tends to include toleration of some behaviors or beliefs that fundamentalists find objectionable. It is there that the fundamentalists' problems with public schools arise.

In attempting to correct this problem, fundamentalists attempt either to censor some liberal views or to promote their own views in the public schools. Fundamentalists' frustrations with public schools point toward a deeper problem: Americans expect to have one unified public school system. American public education grew out of an America dominated by Protestants who originally developed a single public school system congenial to their own views. Fundamentalists, of course, are also Protestants. Thus they are of two minds in relation to American culture and its schools.

On the one hand, fundamentalists have a heritage of being sectarian, preaching against the culture and separating themselves from it. Often, they start their own schools. However, because they are Protestants they have very deeply ingrained in their mentality the idea that they ought to be running the culture as birthright heirs. So at the same time that they are sectarian, labeling America as Babylon, they also preach America as being the New Israel. Having an establishmentarian mentality as well as a sectarian one relates to their not having a very good solution to the problems of American public education.

Like other establishmentarians, they believe there should be one dominant educational system with values that everyone should agree on. Here, they agree with many liberal educators and they are consistent with the origins of American education in the 19th century, when the Protestant founders of the common schools made quite a point of saying they were nonsectarian. During the colonial era and in the early days of the Republic, the state had supported church-controlled education and a variety of denominational schools. The problem in the 19th century arose when there was a large Catholic immigration and these new citizens soon asked that their schools be supported by taxes as well. In response, the Protestants argued that everyone had to support the public school system since it was not really religious in its orientation but nonsectarian. In fact, it represented the views of a variety of Protestants. Catholics, therefore, established their own schools.

In order to maintain this ideal of nonsectarianism within public schools, as we moved from the 19th into the early 20th century, the moral ideals had to be broadened, resulting in a lower and lower common denominator. What resulted was a public school system without much of a moral center other than this generalized idea of tolerance.

Today, fundamentalists understand that they are not represented in the public school system, but their solution is essentially to take over the system—which would only mean that the views of other groups would not be represented. One example of that approach was the 1981 Arkansas creation science law. Here the legislature had mandated that whenever the subject of the origins of the universe was taught in public schools, then creation science (defined as holding that the Earth isn't more than some 10,000 years old) would be taught along with a naturalistic evolutionary explanation. I testified as an expert witness against that because if you represent only two views in the public schools, you are not doing much better than representing only one; you are leaving out all those positions in the middle.

Fundamentalists are failing to address the real problem of pluralism. How in public schools can one present a truly pluralistic set of outlooks that represent not only extreme positions but a whole spectrum? What we have now (which fundamentalists are correct in recognizing) is schools having eliminated religious perspectives entirely because they have to be so thoroughly nonsectarian. The real problem is that although we are no longer predominantly Protestant, we still hold to the 19th-century Protestant assumption that you can have one nonsectarian school system that will satisfy all. But how could you represent the many varieties of American religions in public education?

The immediate practical solution if one is working in public education is to try to get as many points of view represented as possible and to take into account that there are going to be minorities that are excluded who also have rights. The other option is to encourage an institutional pluralism in education that, as in many Western European countries, includes tax-supported schools representing a variety of ideological points of view.

There is a growing recognition that public education is in crisis and that American public education would improve if it had more of a competitive dimension to it. Failing this, we will have cycles in which extreme views clash and only temporary truces can be made.

COMMENTARY BY *MICHAEL W. McCONNELL*

I would like to begin with three presuppositions about intensely religious persons in the context of public education. First, we live in a pluralist and multicultural society and we are committed—at least at some level—to having an educational system that is of a similar character. Second, fundamentalist and evangelical students are a significant minority in this country who have important differences from the mainstream. So when we think about multicultural or pluralist education, it is extremely important to think about them.

The third presupposition relates to the institutional constraints imposed by the First Amendment religious clauses upholding substantive governmental neutrality toward religion. The free-exercise clause is directed against the use of governmental power to impede religious belief or practice, and the establishment clause is directed against the use of governmental power to support religious belief or practice. In the public school classroom, the problems are quite practical. One set of questions has to do with how these intensely religious students are to be treated. This is principally, but not exclusively, a question that arises under the free-exercise clause. A second set has to do with how their opinions and worldview should be reflected in the curriculum.

Let's begin with how we must deal with intensely religious children in the public schools. The clearest case that we have had in the federal court system is *Mozert v. Hawkins County School Board*. In this case fundamentalist parents of several children objected to a particular reader assigned in one of the lower grades. Their objection was based, in part, on several passages that seemed to them to express ideas contrary to their faith. They objected, moreover, to the reader as a whole, which they believed was systematically biased against their worldview and would operate as a way of inculcating a belief structure inconsistent with their religious point of view. Initially, the teachers were fairly cooperative, allowing the children to read alternative materials. But, as the matter became public, the school board became involved. The board forbade the teachers from making these accommodations; the parents went to court. The parents won at the lowest level of the federal court system but the decision was reversed on appeal, with the lead opinion being that the mere exposure of a child to different points of view is not a violation of the free-exercise clause.

But where is the line between exposure and indoctrination? Would the court be so unconcerned if the shoe was on the other foot—if secular children or children of other religious beliefs were exposed to a curriculum slanted in favor of Protestant Christianity? All these children wanted was an accommodation—an opt-out. If the objectionable curriculum had been favorable to religion rather than—as these families thought—hostile to it, the remedy under the Establishment Clause would have been to change the curriculum for everyone.

As we address these questions, we are driven to consider even more fundamental ones, such as whether the project of government-operated schools is possible at all within the constraints of the First Amendment and whether you can have a public school system that complies with both the free-exercise and establishment clauses.

The best kind of curriculum, I believe, would be one in which the children would be introduced to a multiplicity of points of view, including those that are expressly religious. Part of the problem with the *Mozert* case was that there were many points of view in the curriculum but *none* of them bore any resemblance to those of the parents. It was not a genuinely open curriculum; it was a selectively open curriculum. The effect on such children, I think, is quite damaging. The message is that there are a whole lot of serious positions out in the world, but my parents' position isnt one of them.

Now, if it is not enough to have your own view fairly presented as one of several points of view, then there is no possibility of having public schools consistent with the Constitution. Here, the only option is for the government to make financial resources available to all schools that meet minimal requirements.

To the extent that you agree with the claim that all education has an inescapably religious component to it (see Leitch, 1985), the idea that we should all go to the same public schools becomes as intolerable as the notion that we should all go to the same church. For those who ask whether the dissolution of the public school system will lead to the breakdown of American community, I remind you that this was the same question that was asked at the beginning of our nation's history. Previously in history, religion itself had been the glue that held most nations together; the experiment of having citizens attend whatever church they wanted was rather a scary proposition. It has worked rather well, and I am inclined to think it would work well for education, too, in that it depoliticizes the culture war. If we privatized education, then the most serious sources of divisiveness, anger, and contention that have occurred when we have had to fight it out in the public arena would be eliminated.

Reference

Leitch, D. (1985). The myth of religious neutrality by separation in education. *Virginia Law Review, 71*(1), 127–172.

CHAPTER 3

Crossing Boundaries and Becoming the Other: Voices Across Borders

James T. Sears

In the summer of 1993 my graduate seminar at the University of South Carolina, "Christian Fundamentalism and Public Education," attracted nationwide attention and reaped a whirlwind of criticism from the highest state official to the simplest church-goer. Some viewed the course as "Christian-bashing," while others saw this criticism as rampant homophobia; some questioned my ability to deliver an "objective" course, while others saw the ensuing controversy as evidence of the Christian Right's growing influence in the state; a few wondered why a public university would ever want to challenge the views of a "majority" of the state's taxpayers, while others waved the tattered flag of academic freedom.[1]

Upon learning about this seminar, religious groups, along with many of the state's politicians and its conservative citizenry, voiced their concerns— amplified through the news media—to university administrators and the board of trustees:

- The Virginia-based Christian Coalition mailed 60,000 first-class letters urging South Carolinians to take action, while the Reverend Pat Robertson decried me as the "Satan of the University" on his popular "700 Club."
- The lead story read in a leading fundamentalist newsletter: "Mr. Sears is a self professing homosexual who wrote the book *Growing up Gay in the South*. An activist for homosexual causes, he is also the publisher and editor of *Empathy*, a journal that acts as an advocate for homosexuals, bisexual and lesbians."

- The editors of *The State*, South Carolina's largest newspaper, wrote "it sounded more like the university was offering a self-defense course in a war against Christians. . . . The course will be taught by a professor who has been an outspoken critic of many positions taken by conservative Christians, in particular their condemnation of homosexuals' demands for special civil-rights protection."
- Leaders in the Southern Baptist Convention lambasted me for "trying to put Christians in the closet."
- Forty-five of the 124 members of the South Carolina House of Representative signed a letter "strongly objecting" to the seminar: "We feel that it is improper for our state-supported [university] to address a very sensitive issue that cannot be discussed in our public schools." A leader of this group, Representative Bob Walker, wrote a personal letter to USC President John Palms threatening not to support USC's budget requests "if this is the direction that you wish to take the university."[2]

An avalanche of telephone calls and letters from 34 states were received by the office of the president and the members of the board of trustees. These letters, running nearly 100 to 1 against me, centered on three major themes: tax dollars to support an antireligious course; my sexual orientation and gay-related writings; and discontinuation of further financial support for the university. Representative of these views were the following:

- "Stick to academics not anti-Christian bigotry."
- "Remove this gay teacher from our school."
- "If you can allow a gay teacher to teach this course, then our support stops. This is telling me you are not a true Christian believer and my prayer is for God to deal with you harshly."
- ". . . a government-sanctioned attempt to bash Christians by an admitted Sodomite."
- "You should have a bigger problem with Sears' homosexual lifestyle and his writings than with law abiding Christian parents who are concerned about their own children's education."
- "This course is not unlike similar courses on other college campuses where the objective is not free inquiry, but rather leftist indoctrination."[3]

Meanwhile, forces on the left ranging from the American Civil Liberties Union to the People for the American Way, as well as various gay newspapers, marshaled their resources for the coming battle. The deputy legal director of the People for the American Way was quoted in the press as stating: "The fact that Religious Right organizations, including the Christian Coalition, have launched such a widespread and vitriolic campaign against the course, based in part on the sexual orientation of the professor, provides the best evidence for the need of the course." A North Carolina gay and lesbian newspaper, citing my course, warned its readers, "As the religious right has become more organized and sophisticated, so have their methods of communication. The direct mail is flying. The phone banks are ringing."

A smaller effort was initiated by those on the left. The National Coalition Against Censorship sent letters to 75 of its South Carolina members under the title "Educator's Course Attacked" and wrote directly to the university president that no "institution of higher education can allow curriculum content to be dictated by individuals and groups with special interests and ideologies." The associate secretary for the American Association of University Professors also wrote the president, noting "we hope that his candidacy for promotion to full professor will be considered by the board of trustees solely on academic grounds." Liberal editorials endorsing the course appeared as far away as Gainesville and San Antonio.[4]

On the eve of the first scheduled class day, *The State* headlines read: "Religion and Schools: Will It Be War?" The faculty senate steering committee had just endorsed the modified course description,[5] its syllabus, and its instructor. The first class was attended by the dozen enrolled students, members of the news media and university officials, and an undercover police officer responding to threats on my life. A week later, an open hearing was held by the board of trustees to decide the course's fate. The chairman of the board retorted: "A homosexual activist . . . could not possibly understand anything about fundamentalists' religious beliefs," while the spokesman for the governor described him as "livid."[6]

Deferring to the judgment of the president, the board took no official action during the heated two-hour meeting—aside from delaying its decision on all university promotions (I was one of 35 faculty members recommended by the president for promotion) and seeking assurances that the university would adopt procedures for reviewing topical seminars.

During the six-week course, nationally known scholars, persons from the religious community, and educational practitioners spoke before the class. Mid-term evaluations completed by the mostly conservative and Christian educators attending lauded the course's content and the competence of the instructor. News media coverage gradually changed from hostile, to neutral, to positive. Under *The State* headline "Controversial Course Deserves an 'A'," one of the seminar's students—describing herself as a "Bible-believing Christian"—concluded:

> The course featured frank, face-to-face discussion of important issues among people who hold widely divergent world views. . . . I was forced to define my own point of view more clearly, and I learned how to disagree profoundly with someone about specific issues without dehumanizing that person. . . . Perhaps the most remarkable feature of the course was its provision of a forum for dis-

cussion among people who might never otherwise encounter each other on such neutral ground. . . . Much of the newspaper coverage of the course directed attention to Sears himself. . . . [Yet] one of the few things we [the students] all agreed about is that Sears did an outstanding job conducting the class.[7]

Interestingly, *The State*, which had originally intended to run a "pro" and "con" set of articles, could find no one who had completed the course with anything negative to say. By the end of the semester, even some of my harshest critics praised the course and, following a three-month delay, the board approved all 35 promotions.

THE TRIBALIZATION OF AMERICA

Since that summer of 1993, the divide between conservative Christians and progressive educators has deepened as calls for the coming "culture wars" and solicitations for monies to arm various factions within the two camps have surged. The shrillness and animosity among factions can be spotted on a Sunday drive, with motorists proudly displaying bumper stickers such as "My Middle School Kid Can Beat Up on Your Honor Roll Child," "Save the Males," and "Redneck and Proud of It!" Technology has seemed to further this divide as Americans once networked among three channels are now scrambled across the television spectrum with choices ranging from Family Values and Empower America to MTV and "gay cable." Similarly, special-interest magazines such as *Vegetarian Times* and *Soldier of Fortune*, desktop-published newsletters such as Call Back, and Generation X 'zines like URB cater to subgroups. Cyberspace, with its myriad of newsgroups, homepages, and listservers, further splinters the citizenry.

The fragmentation of America is also evident in grim economic reports documenting the widening economic gap between rich and poor and the shrinking of the middle class, reaction to national news stories such as the Simpson contradictory verdicts revealing our great racial divide, and polls demonstrating a continued gender gap on social and political issues. Not surprisingly, these racial, social-class, and gender differences are also evident (if not amplified) among various church denominations. From the 36 million Baptists, many of whom are drawn from the rural citizenry and working poor, to the 2.5 million Episcopalians, traditionally composed of upper-income families, the United States also includes millions of persons who practice Judaism, Roman Catholicism, and Islam. And there are divisions even within the denominations: the Southern and American Baptists; the orthodox and the reform Jews; the Sunnis and the Shiites; the African Methodist Episcopals and the African Methodist Episcopal Zions; the Southern Methodist Episcopals and the Northern Methodists.

These reflect a disturbing phenomenon: the tribalization of America. Here complex issues become reified into simplistic slogans (e.g., "Abortion Is Murder," "The Christian Right Is Neither," "When Guns Are Outlawed Only Outlaws Will Have Guns") as a variety of ideological and theological positions get reduced into competing binaries: us/them, right/wrong, win/lose, sinner/saint, left/right.

THE NEW AMERICAN TRIBES

We are quickly becoming a nation of tribes. These tribes may be clothed with gang colors, professorial robes, or clerical collars; these tribes are located in the boardrooms of Manhattan skyscrapers, inside offices of ivy-covered faculty buildings, and on ground zero of our urban jungles; these tribes mount children's crusades for Operation Rescue or engage in the personal terrorism of outing; these tribes speak in the language of the church, the street, or academe; these tribes erect icons such as Louis Farrakhan, Donald Trump, or Camille Paglia.

Although each tribe is distinctive, they have much in common. Each requires "the other" to justify its existence and contest borders in order to warrant its territorial claims: the queer, the filthy rich, the spick, the baby killer, the radical feminist, the fundamentalist, the pointy-head intellectual. Without imagined threats posed by "the other," without the silencing of "the other," without the objectification of "the other," the tribe—whose members are bound by commonly held beliefs, values, and experiences—could not exist.

American tribalization also requires territories and borders: the hallowed halls of academe; the gangland divisions between the Crips and the Bloods; the homosexual sanctuaries of Fire Island and the Castro, the Christian fortresses of Lynchburg and Colorado Springs. Those who choose to cross territories risk the wrath from all sides along the border. Just as it is dangerous for a Cambodian youth flagging his colors to cross Chicago's Broadway Avenue, so, too, it is difficult for an evangelical Christian embracing a Bible to enter a public university classroom of an "avowed homosexual." Without these border-crossers, though, our public square dwindles.

THE CHURCH AND ACADEME:
THE EDUCATION OF A SECULARIST

Scattered throughout the nation, alongside dirt roads or crowded together in small towns, are conservative Christian outposts where networks of family and kin huddle together in worship and prayer. These Christian fortresses guard against the isms: evolutionism, ecumenicalism, secular humanism, multiculturalism.

At the center of these isms, bounded by tree-lined streets and secular enterprises, towers academe. Protected by tenure and promised academic freedom, professors too often isolate themselves from the maelstrom of everyday life, content to erect academic empires, to write in obscurant prose, to engage in academic hucksterism, or to partake in departmental or disciplinary factionalism.

For the conservative Christian, the decades since the 1960s have seen a progressive deterioration of moral conduct as biblical truths and moral absolutes have been abandoned by society. The ship of state—absent a moral compass and ethical rudder (to borrow a phrase from Charles Dunn)—has been scuttled on the shoals of secular humanism. Only through the waters of rebirth and redemption can this ship be righted; only through confessing our willful separation from God—sin—and seeking repentance can our New Zion be reclaimed. No longer content to await the millennium, many of these conservative Christians have returned to the public square from self-imposed exile to mirror tactics of the religious left a generation earlier. As their cause becomes a crusade, their ability and willingness to communicate in civil dialogue in the public square lessens.

My generation of academics, weaned on democratic ideals of a postwar capitalist era, came of age against the backdrop of the Vietnam War, the civil rights movement, and Watergate. Entering into temples of secular wisdom, our deacons included Noam Chomsky, Herbert Marcuse, Albert Camus, Simone de Beauvoir, and Harvey Cox. On altars of radical critique and social activism, our democratic idealism was sacrificed. Within a short time, however, a new intellectual orthodoxy replaced the old. This new orthodoxy reified scholarly discourse and stifled public debate as it diverted valuable intellectual energy and professional activity from the public square (Sears, 1994).

In the late spring of 1993, as a tenured associate professor, I gave little thought to those who opposed my research, politics, or lifestyle. Later, seared by that summer experience, I responded to an official reprimand from the university:

> As I noted at the onset of this course . . . my role was to engage in
> open dialogue and criticism as well as to be open to changing my
> position on the basis of the principles of disciplined inquiry. While I
> remain unalterably opposed to any attempt by a particular religious
> or sectarian group to camouflage its beliefs as universal and impose
> them in the public schools, I have changed my thinking on some
> issues relating to the interrelationship between education and
> religion. For example, the "judicial wall" between church and state is

much more porous than I had understood it to be, allowing for greater opportunity of religious expression within the confines of the public schools. Also, I believe that religious conservatives have indeed been excluded, belittled, or ignored by some public school teachers and administrators. Further, in order to maintain a separation between church and state, in some cases we have exorcised religion from the public school curriculum and, in the process, sacrificed the scholarly integrity of the subject matter itself.[8]

That summer, I began to appreciate the similarities between religious and educational institutions and the importance of engaging with "the other" in a dialogue leading toward understanding, if not reconciliation.

VOICES ALONG THE BORDER

As we engage with others, it is important to understand and appreciate the assumptions and values that those across borders hold. Since this text represents ideas representative of four broadly defined philosophical traditions—categorized here as evangelical conservatism, orthodox culturalism, secular progressivism, and critical postmodernism—these traditions are the focus of the following sections. Following a description of each tradition, the beliefs of each will be voiced by a person who shares them. Along the way, each suggests how conversations across borders may be possible *within* their tradition.

The Evangelical Conservative Tradition[9]

Rooted in the Protestant Reformation, evangelical Christianity has exerted substantial force in shaping the American experience.[10] From the Calvinist orthodoxy of the 17th century, to the evangelical awakenings of the 18th and 19th centuries, to its waning influence throughout most of the 20th century, conservative Protestantism's twin pillars of the saving work of Jesus Christ on the cross and the authority of Scripture have never changed.

There are, of course, substantial differences among evangelical conservatives on matters such as the relation with modernity, the meaning of church/state separation, the application of New Testament gifts, ecumenism, and the legitimacy of government-operated schools. Fundamentalist Christian religious doctrines are rooted in 12 booklets, *The Fundamentals*, published during this century's second decade and edited by Amzi Dixon, Louis Meyer, and Reubin Torrey. Fundamentalism's theological and cultural separatism, well articulated by the founders of Bob Jones University and the

Reverend John Vaughn here, grew out of early-20th-century theological battles with the "modernists" in the churches and seminaries over issues such as the inerrancy of the Bible and the virgin birth of Christ as well as struggles in the public arena regarding the teaching of evolution.

Charismatic evangelicals, like Pastor Bob Shearer in this volume, though clearly troubled by the tenets of modernism, choose to selectively embrace the modern world. Placing a strong emphasis on the ministry of the Holy Spirit, charismatics practice New Testament gifts such as speaking in tongues and healing through faith. Finally, self-styled "neo-evangelicals," popularized by post–World War II fundamentalists such as Harold Ockenga and Carl Henry and personalized by the contributions of James C. Carper in this volume, engage the secular world through organizations such as Campus Crusade for Christ, InterVarsity Christian Fellowship, the Christian Society, and publications such as *Christianity Today*. Distancing themselves from the historical fundamentalists in their willingness to assess carefully and, in some cases, incorporate modern biblical scholarship yet uncomfortable with charismatic claims of New Testament gifts, these mainstream evangelicals have entered into ecumenical alliances with traditional Catholics and orthodox Jews in order to address common concerns about current social issues such as abortion.

Although differing on some theological issues and holding varying perspectives on the role of the faithful in a secular society, conservative Protestants generally view public education as an institution where the needs of society have triumphed over the individual and secularism has subjugated theism. Although rooted in 19th-century Protestant culture, public education has placed the power of the state above that of the family as the educator's authority transcended that of the parents. The development of the modern high school and the educational principles outlined by the Cardinal Principles of Secondary Education, the progressives' concern with the whole child, the new science and mathematics curriculum of postwar America, and the movement toward values education and outcome-based education during the 1970s and 1980s all evidence this trend toward a secular life.

A Historical Fundamentalist Voice—John Vaughn. Many have promoted the idea that a fundamentalist basically means "dangerous religious extremist." I am a Christian fundamentalist—a biblical fundamentalist in the historical sense. I am one who takes his Christian roots—fundamentals—from the 1920s, the time when modernism or German rationalism had begun to bring a more liberal view into American Protestantism. Fundamentalism was a reaction to that drift from historical biblical to rational principles.

By fundamentalism, we mean irreducible minimums—fundamentals—beyond which you cannot have Christianity. We hold the basic, a priori metaphysical assumption that God exists. We accept this on the basis of faith in a self-evident truth, not on the basis of scientific investigation or of logical or rational conclusion. A second foundational assumption is that God has revealed Himself generally to us in the natural creation and in the moral nature of human beings. Everything created—human beings especially—bears the signature of the Creator. He also reveals Himself specially by the spiritual communication that He makes to the spirit of man. Of course, there is wide divergence of opinion as to what God has actually said, to whom, and how. For the Christian fundamentalist, God communicates to us through Scripture—our most objective source of information about God, since it is available for examination. Faith, therefore, is not leaping blindly but accepting the evidence—the Bible is our evidence.

Belief in the Scriptures as divine revelation is not arbitrary. It is based on the Resurrection of Jesus Christ (the fundamental of all Christian fundamentals). First, it is based on the objective historical fact of the Resurrection. The Resurrection validates Jesus' claim that He is God. It therefore validates the entirety of His message, including His teaching on the authority and inerrancy of the Old Testament, as well as the divine enablement and authority of the Apostles from which the New Testament derives its authority. No other book can claim such a basis for its authority. Second, the authority of the Bible also rests upon the subjective fact of the Resurrection in the life of the believer. When a sinner hears the gospel message (derived directly or indirectly from the Scriptures) and is "born again," he recognizes the voice of Christ not only in the "good news" of salvation but also in the Bible as a whole. The Bible is therefore affirmed both in the objective fact of Jesus Christ's Resurrection and in the subjective appropriation of that fact by the believer.

Principles evidenced in the Bible are objective truths as revealed by God. When we read the Bible, we believe that we are truly reading the words that God has breathed out and that were written down by holy men of old moved by the Holy Spirit. The Bible is His voice. The Bible therefore is not simply a historical record but the living Word. When we read it, we believe that we are engaged in a conversation with God Himself.

One principle about God's revelation that historical Christianity has held to is inerrancy. That means that God made no mistakes when he transmitted the Bible to us, that everything He wanted is in it, and that everything that is in it is perfect.

Another principle we hold to is authority. We believe that the Bible is the final authority for faith and practice. God has given us a book of answers, and it remains for the problems of life to furnish the questions.

Although many events that can occur in life are not specifically addressed in the Bible, there is nothing that can occur which is not dealt with *in principle* in the Bible.

When speaking of the fundamentals of faith, we can be dogmatic and unyielding. There are doctrinal truths, such as the Trinity, the virgin birth, or the Resurrection, that we hold as essential. But whenever I start reasoning from the biblical teaching and applying principles derived from the Bible, the possibility of my subjectivity enters in. Biblical teaching is fundamental; our convictions and standards are not fundamental—they are simply our sincere attempts to build on the fundamentals.

Christian fundamentalists approach the Bible very much the way a scientist would approach his measurements. Our principles are derived from the grammatical-historical method of hermeneutics—the field of biblical study through which we try to determine what God actually said. We believe we must take the passage in question and determine objectively what it teaches. In so doing, we assume that the Bible employs language in a normal manner to communicate truth. In our practice, we attempt to use exegesis to explain what a passage says honestly and with integrity. We are often accused of deriving doctrines to support behavior that we want to promote; that is not fair, not honest, and not true.

Since the hostage crises in Iran and the rise of the Christian Coalition, "fundamentalism" has been used in our culture to describe a wide variety of persons who don't like what is happening in society and want to change it. But that is not historical fundamentalism. Pat Robertson, for example, will talk about a "word from God"; he is not a fundamentalist in the historical sense. He makes subjective claims of spiritual revelation above the revealed word of God. Similarly, Randall Terry of Operation Rescue is an evangelical activist, not a fundamentalist. I oppose abortion as contrary to the Bible, but I also oppose his approach because it is contrary to the Bible.

We are militantly unyielding about what God has revealed, but Christian grace requires us to be patient, humane, and gracious at the level of policy. Unfortunately, most people are as militant at this level as they ought to be at the level of biblical principle. While doctrines are the truths revealed by God—which can be corrupted by our perceptions—we also develop convictions based on those doctrines. This, unfortunately, is where great disagreement, misunderstanding, hostility, and objection to someone else's right to believe often occur. Convictions are subjective perceptions—our beliefs. We establish standards or policies for our lives based on our convictions, which are, in turn, based upon doctrine. When people preach standards as though they were doctrines or when one generation interprets standards passed down from another as doctrine, we run into problems.

A true historical biblical fundamentalist is a separatist who values the accuracy and purity of God's message above political convenience. Because a fundamental tenet of Christianity is salvation by genuine, voluntary belief in Jesus Christ, one of the conclusions that a true biblical fundamentalist must come to is that he has no right—ever—to impose by force his beliefs onto another person even if it might seem the expedient thing to do. A true historical fundamentalist is a person who believes in the exchange of ideas through persuasion, not pressure. I believe in changing society by persuading individuals about the truth that God has revealed about Himself. When they subscribe to those beliefs, God, by His infinite power, will change them.

The Orthodox Culturalist Tradition[11]

The Federalist Papers are the clearest and earliest example of conservative Christian philosophy translated into the American political system. The fear of the unrestrained citizen—sinful in nature—was balanced with a modified Enlightenment belief in the rationality of man. Consequently, republican realism—epitomized by James Madison and rooted philosophically from Burke to Hume—sought to secure human liberties and restrain human excesses through the protection of government while protecting citizens against governmental tyranny or the rule of the mob. Wedding the consent of the governed with natural law and natural rights, constitutional power was divided between the federal and state/local governments, power was split at the federal level, and limited legislator tenure was coupled to limited legislative control. This system reconciled individual liberty and self-interest with a virtuous community and the common good: Power would check power; ambition would temper desire; reason would combat passion.

This system reflects the conservative view of institutions as inherently imperfect. Gradual progress is made through limited government and natural social forces. Government cannot grant or guarantee peace, liberty, or social justice—but it can create the framework in which these can be imperfectly realized. Here, institutions—particularly the family and the church—have a substantive role in mediating between the state and the individual. Thus, as republican virtues such as honor, duty, community, and liberty are stressed, education becomes an instrument for stability not change, preservation not transformation. Given that there is divine intent in history, educators have a responsibility to help students discover the order that inheres in nature and to stress compliance with universal moral laws.

The debate regarding the role of religion and religious values in public education is articulated forcefully by modern-day orthodox conservatives such as former secretary of education William Bennett (1992) and Boston

University president John Silber (1989), while in this volume the position is well articulated by contributors such as Charles Glenn and Richard Baer.

A Politically Conservative Voice—Charles W. Dunn. Sociologist Robert Bellah (1975) tells us that

> any coherent and viable society rests on a common set of moral understandings about good and bad, right and wrong in the realm of individual and social action. It is almost as widely held that these common moral understandings must also rest, in turn, on a common set of religious understandings that provide a picture of the universe in terms of which the moral understandings make sense. (p. ix)

American values are now kaleidoscopic because of an increasing disagreement on the common set of religious and moral understandings. Indeed, there never was a time when total agreement existed, although agreement was far more common earlier in our history. From uniformity to diversity, from simplicity to complexity, these have been the directions of our values.

Conservatism's influence on American history includes authoritarian conservatism, represented by Alexander Hamilton's governing elites; economic conservatism, with its emphasis on capitalism; international conservatism, represented by power politics; political conservatism, emphasizing liberty; populist conservatism, which stresses morality; religious conservatism, which emphasizes orthodoxy; and social conservatism, with its emphasis on order. These various manifestations of conservatism can still be found in today's society.

Early government charters such as the Mayflower Compact generally drew their ideas and sometimes their precise wording from the Bible. The theorists who influenced the formation of American government were themselves either of conservative religious persuasion or significantly influenced by it. Divine/natural law was commonly applied. Principal writers about the Founding Era, such as Harvard University historian Samuel Eliot Morison, acknowledged the pervasive, conservative religious influence. In his *Oxford History of the American People*, Morison (1965) wrote: "Puritanism was a cutting edge which hued liberty, democracy, humanitarianism, and universal education out of the black forest of feudal Europe" (p. 74). The early Thanksgiving Day proclamations—in fact even into the 1930s—expressed a desire "to cause the knowledge of Christianity to spread over the earth."

Not until the mid-1960s did conservative Christianity feel seriously threatened politically and socially. The government's overextension of liberal social and economic policies aroused latent conservatism among those who believed in the right of the community to establish and pass along customs and traditions from generation to generation. Community was challenged by individualism. Ronald Reagan, in effect, fostered a marriage between conservative ideology and conservative theology, bringing leaders of both to his campaign for the presidency and, ultimately, into his administration.

Today we see serious divisions within conservative Christianity between those who would like to establish the kingdom of God on Earth and those who do not believe there can be a kingdom without a king. The former believe that the United States was established as a Christian nation and that its religious foundation should be restored. The latter believe that meaningful social and governmental reform should be, first of all, the product of personal regeneration—regeneration of the soul.

Religion, once a part of the glue that held our society together, now appears to be contributing substantially to society's breaking apart. Religious interests have come to compete on the same political terrain with nonreligious interests in attempting to define American public policy. Contrast this to the observation of Alexis de Tocqueville in the early 1800s: "In the United States religion exercises little influence upon the laws and upon the details of public opinion. But, it directs the customs of the community and by regulating domestic life, it regulates the state" (quoted in Alley, 1972, p. 21). The secularization of American politics and society has generally reduced religion to another competing political force.

Nevertheless, I look upon the pluralism of America and this current debate as being healthy. It becomes unhealthy only when we have a lack of respect for other individuals and their views. Conservatism demands that we coalesce lest we tear apart.

The Secular Humanist Tradition[12]

Shaped also by Continental philosophy—that of Spinoza, Kant, and Rousseau—Jefferson held an unabiding faith in human beings and in human intelligence. Hence the role of political, religious, and educational institutions was to permit, preserve, and protect liberty of thought and expression while fostering the betterment of human beings through self-development in community. Rejecting the republican realism in *The Federalist Papers* and championing free schooling against the "tyranny over the mind of man," a Jeffersonian community of farmers, craftsmen, and property owners "could come together in village squares and meeting halls and articulate their concerns in such a ways as to constitute a live, consequential public sphere" (Greene, 1988, p. 27).

The Progressive movement reflects this abiding faith in human intelligence and human progress, represented in this volume by contributors such as Maxine Greene and Nel Noddings. In the 20th century progressivism, acquiescing to the modern industrial order, reluctantly turned to the state in reaction to rising urban despair, political machines, corporate monopolies, and an influx of immigrants. This was the age of populism evidenced in La Follette, greater electoral participation such as direct senatorial elections, the rise of scientific management evidenced in city managers and government bureaucrats, and the rise of professional social services and social sciences personified by Jane Addams and Charles Beard.

Underlying progressive social thought was the philosophy of pragmatism. In the mid to late 19th century Charles Peirce and William James established its philosophical framework. In an 1877 article that appeared in *Popular Science Monthly*, Peirce—mathematical and objective—advocated scientific inquiry as the most valid method for arriving at beliefs. James, psychological and subjective, popularized pragmatism, asserting that the adequacy of any meaning or value, truth or theory, belief or doctrine lies in its practical consequences. More than any other intellectual, though, John Dewey articulated the philosophy of pragmatism, rooting it in the psychological and the logical while coupling it to a theory of progressive education. Advocating "instrumentalism," he asserted that values are tested through problem solving and experience. Endorsing social planning and state direction, he viewed public schools as a social instrument—an "embryonic democracy" in which future generations would learn through experience in communities of inquiry.

Dewey's scientific humanism represents one manifestation of humanism. Unlike many other scientific humanists, he also considered himself a religious humanist (like other distinguished thinkers such as Rabbi Mordecai Kaplan), championing reason over revelation and defining God as the highest good. Here faith rests as comfortably with reason as God within Man. In the words of Algernon Black (1973) of the New York Society for Ethical Culture:

> The quest for faith must go beyond the God belief. Man has to face the fact that he does not know the beginning of the beginnings and that he does not know the purpose, and the purpose beyond all purposes, of the universe. . . . Whether we seek new symbols beyond a God or Saviour, beyond a Revelation or Salvation, or whether we remain with the old, we cannot expect to fulfill the human distinctiveness of our species unless we recognize the need for growth and development, the possibilities and potentialities of growth in the individual and in the quality of human relations and in the nature of human society. (p. 73)

A Progressive Voice—William H. Schubert. John Dewey has had a major impact on my deliberations. If we are going to understand Dewey, we must understand the far-reaching impact he has had in epistemology, aesthetics, ethics, and metaphysics as well as politics and education. There are three main points in his philosophy that seem relevant here: faith in democracy, method of intelligence, and rejection of dualisms.

In *Problems of Men* (1929), Dewey wrote: "The foundation of democracy is faith in the capacities of human nature, the power of human intelligence, and in the power of pooled and cooperative experience" (p. 59). Developing democracy is an essential role of public schools. In the classroom, Dewey called for a movement from the *psychological* to the *logical* (see Dewey, 1916). Here you start with the basic concerns and interests of the learners. These need to be taken seriously by the teacher, who inquires about what lies deeper in their concerns. What do their concerns symbolize? What common interests do they represent?

Embedded in Dewey's *psychological* realm, then, are basic human interests that bind people together and help to form a community. When we talk about democracy, we are speaking of a shared living together. A most important observation of Dewey is found in *Education Today* (1940), where he described democracy: "A society of free individuals in which all, through their own work, contribute to the liberation and enrichment of the lives of others, is the only environment where any individual can really grow normally to his full stature" (p. 298).

In *Liberalism and Social Action* (1935), Dewey observed that "the measure of civilization is the degree in which the method of cooperative intelligence replaces brute conflict" (p. 81). The method of human intelligence requires that we continually be reflective about our experience, refining and developing our ideas about what is worth knowing and experiencing. He called for faith in community and people engaging in intelligence discourse. In *A Common Faith* (1934b) he noted: "Faith in the continued disclosing of truth through directed co-operative human endeavor is more religious in quality than is any faith in a completed revelation" (p. 26). When he referred to faith in "intelligence," Dewey (1938) was speaking about human capacity. I would not want the spiritual dimension taken from that definition. He did not believe that an absolute truth could be discovered, but that there are good answers or "truths" for specific situations.

While Dewey advocated scientific learning in *How We Think* (1933), he also recognized that we learn in other ways, such as expressive knowing, in his *Art as Experience* (1934a). And in *A Common Faith* he talked about "reverie"—a spiritual knowing. There are certainly many routes to truth. All of these allow us to be open to possibilities and should become part of the public sphere and discussion within the classroom. None should be debased or exalted. We need to imagine when and where in the lives of human beings different ones of these ways of knowing have credibility.

One of the things that is most worth knowing and experiencing is that which brings most meaning and value to life. If religion fits this, then in the classroom we need to put various positions on the table, keeping an open mind about these alternative beliefs. That may strengthen one's beliefs or raise doubts. But I would draw the line where one seeks to impose what he or she believes to be most valuable or meaningful. This type of authority should not be exercised in the classroom.

In *Reconstruction in Philosophy* (1920/1948), Dewey talked about the dualism of whether the individual or the state is more important. He concluded that there is a correlative relationship between the two in that what is best for the individual and what is best for the state can be the same. The state, for Dewey, was not an autocratic authority; he spoke of community and democratic understanding—resting on the creative process of those people involved.

I am not sure that a debate is the best format for trying to resolve the social or educational problems discussed in this volume. In *Experience and Education* (1938), Dewey wrote in the Preface:

> It is the business of an intelligent theory of education to ascertain the causes for the conflicts that exist and then, instead of taking one side or the other, to indicate a plan of operations proceeding from a level deeper and more inclusive than is represented by the practices and ideas of the contending parties. (p. 5)

This can be done by seeking the main point made by each side and then probing more deeply to see if there is some way to find the best of each that can be brought together to address that *particular* situation.

The Postmodernist Tradition[13]

With applications ranging from art and architecture to theology and education, David Griffin (1988), a leading postmodern religious scholar, characterizes postmodernism as:

> a diffuse sentiment rather than to any common set of doctrines. . . . Revisionary postmodernism involves a new unity of scientific, ethical, aesthetic, and religious intuitions. It rejects not science as such but only that scientism in which the data of the modern natural sciences are alone allowed to contribute to the construction of our worldview. (p. x)

Postmodernism, then, is best understood by its relationship to the concept of modernism—itself born pointing its finger at the limitations of spirituality, prayer, and faith in the unseen. As metaphysical oversoul, modernism sought to improve humankind's ability to confront problems. Rooted in the realization that medieval beliefs were no longer adequate to deal with practical problems, modernism has its intellectual foundation in Enlightenment figures, such as Descartes, Bacon, and Newton, who invited a timid peasantry to understand, predict, and control their physical environment. Wedding nascent capitalism, rugged individualism, and democratic liberalism, modernism via science and technology displaced feudal lords with industrial barons and temple priests with laboratory scientists.

Postmodernism shares with premoderns its distrust of modernist claims of scholarly objectivity and scientific truth and their resulting predispositions toward state control or planning and the inevitability of social or technological progress. As one Christian conservative, noting similarities between the two, observed: "The most foolish thing believers could do is to make concessions now to a modernity that is already bankrupt. . . . [We] must not, at this late date, become scientific, bureaucratic, and technological" (Bottom, 1994, p. 31).

In addition, postmodernism is characterized by its interest in language—particularly the power of language (and culture) to reify reality. Spurred by the philosophical insights generated from the new physics pioneered by Albert Einstein, Niels Bohr, and Werner Heisenberg, Alfred Korzybski (1950) pointed out:

> The Aristotelian structure of language is in the main *elementalistic*, implying, through structure, a split or separation of what in actuality cannot be separated. For instance, we can verbally split "body" and "mind," "emotion" and "intellect," "space" and "time," etc., which as a matter of fact cannot be separated empirically. (p. xxxv)

Critical postmodernists view essentialist concepts such as gender, sexuality, and race as problematic. Sometimes drawing upon the theoretical work of Derrida, Lacan, or Foucault, they underscore how we are born into a world of language (itself shaped by history and culture) that constructs sexual, racial, and gendered oppositions which are viewed as natural and universal yet entail hierarchies of difference that transmit a moral order evidenced in the web of power relations and dominant collectivities. It is here that identities—produced through the constellation of language, power, and ideology—evidence various degrees of marginalization characterized by silenced voices and political disempowerment.

The promise of solidarity comes from a recognition of the ephemeral nature of these identities, the symbiotic relationship between the other and the self, and the necessity to deconstruct identities in order to construct communities. Kwame Appiah (1995), observing that the "existence of racism does not require the existence of races" (p. 105), argues for "disruption of the discourse of 'racial' and 'tribal' differences" (p. 111). Splinter groups along fault-lined identities of race, religion, class, or gender ignore how these inscribed categories of differences blind us to those commonalties that bind us as communities.

A Critical Postmodern Voice—Joe Kincheloe and J. Dan Marshall. In discussing how he moved beyond theoretical impasses in his search for a new physics, Einstein described "thought experiments" in which he freely selected the axiomatic bases of his speculations, permitting himself to transcend centuries-old scientific assumptions. In any conversation, concepts which logically explain physical or social phenomena sometimes gain such authority that their historical genesis is forgotten and they appear intractable (Kincheloe, Steinberg, & Tippins, 1992). The following ideas constitute our Einsteinian thought experiment concerning how new conversations about a democratic and theologically diverse culture might come about.

To begin, new conversations will take place within a "zone of uncertainty" (Slattery, 1995)—an environment that is comfortable with diversity, complexity, and the "vulnerable" dialogue that uncertainty elicits. Within this zone, *all* positions are worthy of analysis and historical contextualization. If we apply these principles to the present conflict between fundamentalist Christians and nonfundamentalists, new forms of dialogue can emerge.

Beginning with a mutual willingness to recognize the limitations of modernist science, Christian fundamentalists and others can begin a *tentative* dialogue about the role of modernist science in everyday life. This context or zone of uncertainty permits seemingly concrete notions to be discussed from a less polarized perspective. Is it possible, for example, that what fundamentalist Christians have labeled secular humanism is directly related to what postmodern critics have called the metaphysical dynamic of Cartesian–Newtonian science? If so, then secular humanism can be conceptualized as something more than an irrational attack on an objective curriculum, for the objective or "scientific" curriculum may not be as innocent as its defenders portray it. For example, perhaps textbooks *do* hold theological implications; perhaps sex education *does* promote unstated agendas.

Modernist political scholars have long argued that the foundation for community has rested on consensus—the sharing of common precepts. Postmodernist Sharon Welch (1991), however, challenges such a concept, arguing that heterogeneous populations with *differing* beliefs and principles may better contribute to the formation of a moral and democratic community. A homogeneous community, Welch contends, is often unable to criticize the injustice and exclusionary practices that afflict a social system. Conversely, criticism and reform often emerge from the recognition of difference—from interaction with populations who do not suffer from the same injustices or who have dealt with a different view of that which we agree is important. Indeed, consciousness itself is spurred by difference in that we gain our first awareness of who we are when we become aware that we exist independent of another or another's ways. Continuing our example, differences between the deeply and not-so-deeply religious can be seen as mutually beneficial in light of social or civic change. Binary differences between the "secular" and "spiritual" can dissipate in conversations focused on the "educational" or "pedagogical" value of specific textbooks and the ways in which they entice students to participate in the immortal human conversation.

But what is to stop this "community of difference" from devolving into warring tribal factions? It is at this juncture that the *ethic of solidarity* enters the discussion. Solidarity has two central features. First, it grants diverse social groups enough respect to listen to them and use all ideas when considering existing social and civic values. Second, it realizes that the lives of individuals in differing groups are ecologically interconnected to the point that everyone is accountable to everyone else. No assumption of uniformity exists here—just the commitment to work together to bring about *mutually beneficial social and civic change.*

Within the ethic of solidarity a space for disagreement appears. In the context of a postmodern community of difference grounded on an ethic of solidarity, we find room for a diversity of perspectives, a variety of cultural logics. In an environment grounded on the precepts of a community of difference, dedicated to interpretation and an ethic of solidarity, educators and fundamentalist Christians can live together. Sectarian disagreements over highly localized interpretations stand a chance of being eclipsed by much larger, more generalized questions of *mutual* long-term benefit. Ours should not be a battle against each other, but one against a highly problematic modernistic understanding of our world.

CONCLUDING REMARKS

Education, like religion, is about the transformation of consciousness. Students entertain doubt, while teachers foster faith in human discourse and intelligence. In the process, individual and social transformation occurs. However, the citadels of religion and academia have replaced doubt with certainty, while faith in the power of democratic dialogue has waned.

In his classic work *Dynamics of Faith* (1957), theologian Paul Tillich warned that even in religiously homogeneous societies, when civil authorities endorse doctrinal beliefs and enforce spiritual conformity they have removed "the risk and courage which belong to the act of faith" (pp. 27–28). If we are to truly engage in dialogue within the public square, then *metanoia* and *pistis* are essential.[14] Community members engaged in conversations for an enlarging public square must allow for a change in mind and be open to "another kind of thinking." To accomplish this, we must listen to other voices and enter other rooms.

NOTES

1. For a more detailed discussion of this controversy, see Sears, in press; Swanson, 1994; Welsh, 1995. Correspondence, newspaper articles, and audio/video recordings of the class are housed in my papers, located in the Special Collections Library, Duke University, cited hereafter as Sears Papers.

2. All materials can be found in Sears Papers. See Reed, M. (1993), "USC 'Combatting' Christians," *Community Standard,* 3(5), p. 1; Editorial, "Study of Fundamentalists Strains USC's Credibility," *The State,* June 4, 1993, p. 10A; Bandy, L., "Baptists Urge USC to Cancel Course," *The State,* June 4, 1993, pp. 1A, 11A; Letter to John Palms from members of the South Carolina State Legislature, June 1, 1993. Sears Papers.

3. Sears Papers.

4. "Look Carefully to the Right," *The Front Page,* June 25, 1993, pp. 11–12; Letter NCAC Friends in South Carolina, June 9, 1993; Letter to John M. Palms from Leanne Katz, executive director NCAC, June 9, 1993. Letter to John M. Palms from Jonathan Knight, associate secretary AAUP, June 22, 1993; "Crackdown on Campus," *Gainesville Sun,* June 1993; "Churches Don't Run Public Universities," *San Antonio Light,* June 13, 1993. Sears Papers.

5. The original course description read:

> An examination of curricular and administrative issues related to the growing influence of Christian fundamentalism in public education. Using insights from psychology, history, theology, law, and sociology, this interdisciplinary seminar will assist school practitioners and others in understanding the fundamentalist phenomenon and combatting its challenge to public education in a secular democracy. Numerous speakers will include educators and policy makers; professionals in law, journalism, religion, and psychology; and fundamentalist activists.

At the onset of the controversy, the university's provost insisted that modifications be made to the original seminar description. Following some negotiations, the word "objective" was inserted into the first sentence and "doctoral students" into the second. Also, the phrase "combatting its challenge" was deleted in the second sentence and replaced by "its impact on," while "fundamentalist activists" was changed to "Christian fundamentalists."

6. Robinson, B., "Trustees Slam USC's Handling of Course," *The State*, June 18, 1993, pp. 1A, 11A: June 4, 1993, pp. 1A, 11A. Sears Papers.

7. Haddad, D., "Controversial Course Deserves an 'A'," *The State*, July 11, 1993, p. 1D. Also see "Controversial Class Makes the Grade," Charlotte *Observer*, July 9, 1993, p. 5A; "Religion Course Gets High Marks," *The State*, July 9, 1993.

8. Letter to President John Palms, August 3, 1993. Sears Papers.

9. For a more detailed description, see Dollar, 1973; Hunter, 1983; Magnuson, 1990, Marsden, 1980, 1984; Neuhaus & Cromartie, 1987; Noll, 1994; Rushdoony, 1972; Sandeen, 1970.

10. See Linder, Shelley, & Stout, 1990, pp. 415–416, 461–465; Marty & Appleby, 1994; Nord, 1995, pp. 54–56.

11. For a more detailed description, see Carter, 1993; Dunn, 1984, 1991, 1996.

12. For a more detailed description, see Hofstadter, 1963; Rockefeller, 1991; Schön, 1992; Schubert, 1992; Sellers, 1933; Westbrook, 1991.

13. For a more detailed description, see Doll, 1993; Griffin, 1988; Lyotard, 1984; Nicholson & Seidman, 1995; Tyler, 1987.

14. The Greek word *metanoia*, meaning "change of mind," has been translated poorly as "repentance"—derived from the Latin *poenitare*, meaning "to feel sorry." Similarly, *pistis*, often translated "faith," is more correctly translated as "another kind of thinking" (Nicoll, 1954).

REFERENCES

Alley, R. (1972). *So help me God*. Richmond, VA: John Knox Press.

Appiah, K. (1995). African identities. In L. Nicholson & S. Seidman (Eds.), *Social postmodernism* (pp. 103–115). New York: Cambridge University Press.

Bellah, R. (1975). *The broken covenant*. New York: Seabury.

Bennett, W. (1992). *The de-valuing of America*. New York: Simon & Schuster.

Black, A. (1973). Our quest for faith: Is humanism enough? In P. Kurtz (Ed.), *The humanist alternative* (pp. 70–77). Buffalo, NY: Prometheus.

Bottom, J. (1994, February). Christians and postmoderns. *First Things*, pp. 28–32.

Carter, S. (1993). *The culture of disbelief*. New York: Basic Books.

Dewey, J. (1916). *Democracy and education*. New York: Macmillan.

Dewey, J. (1927). *Problems of men*. New York: Philosophical Library.

Dewey, J. (1933). *How we think*. New York: Heath.

Dewey, J. (1934a). *Art as experience*. New York: Minton, Balch & Co.

Dewey, J. (1934b). *A common faith*. New Haven, CT: Yale University Press.

Dewey, J. (1935). *Liberalism and social action*. New York: Putnam.

Dewey, J. (1938). *Experience and education*. New York: Macmillan.

Dewey, J. (1940). *Education today*. New York: Putnam.

Dewey, J. (1948). *Reconstruction in philosophy*. Boston: Beacon. (Original work published 1920)

Doll, W. (1993). *A post-modern perspective on curriculum*. New York: Teachers College Press.

Dollar, G. (1973). *A history of fundamentalism in America*. Greenville, SC: Bob Jones Press.

Dunn, C. (1984). *American political theology*. New York: Praeger.

Dunn, C. (1991). *American conservatism from Burke to Bush*. Lanham, MD: Madison.

Dunn, C., & Woodward, J. (1996). *The conservative tradition in America*. Lanham, MD: Rowman & Littlefield.

Greene, M. (1988). *The dialectic of freedom*. New York: Teachers College Press.

Griffin, D. (1988). *Spirituality and society: Postmodern visions*. Albany: State University of New York Press.

Hofstadter, R. (1963). *Anti-intellectualism in American life*. New York: Knopf.

Hunter, J. (1983). *American evangelicalism*. New Brunswick, NJ: Rutgers University Press.

Kincheloe, J., Steinberg, S., & Tippins, D. (1992). *The stigma of genius*. Wakefield, NH: Hollowbrook.

Korzybski, A. (1950). *Manhood of humanity* (2nd ed.). Lakeville, CT: International Non-Aristotelian Library Publishing.

Linder, R., Shelley, B., & Stout, H. (1990). *Dictionary of Christianity in America*. Downers Grove, IL: InterVarsity.

Lyotard, J. (1984). *The postmodern condition*. Minneapolis: University of Minnesota Press.

Magnuson, W. (1990). *American evangelicalism: An annotated bibliography*. West Cornwall, CT: Lost Hill Press.

Marsden, G. (1980). *Fundamentalism and American culture, the shaping of twentieth-century evangelicalism*. New York: Oxford University Press.

Marsden, G. (1984). *Evangelicalism and modern America*. Grand Rapids, MI: Eerdmans.

Marty, M., & Appleby, R. (Eds.). (1994). *Accounting for fundamentalism*. Chicago: University of Chicago Press.

Morison, S. (1965). *The Oxford history of the American people*. New York: Oxford University Press.

Neuhaus, R., & Cromartie, M. (Eds.). (1987). *Piety and politics: Evangelicals and fundamentalists confront the world*. New York: Ethics and Public Policy Center.

Nicholson, L., & Seidman, S. (Eds.). (1995). *Social postmodernism*. Cambridge, England: Cambridge University Press.

Nicoll, M. (1954). *The mark*. London: Stuart & Watkins.

Noll, M. (1994). *Scandal of the evangelical mind*. Grand Rapids, MI: Eerdmans.

Nord, W. (1995). *Religion and American education*. Chapel Hill: University of North Carolina Press.

Rockefeller, R. (Ed.). (1991). *Religious faith and democratic humanism*. New York: Columbia University Press

Rushdoony, R. (1972). *The messianic character of American education*. Nutley, NJ: Craig Press.

Sandeen, E. (1970). *The roots of fundamentalism*. Chicago: University of Chicago Press.

Schön, D. (1992). The theory of inquiry: Dewey's legacy to education. *Curriculum Inquiry, 22*(2), 119–139.

Schubert, W. (1992). Neo-Deweyan interpretation of curriculum development. *New Education, 14*(2), 61–64.

Sears, J. (1994). The second wave of curriculum theorizing: Labyrinths, orthodoxies, and other legacies of the glass bead game. *Theory into Practice, 31*(3), 210–218.

Sears, J. (in press). In[ter]ventions of Male Sexualities and HIV Education: Case Studies in the Philippines. In D. Epstein & J. Sears (Eds.), *A dangerous knowing: Sexual pedagogies and the master narrative.* London: Cassell.

Sellers, R. (1933). Religious humanism. *The New Humanist, 6*(3), 7–12.

Silber, J. (1989). *Straight shooting: What's wrong with America and how to fix it.* New York: Harper & Row.

Slattery, P. (1995). *Curriculum development in the postmodern era.* New York: Garland.

Swanson, N. (1994). *Christian fundamentalism, academic freedom, and controversy.* Unpublished honors thesis, University of South Carolina, Columbia.

Tillich, P. (1957). *Dynamics of faith.* New York: Harper.

Tyler, S. (1987). *The unspeakable: Discourse, dialogue, and rhetoric in the postmodern world.* Madison: University of Wisconsin Press.

Welch, S. (1991). An ethic of solidarity and difference. In H. Giroux (Ed.), *Postmodernism, feminism, and cultural politics* (pp. 83–99). Albany: State University of New York.

Welsh, M. (1995, Summer/Fall). Combatting Christian fundamentalism. *Case Research Journal,* pp. 174–188.

Westbrook, R. (1991). *John Dewey.* Ithaca, NY: Cornell University Press.

CHAPTER 4

Dialogue, Religion, and Tolerance: How to Talk to People Who Are Wrong About (Almost) Everything

Kenneth A. Strike

In his book *Culture Wars* (1991), James Hunter describes an America divided into camps labeled *orthodox* and *progressive*. What defines the orthodox is a commitment to an "external, definable, and transcendent authority" that provides "a consistent unchangeable measure of value, purpose, goodness and identity" (p. 44). Progressives are those attuned to the modern age whose spirit is rationalism and subjectivity and for whom truth is an unfolding process. *Are these outlooks reconcilable? Can there be a moral conversation between outlooks so diverse?*

I answer these two questions differently. The differences, Hunter notes, run deep, although, as I will argue below, his formulation is too extreme. If a just and peaceful civic life depends on achieving a widely shared and noncoercively achieved consensus about them, there is little hope. I believe it does not. We have survived other deep divisions. Catholics and Protestants fought for political domination for centuries after the Reformation. These struggles were "resolved" sometimes by political partition and sometimes by religious dominance. However, in free and religiously pluralist societies, such "solutions" as these, which achieve a shared faith by means of political dominance or coercion, are untenable. The alternative to the political dominance of a privileged religion is to seek a shared civic morality, a fabric of "public reason," that can be described in ways consistent with various faiths but that privileges none. It is this solution I wish to describe and advance as a conception of public dialogue suitable for a pluralistic and noncoercive state.

A central part of its strategy is to take certain deep disagreements off the public table. We can only reconcile religious diversity with civic justice and social peace if no religion is privileged in conversation in the public sphere. Minimally, this strategy requires that government not base its decisions solely on convictions that are distinctive to a particular creed. It does not, I shall argue, require that religious issues be altogether avoided in all public contexts. Nevertheless, the key to public dialogue in pluralistic societies is to conduct it so as to respect this fabric of public reason and, pursuantly, to avoid partisan arguments. If we are to respect public reason, we must, in some contexts, be willing to set aside some of our deepest convictions for conversational public purposes.[1]

In an era when our fundamental convictions are no longer necessarily religious, this nonaggression pact needs to be broadened. Thus we should expect this governmental neutrality to apply to any religious or philosophical perspectives that run deeply enough to function as people's central convictions. We must apply an expectation of neutrality to those various Enlightenment doctrines—utilitarianism, neo-Kantianism, and secular humanism (if there is such a thing)—that often seek the status of the official public philosophy.

This strategy requires that arguments within the public sphere be framed by a view of public reason that is religiously and philosophically "shallow." Its content should be such that it does not assert or assume doctrines that are distinctive to some particular religious or philosophical perspective. Instead, it should represent a dialogically achieved "overlapping consensus." An overlapping consensus should consist of claims that can be accepted by all reasonable people regardless of differing religious or philosophical perspectives. That this overlapping consensus be dialogically achieved means that we must regard it as produced by argument between interlocutors with diverse religious and philosophical perspectives and that we regard it as an object of renegotiation. My view of the character of an overlapping consensus and especially the nature of the argument for it differs somewhat from John Rawls's (1993) view that public reason should be philosophically shallow (Strike, 1993b, 1994).

By a fabric of public reason or an overlapping consensus, I am not speaking of an extensive and detailed set of moral claims as much as I am about basic, and perhaps vaguely formulated, moral assumptions that frame discussion. This is one role played by constitutional principles such as due process, the right to privacy, and democratic decision making. That human beings are free and equal in their role as citizens is an essential part of an overlapping consensus. The phrase "in their role as citizens" means that while people must respect one another's equality and liberty in the public arena, they may operate on different assumptions in their nonpublic associations. For example, that people as citizens are free and equal means that women and men equally may vote and hold public office. But Catholics may also, if they choose, deny the priesthood to women. The boundaries between the public arena and nonpublic associations are notoriously difficult to negotiate. However, I suspect that few whose religious views espouse different roles for men and women find this a reason for denying women the right to vote or to hold office and that few champions of women's equality wish to use the power of the state to install women in the Catholic priesthood. If so, this suggests that, despite their complexities and ambiguities, the assumptions underlying my treatment of these examples are widely shared. This degree of agreement does not resolve all issues, but it is sufficient for an overlapping consensus to function as a framework for public argument.

What is the content of this fabric of public reason? Briefly, its central components are (1) a political conception of people as free and equal in their role as citizens; (2) basic constitutional principles such as free speech, a free press, religious liberty, due process, equal protection of the laws, and democratic decision making; (3) widely accepted views as to the nature of human goods; and (4) broadly accepted claims of the natural and human sciences. Public reason seeks to respect those features of our political culture that are broadly accepted (in some measure because they have both diverse religious and secular antecedents) and "facts" that are viewed as facts by broad and diverse segments of our culture. It does not privilege any epistemological account (positivism, for example) as to what counts as a fact.

Of course, some public issues are more resistant to dialogue rooted in an overlapping consensus than others. Abortion comes to mind. But even here we should remind ourselves that this debate is conducted within a framework of some shared moral commitments. Pro-life advocates do not reject the very idea of privacy. Nor do pro-choice proponents advance a broad policy of murder. We agree that human beings are entitled to some privacy and that it is wrong to kill them. That we cannot agree on what counts as a human being is no small matter, but we should not lose sight of the shared content of the debate either.

Nevertheless, dialogue is not easily achieved. Several years ago, I asked a group of principals to design dialogue forums to discuss two controversial issues that might emerge in their schools. The first concerned the teaching of evolution; the second was an issue of multiculturalism. Two things struck me about the forums these principals designed. First was their need to control any forum. These principals had little confidence in the ability of participants to be reasonable. Thus they wanted strict rules of participation, control over microphones, and citations for facts asserted. The second was that these principals said they would be unwilling to attempt such a forum. They viewed the attempt as a ticket to unemployment. Dialogue received much support in the abstract—but not in "my school." There was every expectation that people would be unreasonable.

We can do better. If we are to do better, we must have a clearer understanding of the dialogical requirements of what I have referred to as "setting aside" some of our deeper convictions. What must we set aside and in what contexts? And we must disabuse ourselves of some antidialogical notions. To this end, in what follows, I describe several ideas that are important for public (and educational) dialogue among citizens of a nation that will continue to be deeply divided but who share something of a fabric of public reason. Briefly stated, these ideas are:

1. Public dialogue should be governed by conversational restraint.
2. Tolerance does not depend on moral relativism, nor does it convey acceptance of the views tolerated.
3. Absolutism and relativism are not useful concepts.
4. We need to be better at distinguishing between what schools can discuss and what they can advocate.
5. Dialogue depends on an adequate grounding of people in their own perspectives.
6. Dialogue depends on the virtue of reasonableness.

PUBLIC DIALOGUE SHOULD BE GOVERNED BY CONVERSATIONAL RESTRAINT

Regulating discussion by an overlapping consensus requires people to show restraint about how they argue and what they argue for in public contexts. Public dialogue will not long survive the habit of insisting that public acknowledgment be granted to our deepest convictions. Nor will it survive the attempt to decide whose fundamental convictions are true. The strategy of tolerance I have described requires that we be willing to take some things off the public table, to set them aside, to be pursued with the like-minded in private.

However, it is also unacceptable simply to forbid people to express their deepest moral convictions in public forums. Such a prohibition would be inconsistent with free speech. It would also foster claims that the understanding of the overlapping consensus is unfair. Thus,while conversational restraint seems important, it is hard to say exactly what it consists of. It seems to require that we balance two inconsistent notions: that we take some ideas off the table and that we respect free speech. I would propose the following formulation: Public debate should be conducted on the assumption that eventually public decisions must rest on public reasons; otherwise they are illegitimate. It is thus a matter of prudence to argue from premises that have public standing and to avoid arguing from premises that are religiously or philosophically controversial. This formulation forbids no form of speech. However, it recognizes that in a religiously pluralistic society, public policies that have only religious (or similarly partisan) justification cannot stand, and it asks us, in the light of this fact, which is a common interpretation of the establishment clause of the First Amendment, that we emphasize public reasons and deemphasize partisan ones in our public speech. Thus it balances "setting aside" and free speech by focusing legal attention on the basis of public decisions, not on speech. Second, it views restraint on speech as a matter of prudence, not law. Thus it does not propose that conversational restraint be backed by any form of legal enforcement. Rather, conversational restraint is viewed as a public virtue and as an important part of public civility. Also, it does not forbid policies that have deep religious or philosophical justifications in the minds of their advocates. It does, however, forbid policies that can find no form of public justification in addition. Finally, it does not ask that anyone reject their deepest religious or philosophical convictions. Instead, it asks them to emphasize public reasons in forums where these convictions are not shared (e.g., Ackerman, 1989; Benhabib, 1989; McCarthy, 1994).[2]

TOLERANCE DOES NOT DEPEND ON MORAL RELATIVISM

One of the programs that has most alienated religious people from public schools has been values clarification (see Raths, Harmin, & Simon, 1966). One reason is that values clarification grounds tolerance in relativism. This view is historically wrong and is disastrous for dialogue. Historically, religious tolerance was not rooted in the presumption that religious truth is relative. Indeed, people were asked to tolerate those whose views they regarded as damnable. The essence of religious tolerance is that all religions and their adherents are equal before the law, not that all religions are equally true. A view that grounded tolerance in relativism could not be the basis of religious toleration, since it would discriminate (as values clarification does) against those who believe their religion to be true (see Strike, 1990, 1993a) and compel their approval of doctrines they believe to be false.

Similarly, dialogue rooted in an overlapping consensus does not require that we regard all cultures, convictions, or lifestyles as equally praiseworthy. In school contexts, the implication is that we should teach that people should respect the rights of others regardless of whether we approve of their convictions or their lifestyles. However, teaching that all religions or lifestyles are equally deserving of approval may constitute the violation of the liberty of those who think otherwise.

Pervasive moral skepticism is inconsistent with dialogue. Its consequence is to undermine the meaningfulness of any claims of worth (Taylor, 1992). Dialogue assumes that people can give one another reasons that count as grounds for altering belief or behavior. Dialogue takes Mill's (1859/1956) perspective that truth is sought through free and open debate. Skepticism rejects the view that there is any truth to be sought. It reduces dialogue to bargaining or, as with values clarification, to a means of personal choice instead of reasoned consensus. And when it is discovered that in some cases some values must prevail, it leads to moral authoritarianism since the possibility of reasoned consensus is precluded (see Strike, 1993a).

ABSOLUTISM AND RELATIVISM
ARE NOT USEFUL CONCEPTS

It is not true that religious views, even orthodox ones, are absolutist. Consider Paul's idea that we are under grace, not law; or Augustine's aphorism "Love and do what you will"; or the fact that those who believe in the Ten Commandments have found it necessary to write thousands of volumes interpreting them and applying them to novel circumstances. Is the command "Thou shalt not kill" an absolute when it requires volumes of just-war theory to explicate it? What are Christians to make of Christ's comments about the Sabbath being made for man and not man for the Sabbath? Is man the measure of this absolute? It seems that religious people must search hard to discover the real meaning of their absolutes, expend intellectual labor to apply them to diverse contexts, and look for ordering principles when absolutes conflict. If so, what does it mean to call them absolutes?

Nor are secular views inherently relativist. Plato and Kant are surely worthy of the label "absolutist" if it means anything at all. They attacked the relativists of their day. Plato's (1957) target in the *Theaetetus* is Protagoras, whose aphorism, "Man is the measure of things," remains the quintessential definition of relativism. Nevertheless, Plato and Kant also formed their views in opposition to the dominant religions of their day. Ironically, Augustine and Jesus seem more deserving of the label "relativist" than they. Finally, consider utilitarianism. It holds that pleasure is the good and defines justice as the greatest good for the greatest number. Absolutism? Yet it also claims that people find their happiness in different things and that we must appraise each act in terms of its consequences for human happiness. Relativism? Here the words lose their grip on any matter of significance.

The words *relativism* and *absolutism* defeat dialogue. They identify who is beyond reason. They close minds. They lock us into mindless and dismissive stereotypes. We should give them up. We need to listen to the reasons people give us and respond with those we have. Categorizing our interlocutors or ourselves as relativists or absolutists defeats the possibility of meeting our interlocutors on their own terms. It distorts conversation.

What is essential to both religious and secular ethics is *not* moral absolutism, but moral objectivity—the belief that moral claims can be justified by reasons. What unites Paul, Augustine, and Jesus is their unwillingness to treat rules of conduct as absolute and their willingness to judge rules in terms of the ultimate good of the objects of their love. They, along with many secular sources, believed that rules must be judged by their consequences for the good. To believe this is to believe that moral judgments are objective, but not absolute. Note that once it is granted that the interest of religious people is in objectivity, not absolutism, we will have discovered that they have much common ground with those several writers who also believe in moral objectivity. And we will have found reason to abandon Hunter's formulation of the culture wars. Of course, religious and nonreligious people will continue to disagree about the nature of the human good. However, once they get beyond the categories of relativism and absolutism, they may find that giving one another reasons for their views and inquiring into the grounds of their real differences is a productive activity.

Is public reason the new absolute? Of course not! The features of public reason are dialogically achieved and remain contestable and rebuttable. But they have the kind of provisional objectivity of any view that has been well argued—and the same claim to our allegiance.

What is critical is that the tendency to divide the world into absolutists, the good guys, and relativists, the bad guys, may distort what is central in religious traditions. The ideas of reconciliation and redemption are central to the Christian gospel. When religious people come to think of themselves as absolutists and others as relativists, they may, as a consequence, find unquestioning obedience to a set of moral prescriptions as central to their ethic. And they may abandon the work of redemption and reconciliation in favor of an inhumane adherence to an unreflective code. Redemption and reconciliation are no enemies to dialogue. Religion has often incorporated within itself a struggle between those who would control God through ritual and control others through demands for obedience to their absolute rules and certainties and those who can say with Micah, "And what does the Lord require of thee . . . but to do justly, and to love mercy, and to walk humbly with thy God" (Micah 6:8) and with Jesus, "Blessed are the peacemakers"

(Matthew 5:9). Those who follow Micah and Jesus are no propounders of absolutes and no foes of dialogue.

DISTINGUISHING BETWEEN WHAT SCHOOLS CAN DISCUSS AND WHAT THEY CAN ADVOCATE

That civic dialogue requires us to practice conversational restraint in public dialogue constrains the ideas schools can advance. We will be unable to advance doctrines that can have no public justification. Moreover, the idea of conversational restraint should inhibit us from appealing to our more partisan views in arguing for public educational policies. However, it is crucial to note that this places no restrictions on what can be discussed in educational contexts. Unhappily, we often treat curricular decisions as questions about what truths (and pursuantly, whose truths) will be taught. That doing so will produces intense battles about the curriculum is evident. If we insist on viewing the curriculum as a collection of truths to be advanced rather than as a set of topics to be discussed, it is hard to see that we will be able to deal with many issues at all. What view shall we advance about homosexuality—that it is a sin or an alternative lifestyle? It hardly seems that we can say either.

From this reasoning, we could advance neither view since it is unlikely that an educational policy to advance either view could be justified apart from some partisan and nonpublic grounds. Note, however, that it is possible to argue for gay rights on public grounds apart from any convictions about whether homosexuality is a sin or an alternative lifestyle, just as it is possible to argue that Protestants and Catholics have equal rights apart from any convictions about transubstantiation.

Educational dialogue is an alternative. Dialogue requires us to view the curriculum as questions and resources for their discussion, not as truths to be taught. Such an approach to the curriculum will be difficult and threatening. The difficulty lies in finding ways to represent the many diverse voices on the many issues we need to discuss in a way that is broadly seen as fair to different views.

Educative dialogue, unlike civic dialogue, is not subject to dialogical restraint. Civic discussions are ultimately about the use of public power. The virtues of conversational restraint and an overlapping consensus are that cooperation becomes possible despite enduring and deep disagreement because public decisions are made in a way that avoids coercing people's deepest convictions. Freedom of conscience is the core value. However, educative dialogue need not coerce. I am not so naive as to suppose that there are no issues of power involved in dialogue. However, that something is put on the table for open discussion coerces no one's belief or action.

Freedom of conscience is not threatened. Indeed, it is abetted. Unrestrained dialogue provides us an opportunity to test our convictions and to change them if need be, but it does not coerce belief. It may help us to understand and to tolerate those with whom we disagree, but it does not compel belief. It is threatening only if we cannot find fair ways to represent a diversity of voices. It is threatening only to those who are unwilling to have their views subjected to criticism.

It needs to be emphasized that conversational restraint does not take controversial issues off the table even when issues of public policy are being debated. Rather it seeks shared ground for discussing them. And it most assuredly does not require or ask that we avoid controversy in public educational forums when no public decision is envisioned. Indeed, in such contexts, it does not even restrain us from arguing from a partisan perspective. In educational debates what is sought is mutual understanding and the truth of the matter. Such debates often must argue about and from basic principles and commitments.

DIALOGUE DEPENDS ON AN ADEQUATE GROUNDING OF PEOPLE'S PERSPECTIVES

It is commonly observed that dialogue is difficult if people cannot be gotten to understand the views of their opponents. Surely this is true. It is less commonly noted that dialogue is also difficult if people do not know their own traditions. I have found that many of those with intense feelings about abortion are unable to get beyond asserting clichés about baby killing or women's right to control their bodies to a coherent articulation of the metaphysics of the fetus that is assumed by their claims. I have had numerous discussions with Cornell undergraduates, an otherwise bright and well-educated group, that suggest that religious students (and certainly not they only) have only the most superficial grasp of the richness, depth, and complexity of their own traditions and how these traditions might apply to perplexing moral issues.

No doubt there are many causes for such ignorance. We should consider whether one of them is the absence of educational forums in which the substance of our most central commitments are discussed and debated with others who do not hold them. Mill (1859/1956) reminds us that ideas that are not regularly debated degenerate into clichés and lose their meaning even to their own adherents. Perhaps one of the costs of a society in which the slogans of our various faiths are screamed as soundbites on the evening news, but not discussed and debated in its educational institutions, is the degradation of the cognitive contents of these faiths. And perhaps the absolutism and certainty exhibited in such contexts is not only a political weapon but also a veil for ignorance of the grounds of conviction.

DIALOGUE DEPENDS ON
THE VIRTUE OF REASONABLENESS

The key to dialogue is the virtue of reasonableness. We can have dialogues about civic matters that do not threaten freedom of conscience despite the fact that we disagree, if we are willing to argue within the confines of an overlapping consensus and exercise dialogical restraint. We do not need to stereotype each other with labels such as "relativist" and "absolutist." Instead, we can listen to what we actually have to say to one another. We can competently educate if we are willing to allow our children to discuss matters of importance and not feel the need to determine the truth for them in advance. We can value truth more than ideological victory by taking the risk of real argument. If any of these things are to happen, we will need to cultivate the virtue of reasonableness. Reasonableness is the willingness to regulate one's conduct by a dialogically achieved overlapping consensus. It requires us to listen, to argue our view while respecting the bounds of dialogical restraint, to value truth and reasoned discussion, to be willing to cooperate when our view does not prevail and when others respect the overlapping consensus, and to treat others fairly when they are not of our group. It seems of late to be in short supply, but it is the key to a just and stable political order and to good education.

NOTES

1. Here my purpose is to describe more fully the requirements of respecting a fabric of public reason. However, such respect does require people, in some contexts, to set aside their fundamental convictions in order to participate in public dialogue. It might be objected at the outset that this setting aside of convictions already gives the victory to those Hunter calls progressives. Does it? Much depends on the details of a fuller characterization of public reason and on what must be set aside when. Here note: (1) No one is asked to set aside their fundamental convictions so far as their own lives are concerned. Asking people to set aside their fundamental convictions for public purposes means asking them to refrain from making those convictions obligatory or from privileging them for the lives of those who do not share them. (2) All people are asked to set aside their fundamental convictions. Whatever is required is equally required of the progressives, not just the orthodox. (3) This setting aside inherently privileges progressives over the orthodox only if one assumes that tolerance is a progressive, but not an orthodox, doctrine.

Does this setting aside inherently disadvantage anyone? In fact it disadvantages the kind of communitarian who believes that an adequate moral community cannot exist unless its assumptions are the ruling assumptions of the polity. There are a variety of such communitarians. When their moral community is rooted in some national culture, we call them fascists. When it is rooted in religious assumptions, we call them theocrats.

2. Are religious views thus ruled out of the public sphere *ab initio*? And is this consistent with neutrality? Consider what is not ruled out. No view is ruled out of private practice or private speech because it is religious. No policy is ruled out because it is held by some for religious reasons. No policy is ruled out because its justification has historical antecedents in religion. (Since the idea of the separation of church and state, a belief in religious tolerance, and the claim that people are free and equal all have such antecedents, this would seem a compelling requirement.) What is ruled out is political decisions that can have only deeply partisan justifications. What is requested is that this be considered in dialogue.

We must also be clear that insofar as an overlapping consensus is dialogically constructed, arguments that it privileges or disadvantages religious interests must be considered. Thus religious claims must be considered in the construction of any view of public reason.

REFERENCES

Ackerman, B. (1989). Why dialogue? *Journal of Philosophy*, 86(1), 5–22.

Benhabib, S. (1989). Liberal dialogue versus a critical theory of discursive legitimation. In N. L. Rosenblum (Ed.), *Liberalism and the moral life* (pp. 143–156). Cambridge, MA: Harvard University Press.

Hunter, J. (1991). *Culture wars: The struggle to define America*. New York: Basic Books.

McCarthy, T. (1994). Kantian constructivism and reconstructivism: Rawls and Habermas in dialogue. *Ethics*, *105*(1), 44–63.

Mill, J. S. (1956). *On liberty*. New York: Bobbs-Merrill. (Original work published 1859)

Plato. (1957). *Theaetetus* (F. M. Cornford, Trans.). Indianapolis, IN: Bobbs-Merrill.

Raths, L., Harmin, M., & Simon, S. (1966). *Values and teaching: Working with values in the classroom*. Columbus, OH: Merrill.

Rawls, J. (1993). *Political liberalism*. New York: Columbia University Press.

Strike, K. A. (1990). Are secular ethical languages religiously neutral? *The Journal of Law and Politics*, 6(3), 469–502.

Strike, K. A. (1993a). Against values: Reflections on moral language and moral education. *Educational Policy Analysis Archives*, *1*, 13.

Strike, K. A. (1993b). Liberal discourse and ethical pluralism: An educational agenda. In H. A. Alexander (Ed.), *Philosophy of education 1992* (pp. 226–240). Normal: Illinois State University, Philosophy of Education Society.

Strike, K. A. (1994). On the construction of public speech: Pluralism and public reason. *Educational Theory*, *44*(1), 1–26.

Taylor, C. (1992). *Multiculturalism and the politics of recognition: An essay*. Princeton, NJ: Princeton University Press.

PART II

Textbooks: Whose Stories Are to Be Told?

While curriculum scholars have long lamented the reliance on textbooks and despite the emergence of educational technologies ranging from educational television to the Internet, classroom instruction largely remains textbook-driven. Given the centrality and visibility of the text as the principal artifact of the teaching–learning process, it is not surprising that conservative Christians have focused much of their resources during the past few decades on asking, "What stories ought our children be told?"

Here, noted textbook authority Gilbert T. Sewall casts a discerning eye on the failures of earlier textbook critics, such as the "eccentric campaigns" of the Gablers. Arguing that "'Christian' curriculum reform is too often intertwined with cracker-barrel philosophy, folk wisdom, and nativism," Sewall thoughtfully examines contemporary social science textbooks, which, though no longer omitting religion, have fallen prey to presentism, reductionism, and simplification. It is at this juncture that J. Dan Marshall and Joe Kincheloe extend the argument to underscore the reductionism evident in textbook controversies themselves, which have created "oppositional identities" and artificial either/or positions, precluding substantive discussions on how we can "collectively shape questions about public schools, parents' rights, and civic responsibility."

During the dialogue, participants build upon these essays to explore the complexities of textbook use, reactions and accommodations to parental concerns, and the community politics of teachers and texts, as well textual certainties and uncertain conversations.

CHAPTER 5

Religion and the Textbooks

Gilbert T. Sewall

The arrival of such different books as William J. Bennett's *The Book of Virtues* (1993) and James Q. Wilson's *The Moral Sense* (1993)—both sensitive to topics of religion and moral feeling—confirm broad public interest in character morality and ethical training. But controversies about religion's role in public life—and particularly in schools—remain unresolved, as illustrated in the perennial school prayer amendment crusade and multiple curriculum disputes, especially involving "values" and sex. The secular and religious speak radically different civic languages. They rely on different sources of authority—one constitutional, the other theological—to justify their views. The legal nature of separation of church and state is a subtle subject, the range of honorable outlook and disagreement is wide, and no easy meeting of minds is upon the culture and society.

In covering religion's role in history and human life, social studies and health textbooks touch upon sensitive and unsettled issues, both public and private, often with a moral dimension. History and social studies textbooks contain descriptions and judgments about the course of events, societal norms, and personal ideals, subjects on which scholars, educators, and school clients disagree. Many of these disputes are framed around religion.

Some school clients think that moral authority comes from God-given absolutes and the Judeo-Christian canon. Others subscribe to values that emphasize secular experience and the capacity of humans to transform their lives. The contestants are increasingly media-wise and disdainful of their adversaries. Each understands the importance of ideas and beliefs as determinants of prevailing morality, and each is convinced of its moral superiority in decreeing a framework for the nation's children. There are abundant flaws in the Bible-based educational vision articulated by politicized Christian activists. But first, consider the modern spiritual conditions against which conservative Christians are reacting.

For several decades, evangelicals and fundamentalists have suffered great disrespect in the educational and popular press. "True believers usually materialize as a strident voice in favor of a turn-back-the-clock orthodoxy as our only hope against the sinister forces of modernism and progressivism in education," the education writer George R. Kaplan (1994) writes with scorn in the *Phi Delta Kappan*. "If you aren't with them, you might as well be the Antichrist." Kaplan (1994, p. K2) asserts that "clean living, solid academic grounding, and respect for the family" is a descriptor of the Christian Right, whom he calls "paleolithic spear throwers" and many other unpleasant names. He concludes that "there is the suspicion that elements of the Christian right, including some who are active in school matters, are kissing cousins of David Duke, the Posse Comitatus, and various other explicitly racist or 'Aryan' groups and individuals."

The American Civil Liberties Union, People for the American Way, Americans United for Separation of Church and State, Sex Education Information Council of the United States, National Council for the Social Studies, Planned Parenthood, Children's Defense Fund, and PTA have strong views about religion, the social studies curriculum, and the nonacademic mission of schools. In curriculum revision and counsel, these are the agencies that the Association for Supervision and Curriculum Development, American Association of Publishers, and American Library Association heed. Their reach is powerful, for unlike religious conservatives, they have the concordant ear of textbook publishers. Secularist bias permeates the "cultural orientation of a larger category of cultural elites—not only those who design educational curricula, but other arbiters of social taste and opinion," James Davison Hunter (1987, p. 102) observes. But what is that cultural orientation?

Since the 1970s character development has emphasized self-actualization. Therapeutic approaches to education have grown popular. Educators generally feel that subject matter should emphasize and nourish personal choice. They endorse self-expressive behavior. These preferences are rarely questioned by textbook editors and authors. More likely than not, like educators to whom they sell books, textbook makers are inclined to see spirituality through modern or postmodern eyes. Thus *Holt Heath*, a standard high school textbook, presents the religious experience as such:

> Organized religions can help people deal with stress not only by offering spiritual guidance, but also by helping people feel part of a community. In this way, members of churches, synagogues, and other religious communities may find the support group they need to cope with the stressors in their lives. (Greenberg & Gold, 1994, p. 208)

Powerful cultural icons challenge and mock older religious traditions. When Madonna frolics among burning crosses on MTV, her producers understand full well the shock and power—and appeal—of desacralization. Raw, rebellious, and violent spectacles buzz into everyday life, on television and in the shopping mall, they act as graphic primers of popular culture. They tumble into public schools. More vividly than textbooks, they provide unpleasant lessons about "secular" society, behavior, habit, and inclination.

As a result, many conservative Christian parents—as well as a smaller number of Jewish and Muslim ones—seek textbook reform or, perhaps, private educational alternatives, where closed moral systems are protected by law. Some turn to home schooling. It is easy to pretend that religion is only a matter of taste, a "lifestyle," but any clear reading of history proves otherwise. From religions flow legend and lore, moral systems, and aphorisms of life. Hunter (1987) has observed:

> For the individual, religion provides a meaning system offering a sense of purpose and meaning, a stable set of moral coordinates to guide everyday life, as well as mechanisms to help the individual cope with the traumatic experiences of suffering, pain, and death. (p. 109)

What activates "people of faith" are orchestrated legal and institutional challenges that seek to expunge their deepest beliefs from the nation's schools. Organizations such as the American Civil Liberties Union (ACLU), the National Education Association, and even the National Council of Churches have been effective in using the federal courts to secularize public education. Many Christians of various denominations now believe that the ACLU and its allies have purposively driven Christmas and all things Christian out of schools, a false perception that nonetheless has profound political repercussions. The religious component of Thanksgiving seems also on its way out of the curriculum, but Kwanzaa, an African harvest celebration, now seeks equal time in some urban schools. Some Christians believe that holy days are consciously undermined by pagan countercelebrations, and as a result of these protests, strangely, Halloween is becoming a taboo holiday in some jurisdictions.

For more than a decade, religious conservatives have complained that schools, the news media, and the courts have discriminated against them in a way that would not be tolerated if ethnicity, disability, or sexual orientation set them apart. In their children's textbooks and classrooms they have seen that the Ten Commandments are out and Native American creation myths and self-esteem pledges are in. They worry that schools are deleting religion from history and social studies and, in the process, are denying children the opportunity to learn how religion has affected the development of this country and world events, past and present.

THE GABLERS AND THE RUTHERFORD INSTITUTE

An early spearhead of the Christian fight against secular humanism and the pollution of textbooks was the Education Research Associates of Longview, Texas. In the late 1970s Mel and Norma Gabler, Christian folk heroes, became eponyms of right-wing textbook "extremism" and "censorship" in the national press. They have conducted campaigns against secular humanism and textbook accuracy. Until well into the 1980s the Gablers were able to exert virtual veto power over the Texas Education Agency, the largest purchaser of textbooks in the nation. Christian activists like the Gablers view secular humanism as an assault on sacred truth, part of a conspiratorial program of indoctrination in the schools to wean children away from God and moral right. "Humanism is faith in man instead of God," says one Gabler (1988) publication entitled *Humanism/Moral Relativism in Textbooks*. According to the Gabler schema, humanism has promoted situational ethics; evolution; sexual freedom, including public school sex education courses; and internationalism. In 1988, another Gabler broadside maintained that secular humanism promotes a Darwinian, anti-biblical, individualistic, relativistic, sexually permissive, statist, materialistic, and morally dissolute mindset.

The Gablers have done curriculum reform no service, from their deformation of the Texas market in the 1970s to their specious crusade against textbook accuracy in 1992. Their reductive definitions and eccentric campaigns long ago offended and alienated discerning intellectuals, including "people of faith." They have reinforced moderate and liberal prejudice against the "Christian" educational complaint. The Gablers' populist crusade has been superseded by high-technology, computer-based, direct-mail, action-oriented enterprises, often Pentecostal in spirit, eager to make textbooks conform to what they determine to be "Christian" values in a "Christian" nation, making skilled appeals aimed at believers who are impressionable or ill-educated or who resist modernity. This Christian resistance is no longer new, but it is still not well understood by educational leaders or textbook publishers, concentrated in research universities and cosmopolitan areas, who exhibit their own provincialism, driven as they often are by their own ideologies and crusades. Such Christian activism misunderstands or resents the loss of Bible-backed character education in schools, curricula, and textbooks, as well as in the "extracurriculum" and "ethos" that determine campus "climate." It manifests its anxieties and desires sometimes in peculiar ways that make traditional and "mainstream" Christians uncomfortable with their coreligionists' reductive program of educational reform. At the outer margins, these Christians provide an easy target for "Christian-bashers" and repel nonreligious parents who may share Christian complaints about school ethos and lessons.

The Rutherford Institute, based in Charlottesville, Virginia, is the most active Christian legal group in the nation, according to *The Wall Street Journal* (Gerlin, 1994). Like all change agents engaged in political-cultural discourse, the institute tries to use the legal system as a lever of policy, and it funds itself through direct-mail campaigns. The bulk of the legal work is done by a nationwide network of more than 500 legal volunteers, mostly conservative Christian men who share a belief that modern society has grown increasingly hostile to religious people. The Rutherford Institute is nonpartisan only in name, using "worst-case" stories to make "pro-family" appeals, and from sex education to parental rights, its focus is often on the local school district. In 1991, the Rutherford Institute generated $5 million in revenues from unrestricted public donations, of which $2.8 million was spent for informational materials and activities that included fundraising appeals, a direct-mail effort that generated a surplus of about $275,000 in income over expenditures according to its published records.

Since 1990, the Rutherford Institute has helped to orchestrate a textbook war against school boards all over the nation, charging that an elementary language arts textbook series, entitled *Impressions*, originally published by Holt, Rinehart & Winston in 1987—which includes stories about witches and magic—contains a demonic subtext. In this claim the Rutherford Institute was joined by Focus on the Family, which during the 1990–1991 academic year ran several prominent articles in its publication, *Citizen*. The Rutherford Institute was also joined by Citizens for Excellence in Education, an organization based in Orange County, California, and committed to Christian activism in school board policy. (Citizens for Excellence in Education gained attention during the 1990 California textbook adoption hearings, as it objected to the lack of Christian advocacy in the Houghton Mifflin textbook series.)

The *Impressions* series for elementary school children, developed in Canada in the early 1980s, was one of 17 programs adopted by California in 1987. Most of the reading selections were innocuous, and a few, charming. At the very worst, in the effort to be lively, up to date, and vivid, one volume was guilty of a minor lapse of taste in a parody of "The Twelve Days of Christmas." What happened in Walla Walla, Washington, and many other school districts between 1990 and 1992 demonstrates the intensity and wrong-headedness of some Christian-inspired textbook wars.

In 1991, in the Walla Walla school district, 2,769 children attended grades K–5. A local group calling itself Citizens for Active Responsibility in Education (CARE), a group of 45 parents, objected to the *Impressions* series. CARE was represented by attorney John Herrig, who made formal charges to the school board, in the name of the Rutherford Institute of Washington, that the language arts series promoted witchcraft in its readings. Moreover, Herrig contended that witchcraft is an established religion. Thus, he maintained, the use of the series violates both law and district policies that prohibit the promotion of any religion in public schools. On March 29, the Walla Walla school district heard an appeal to remove the *Impressions* series.

Herrig presented his charges to an eight-member committee of district administrators and staff, who refuted witchcraft charges in a standing-room-only event. Threatening a lawsuit, Herrig reminded the district that a court battle would cost them an estimated $250,000. Within the week, a political scientist at a local liberal arts college threatened to sue the Walla Walla school district if the *Impressions* series was removed from district classrooms. He alerted and sought legal assistance from the ACLU. Four days later, the panel unanimously recommended that *Impressions* be maintained in classrooms, a view that the school board certified several weeks later. CARE had by then identified 170 objectionable passages in *Impressions*, including stories that were "occult, fear-producing and depressing" (Walla Walla *Union Bulletin*, 1991, p. 2). The superintendent attempted to placate parents who opposed *Impressions* by offering to excise material from the series or present alternative material. The *Impressions* battle has now been fought in many locales, including California, New Mexico, Mississippi, and Maryland, at great cost and to no valid purpose.

The Rutherford Institute, Citizens for Excellence in Education, and other partisan Christian groups have cited the following curricula as part of an agenda to undermine the fiber and wholesomeness of American children: drug education, death education, values clarification, global education, the study of socialism, the theory of evolution, and the look–say method of reading. In the literature of the Christian Right, environmentalism, feminism, abortion, disarmament, and animal rights are also declared anathema. To repeat, such rallying points on the political edge do not generally reflect—in fact, they distort—the normative desires of most traditional Christians in school reform, who are more interested in academic rigor, good manners, and human decency than in militant creationism.

No doubt a few Christians really believe such things, but inflammatory charges excite the ignorant and have the unfortunate side effect of allowing antireligionists to dismiss the devout collectively as ignorant or deranged. "Christian" curriculum reform is too often intertwined with cracker-barrel philosophy, folk wisdom, and nativism. It can be resentful or hostile toward science, philosophy, modern knowledge, and, occasionally, the constitutional premise of American religious pluralism. By chasing phantoms or worse, high-profile Christian fundamentalists alienate nonreligious parents, who may share their distress about the moral confusion in today's classrooms.

On the other hand conservative Christians have alerted a broader public to trendy subject matter, ideologies, and thought systems introduced into educational materials, notably nonhistorical social studies textbooks that are indifferent or hostile to traditional creeds and mores.

A CONTEMPORARY CRITIQUE OF CIVICS AND HISTORY TEXTS

In 1985, and again in 1990, critiques of textbooks from Paul Vitz of New York University and Warren A. Nord of the University of North Carolina gained wide attention from scholars and educators. The 1989 bicentennial of the Bill of Rights commemorated U.S. religious freedom as the "first right," and celebrated it in the spirit of American pluralism and "diversity." Statements issued at that time by influential First Amendment organizations such as People for the American Way and Americans United for Separation of Church and State complained about the diminution of religious content in textbooks (in several subjects and at all grade levels, not only in social studies). The state of California responded in a nationally recognized effort to restore and amplify the subject of religion in the state social studies K–8 curriculum, then under revision.(California's 1987 history framework for elementary and secondary grades included lessons on five world religions—Christianity, Judaism, Islam, Hinduism, and Buddhism.) In developing a new series to fit this state content mandate, Houghton Mifflin produced a series that treated world religions in depth and, by common agreement, with success. (At the California textbook adoption hearings in 1990, the books nonetheless came under sharp attack from isolated Christian, Jewish, and Muslim activists.) In history textbooks and curricula, the study of religion has expanded in the last 10 years.

Despite this progress, most Christian activists remain deeply disturbed by textbook content in history and the social studies. A few are upset because textbooks do not emphasize Christianity in U.S. and world history; many more are upset because nonhistorical social studies textbooks acquiesce to or promote lifestyles at variance with old-fashioned standards of personal conduct. In March 1994, religion fueled a Texas-based textbook controversy, which led Holt, Rinehart & Winston to withdraw a newly revised health education text from consideration for state adoption after organized Christians convinced the Texas Education Agency to tone down text and remove graphics (e.g., on anal sexuality). This exit was an unprecedented move in the nation's largest state market. It indicated that mass-market school publishers were increasingly willing to downsize and aban-

don controversial areas of curriculum when the multiple demands of interest groups, increased costs, and changing state mandates made some curriculum areas economically unattractive.

Beginning in 1992, the American Textbook Council asked reviewers—
authors, historians, education analysts, and teachers among them—to examine 19 leading secondary-level civics and history textbooks to see what
changes and improvements, if any, have been made in the way these textbooks deal with religion. The Council wanted to know whether current
civics and history textbooks recognize religion's role in individual human
action, in communities, and in cultures, past and present, or whether, as
some claim, religion has been banished from the classroom.

"Nonhistorical" social studies courses—covering topics such as psychology, family life, and personal awareness—seem to be edging out the study
of history in many U.S. schools. Thus, the reviewers also evaluated so-called
alternative social studies textbooks—especially those dealing with environmental awareness, health, psychology, self-esteem, and values—and sought
to determine how these materials were affecting the study of ethics, moral
behavior, and other issues that traditionally have been religion's domain.

According to the survey, the most widely used U.S. and world history
textbooks cover major religious events and movements—including non-
Western religions—more thoroughly than they did as little as 10 years ago.
Indeed, the public perception—often cited by those on the Christian Right—
that religion is omitted from U.S. and world history textbooks is simply out
of date. In the 1980s publishers responded to complaints from textbook
critics and First Amendment groups alike and introduced history textbooks
with expanded, if imperfect, coverage of religion.

What can today's students expect to learn from these texts? For one
thing, they can learn that the founding of America's original colonies came
about because English Puritans, Roman Catholics, and other Christian dissenters emigrated from England in search of tolerant surroundings. For
another, they can learn that religious passion in different forms shaped the
thinking and actions of social reform movements and social reformers from
the Abolitionists to Martin Luther King, Jr.

In world history classes, students can learn that Christianity reigned
supreme from the time of Constantine to the time of Martin Luther—a full
12 centuries of influence on European affairs and culture. And they can learn
that Islam and its theocratic system of government swept through the Eastern world into Africa and Spain beginning in the 7th century; that the Scientific Revolution and the Enlightenment of the 18th century challenged a
religious way of looking at the world; and that Buddhism and Hinduism have
shaped the cosmologies of diverse Asian cultures and remain profoundly
influential in the lives of believers around the world today.

A look at the entries under the word *religion* in textbook indexes is revealing as well. In Scott, Foresman's 1992 edition of *American Voices*, for example, the index item for the topic "religion" includes references to the Anglican Church, anti-Catholic and anti-Semitic bigotry, the Church of Jesus Christ of Latter-Day Saints, religion and the constitution, religion and immigrants, the Yom Kippur War, and Zen Buddhism, among others. As for world history texts, Harcourt Brace Jovanovich's 1990 edition of *World History: People and Nations* and Scott, Foresman's 1990 edition of *History and Life* provide fairly extensive coverage. Among the entries to be found in these texts: religion in Babylonia—and in Safavid Persia—as well as religious liberty in England, the Mogul Empire, the Netherlands, Palestine, and Prussia.

Even a cursory glance at today's history textbooks shows that the texts cover Christianity and other world religions more completely than in the past. This doesn't mean, however, that there are no problems with the way history textbooks treat religion. Textbooks seldom explain religion's role in shaping human thought and action or as a motivating agent of culture, politics, and ethics. Yet without such a discussion of religion, educators are asking students to work a jigsaw puzzle with a few of the pieces missing.

In addition, textbooks commonly try to sidestep any discussion of religious-inspired hatred (the Holocaust is only one example). Religion is almost always presented as a political or social entity, rarely as an intellectual or moral force with individual and public consequences. And because textbooks tend to summarize complex theology rapidly with an eye toward not offending anyone, the passages on religion sometimes are hard to understand.

In world history books, explanations of how Christianity grew from its 15th-century confines in Europe and the Mediterranean to the world's largest religion today are cursory and opaque. In the case of their treatment of missionaries in the Americas, Asia, and Africa from the 16th century onward, these textbooks are also biased. They typically reduce such missionary zeal to a mere example of Western cultural imperialism.

Textbooks cover contemporary religion in oblique and misleading ways, too. In fact, reviewers found that textbook coverage of contemporary religion in the United States is uniformly scant, usually unsympathetic, and sometimes inaccurate. History textbooks are flawed by presentism—that is, interpreting the past by contemporary standards. The result is failure to appreciate vast differences regarding time, place, and culture. Presentism is offensive—trivializing and cheapening the role of religion in the human past—when it attempts to recast the religious impulse into the secular experience of contemporary American youth. One text, for example, includes this misguided activity exercise: "Martin Luther's 95 Theses listed his ideas and criticisms of the Catholic Church. Think of ways your school could be improved.

Write a list of theses describing your ideas and encouraging your classmates to support your reforms. Try to include possible reforms that would affect everyone at school, not just you" (Holt & O'Connor, 1990, p. 289).

What about so-called nonhistorical social studies texts and materials— the kind used in psychology, self-esteem, family life, and personal awareness classes? More and more, these subjects are displacing history in the curriculum. And more and more they are a cause for worry. These texts contain material that a large number of parents, especially religious ones, complain about, saying that the content of these courses challenges not only what they hold to be sacred but what they consider to be private.

Textbooks in psychology, human awareness, self-esteem, and other nonhistorical social studies often challenge traditional belief systems. They frequently champion "insurgent" values "largely concerned with the rights of the individual—with freedom from oppression, from confinement, from hierarchy, from authority, from stricture, from repression, from rigid rule-making, and from the status quo," as Thomas Byrne Edsall and Mary D. Edsall (1991, p. 61) have described them.

Such texts contain prescriptive moral advice that some school clients are certain to find tasteless, perhaps even offensive or profane. Social workers, counselors, psychologists, and nutritionists—a faculty who are not much interested in history and civics per se—seek therapeutic materials in schools that tolerate—or even demand respect for—coarse and hollow lifestyles. Moreover, these "affective" materials are usually blind to cosmic and transcendent issues that have perplexed and fortified civilizations since their beginnings, issues that are better studied through the lens of history and philosophy. Health textbooks emphasize matters very private to most students, at least when they are in public places, like school classrooms. Objections by parents to sex education textbook content often involve some that are broader than religious in nature. The matter may begin with religion— since Christianity, Judaism, and Islam all teach that sex is a sacred treasure to be enjoyed inside the bond of marriage, and since certain moral principles are imbedded in Mosaic and other religion-based law—but these issues extend to matters of lifestyle, decorum, and probity. Many parents who are not religious at all seek to protect the innocence and virtue of their own children—and bridle at what passes for "realism" in "affective education."

These parents simply don't like curricula that convey a problem-filled view of the world, or very possibly of a libertine world in which promiscuity, drug use, and various forms of depression and abuse are taken to be basic, ubiquitous aspects of juvenile life. *Holt Health* asks students a "critical thinking" question: "Why might a person who has abused a drug be more likely to get AIDS than a person who has not?" (Greenberg & Gold, 1994, p. 249). For parents who oppose condom distribution, in fact, who expect their children to learn how to read and write at school, not how to avoid AIDS or behave sexually, such inquiries are inappropriate and objectionable, likely on religious grounds. Can it really be surprising that some people act out their opposition in organized church groups and district-level school board coups?

CONCLUSION

Religions include the effort to define, codify, and promote the good life, to separate right from wrong, to explain the cosmos and the soul. Religions have provided systems by which to live, which is why people defend or denounce them more passionately than mere facts and ideas. Because of their claims on the human spirit, religions will inevitably affect the workings of a community and the quality of public life.

Religions provide rituals and compasses, giving meaning and direction to life. "For the vast majority of people, today as always in human history, the ground of their morality is religious," Peter L. Berger (1989, p. 34) has said. "Most of contemporary humanity, including most Americans, derives its morality from religion." As Stephen L. Carter noted in *The Culture of Disbelief* (1993), a double standard now operates in society and culture, whereby media and courts, sympathetic to the claims of ethnicity, disability, or sexual orientation, for example, vigorously exclude traditional religious thought from respectable discourse on public life and the education of the young. Textbooks are important cultural signifiers, and as symbols they generate a great deal of controversy, especially in an age of moral and ideological conflict. Given the ideals and aspirations of many Americans, jurists and educators trying to litigate Judeo-Christian—and all religious— traditions out of school life will face unrelenting resistance.

REFERENCES

Bennett, W. (1993). *The book of virtues.* New York: Simon & Schuster.

Berger, P. (1989, October 22). Salvation through sociology [Review of *Whose keeper? Social science and moral obligations*]. *The New York Times,* p. 34.

Carter, S. (1993). *The culture of disbelief: How American law and politics trivialize religious devotion.* New York: Basic Books,

Edsall, T., & Edsall, M. (1991). Race. *Atlantic, 267*(5), 61.

Gabler, M. (1988). *Humanism/moral relativism in textbooks.* Longview, TX: Educational Research Analysts.

Gerlin, A. (1994, February 17). With free help, the religious turn litigious. *The Wall Street Journal,* p. B1.

Greenberg, J., & Gold, R. (1994). *Holt health*. Austin, TX: Holt, Rinehart & Winston.

Holt, S., & O'Connor, J. (1990). *Exploring world history*. Englewood Cliffs, NJ: Globe.

Hunter, J. (1987, Fall). "America's fourth faith": A sociological perspective on secular humanism. *This World, 19*, 101–110.

Kaplan, G. (1994). Shotgun wedding: Notes on public education's encounter with the new Christian Right. *Phi Delta Kappan, 75*(8), 1–12.

The Rutherford Institute. (1991). *Statement of support and revenue, expenses, and changes in fund balances*. Charlottesville, VA: Author.

Walla Walla *Union Bulletin*. (1991, May 21).

Wilson, J. (1993). *The moral sense*. New York: Free Press.

CHAPTER 6

It's Not About the Books:
Textbook Controversies and the
Need for Uncertain Conversations

J. Dan Marshall and Joe Kincheloe

The combination of compulsory public schooling, diversities (geographic, cultural, economic, spiritual, etc.) among and within the public they serve, and the need to produce and select curricula for use in these schools has always resulted, and will continue to result, in controversy over textbooks in this country. We see this conflict as both important and problematic: Important because it offers an opportunity to engage in dialogue crucial to the health and success of the public schooling mission within a changing culture; problematic because textbook conflicts have become polarized to the point of preventing these crucial dialogues. Without a collective commitment to engage in "uncertain conversations" and a willingness to transcend their current, deeply oppositional nature, textbook decisions will continue to float rudderless on an ever-changing sea of popular preference, political piety, and professional prerogative.

Regardless of one's status or particular perspective(s) on the matter, any serious search for information related to school textbook choice yields titles like "Confrontation and Alienation," "The Textbook Wars," "Are Textbooks Harming Your Children?," and "Public Education in Shreds." The times and places where varied groups come together to discuss public school textbook selection and use have indeed become battlegrounds. Because textbooks serve as the de facto curriculum in so many schools, they have become manifestations of basic curriculum decisions (i.e., decisions related to the knowledge and experiences determined to be most valuable for students). And no less important than the particular knowledge and experiences contained within what James Moffett (1988) calls this "purchased curriculum" are the values, attitudes, and beliefs that textbooks represent. Thus selecting textbooks—indeed, choosing any curricular materials—requires value-oriented decisions, for all curricula come value-laden. These are not offered as pedagogical secrets but rather as presuppositions important to our position here.

Because all curricula are value-laden, we understand conflicts over textbooks as representations of difference among people's values and understandings of their world—not as specific concerns about certain stories, pictures, or words per se found in textbooks. In short, it's not about the books! Rather, these are struggles about foundational questions concerning that which is true, good, or "real" not only about textbook content but about public schooling and civic life itself. Moreover, these are confrontations about the balance of power and authority concerning the educational rights and responsibilities of families, schools, and communities. As such, textbook controversies play a necessary role in a democratic nation's effort to educate its youth. However, when understood as battles, these occasions are quickly reduced in scope and become oppositional in nature; interest in questions about shared reality, cultural change, or the civic good turns into contests of us versus them, good versus evil, orthodoxy versus progressivism, right versus wrong, pressure groups versus censors, and, more often than not in recent years, the righteous versus the godless.

CREATING OPPOSITIONAL IDENTITIES

This reduction to dichotomous binaries is predictable, in part, because of the identities that are given to and sometimes accepted by textbook protesters. Sewall's illustration (Chapter 5) of George Kaplan's caustic hyperbole makes this point well with respect to conservative Christians. Religious believers who protest textbooks seem to have made it easy for others to *deridingly* name them as conservative, fundamentalist, born-again, or evangelical. Religious protesters, conversely, often find it as seemingly easy to name their opponents, most commonly as liberal educators, social engineers, or secular humanists. Ironically, such naming practices ignore the important differences of members not only within each side (e.g., few Baptists or Catholics would agree that members of their faith could be understood as a single entity) but between each side (e.g., public schools are populated by a good many teachers who would identify themselves as religious).

Regardless of the issue, these now-labeled participants are identified as either part of the problem or part of the solution—depending, of course, upon one's position. With warring factions in place, textbook protests inevitably *prevent* conversation because these sides, as in the courtroom, must now represent oppositional positions relative to a situation in which a decision (e.g., how to represent women in textbooks) must be made in either/or fashion. With this a priori negation of any real common ground or ability to complicate the nature of the discussion, participants find themselves with no alternative but to press their oppositional views. As Bates (1993) puts it: "What PAW [People for the American Way] considers a derogatory, hidebound portrayal of women, Concerned Women for America [CWA] finds positive and appropriate" (p. 226). These oppositional identities—necessary in every war and courtroom—have by now become overly simplistic caricatures that enable us to *un*complicate not only the people involved but the ideas and questions of central concern. As long as textbook protests remain binary and oppositional, such caricatured oppositional identities for their participants will remain prerequisite, winning will remain the primary purpose of the interaction, and the issues at hand will remain overly simplistic and peripheral to more important and substantive ones.

SIMPLIFYING THE ISSUES

Along with the uncomplicated oppositional identities of their participants, the corresponding oversimplification of questions and issues at the heart of textbook controversies is another of the predictable aspects of such protests that work to ensure their dichotomous and oppositional nature while simultaneously hiding their deeply complex and important nature. "Secular humanism" provides a good example of this.

One can find numerous sorts of content-based textbook criticisms offered by a growing number of proponents and opponents, many of whom represent conservative Christian groups. Often, specific textbook criticisms serve as concrete manifestations of what many call secular humanism. Secular humanism is said to be a religion (or at least a coherent philosophical belief system) that represents the antithesis of theism and is believed actually to be an anti-Christian perspective on life. Its existence is said to be manifested in most contemporary U.S. cultural, social, and political changes—ranging from legalized abortion and evolutionary theory to respect for pluralism and laws banning school prayer—although it has no identifiable leadership or practitioners (beyond members of the American Humanist Association and signers of the 1933 *Humanist Manifestos I* and the 1973 *Humanist Manifesto II*).

Belief in the existence and nature of secular humanism encourages conservative Christian textbook protesters to overly simplify and reduce the concerns they have about actual textbook content as well as the values, beliefs, and attitudes such content represents. Here's one simple example of how it usually works: Caring, honest, sincere parents and citizens rapidly move from (1) concerns about a story in which a young person steals an item and is not punished, to (2) concerns about a storied situation that appears to encourage readers to ignore questions of "right and wrong" in lieu of considering the context and circumstances of some decision-making situation, to (3) the eventual position that such stories are representations of secular humanism. In the end, the entire encounter—and all that it might possibly represent—is tragically shrunken in essence, with little more than a set of test questions about "secular humanism" remaining.

CREATING SILENCE

Allowing important public discussion about our changing American culture and the associated issues of power, authority, and civic responsibility relative to public schooling to devolve into a litigious duel over the existence of secular humanism or various other common and perennial textbook concerns is a problem shared by everyone participating in textbook protests. Preventing such discussion often leads to forced silence. It may be helpful to note that the very court decision which first led to the legal ruling that (temporarily) *established* the existence of secular humanism was itself prompted by a form of legal silencing.

In brief: Ishmael Jaffree, an African American attorney in Alabama, sued the Mobile County School District in 1983 because his children were being asked to pray in school. He was opposed in this case by a group of self-identified born-again Christians who argued that humanism, not school prayer, was the central issue in the trial. The judge, Brevard Hand, ruled against Jaffree "and in a footnote warned that if he was overturned, he would reopen the case, rearrange the parties, and try the born-again parents' claim that humanist religion had infected the schools. In 1984 he was overturned" (D'Antonio, 1989, pp. 119–120).

The case resulting from Judge Hand's promise, *Smith et al. v. Mobile County School District*, was tried in 1987. In a class action which the plaintiff's lawyers described as a "civil rights case," the suit alleged "that the district was using books that undermined Christianity and promoted an ungodly religion, which they called 'secular humanism'" (D'Antonio, 1989, p. 97). After presiding over *Smith*, Judge Hand ruled in favor of the plaintiffs, determining that secular humanism, as a coherent set of religious ideas, must be barred from the schools along with Christian prayer. Although eventually overruled by the U.S. District Court of Appeals in Atlanta, Hand successfully used his court to force a broadening of discussion and to take seriously the previously silenced Christian issues.

VIEWING THE HALF-FULL GLASS

Over time—and usually in retrospect—the value of creating oppositional "camps" wears thin. One of this country's most disruptive textbook controversies in Hawkins County, Tennessee is illustrative. In *Mozert v. Hawkins County Board of Education* plaintiffs challenged a Holt, Rinehart and Winston Basic Reading series "on the grounds that repeated exposure to the reading series offended their religious beliefs" (Gaddy, Hall, & Marzano, 1996, p. 255). Specific objections included a poem describing imagination as a vehicle for seeing images not observed by our eyes. Here a parent shared her fear that this "was an 'occult practice' for children to use their imagination beyond the boundaries of the Scriptures" (Gaddy, Hall, & Marzano, 1996, p. 34). Despite the community acrimony, one veteran of this textbook conflict concluded that the protesters "were not monsters; they were parents who wanted what they believed was best for their children" (DelFattore, 1992, p. 50). The ultimate and immediate value in naming "us" and "them" rests in its service to the related element of textbook struggles: simplifying the issues. In Hawkins County, the entire controversy centered on the belief in "only two ways to look at reality—Biblical absolutism and secular humanism—and that both are valid to the same degree and on the same terms" (DelFattore, 1992, p. 59).

Yet, as we've pointed out, the resulting forced-choice test questions about the existence of secular humanism (yes/no?), its status as a form of religion or coherent philosophy (yes/no?), or its presence in school curricula and textbooks (yes/no?) successfully serve to side-step far more substantive issues concerning the selection and use of textbooks in schools. As Moffett (1988) notes, in his exploration of the 1974 Kanawah County textbook controversy, textbook protesters

> should *not* have had . . . books crammed down their throats. Avis' daughter should *not* have been forced to do a book report on evolution. A metropolitan school district should *not* have ignored the known feelings and views of part of their constituency. . . . The curriculum should *not* be a standardized thing forced on all alike. (pp. 103–104)

While secular humanism has played an important role in that and other textbook controversies, the issues noted above virtually disappeared from consideration.

Moreover, textbook protests centered on questions of the existence and (religious) nature of secular humanism, to use our example, have silenced dialogue regarding the sacred, spiritual, religious, and metaphysical health of Americans in general and the role of public schools in promoting and sustaining such health. Few deny that ours is a religious nation populated largely by people who believe in some power(s) greater than themselves. Yet this reality—these very beliefs and their integral ties to the social, political, cultural, and economic lives of our country's many and varied believers—is ignored or, as Sewall explains in Chapter 5, confusingly presented in school textbooks.

The time has come for a brave step forward. What if we could agree to discuss the idea that rather than a *religion*, secular humanism is a *vocabulary or language* (Hammond, 1992) employed in textbooks designed to be used in public schools throughout a country with an increasing religious plurality (Corbett, 1994) and a deepening litigious sensitivity to the "wall" between church and state. Such an uncertain conversation would allow all serious discussants to struggle together over a different and more essential set of questions, such as: Is such a language necessary? Is this the preferred or most appropriate vocabulary? Should public schools be empty of religious or spiritual talk? Is it appropriate to hope that schools can, in Nel Noddings's (1993) words, educate for intelligent belief or unbelief?

Name-calling, oversimplifying, and silencing others' voices are damaging habits that all participants must overcome if we are to resurrect our ability to collectively shape questions about public schools, parents' rights, and civic responsibility around the selection and use of public school textbooks. We must begin to build upon the lessons we've learned the hard way. Christian protesters have, as Sewall notes, helped raise everyone's consciousness about textbook content in general and its religious content in particular. Furthermore, despite his disagreement with the visions and actions of those he terms "ultra-fundamentalists," Provenzo (1990) recognizes that their contemporary involvement in textbook protests has

> raised important questions concerning the role that the public schools play in promoting specific political and social ideologies; the rights of parents to determine what their children will learn; and whether or not the schools should teach values. (p. xii)

Sadly, we seldom address such questions these days when considering public school textbooks, largely because textbook conversations have become controversial "culture wars" and "holy wars" featuring easily identifiable and pitifully caricatured protagonists and positions. Each side remains determined to win at all costs—including the intellectual well-being of young people and the overall public good. Ironically, it's not about the textbooks any more; it's about our inability to explore the changing relationships between culture and schooling around questions of stability and change, meaning and truth, modernity and postmodernity. The time for uncertain conversations about school textbooks has arrived.

REFERENCES

Bates, S. (1993). *Battleground: One mother's crusade, the religious Right, and the struggle for control of our classrooms.* New York: Poseidon.

Corbett, J. M. (1994). *Religion in America* (2nd ed.). Englewood Cliffs, NJ: Prentice-Hall.

D'Antonio, M. (1989). *Fall from grace.* New York: Farrar, Straus, & Giroux.

DelFattore, J. (1992). *What Johnny shouldn't read: Textbook censorship in America.* New Haven, CT: Yale University Press.

Gaddy, B., Hall, T., & Marzano, R. (1996). *School wars: Resolving our conflicts over religion and values.* San Francisco: Jossey-Bass.

Hammond, P. E. (1992). *The Protestant presence in twentieth-century America: Religion and political culture.* Albany: State University of New York Press.

Moffett, J. (1988). *Storm in the mountains.* Carbondale: Southern Illinois University Press.

Noddings, N. (1993). *Educating for intelligent belief or unbelief.* New York: Teachers College Press.

Provenzo, E. F. (1990). *Religious fundamentalism and American education: The battle for the public schools.* Albany: State University of New York Press.

Questing for Certainty and Uncertainty: The Role of Teacher and Text

Pritchett: Are the controversies over particular textbook selection caused by the limited choices or the certainty of one's view of the world?

Carper: When we think of texts, there is reason to think of subtexts. In the conflict in Hawkins County, Tennessee, it appears that some were complaining about stories related to witchcraft in the mandated *Impressions* literature series. But it was an underlying certainty of thinking about the world that was most upsetting to these people. Undergirding these stories was an agnostic, existential view of the world.

Pigford: It is not enough for people to accept "I have a right to my truth." They must also accept "I do not have the right to impose my truth on you."

Pritchett: From where I stand the attitude seems to be either "Leave me alone and let my little group and my family have what we want" or "We know what's best for you." Some are more concerned about intrusion; others are more concerned about imposition.

Lindsey: The reason we have a textbook problem is because textbooks are tangible. Parents can grab them. But there is a much larger issue. When I was first teaching in the 1960s, parents did not feel that they had any right to question public schools. As problems have arisen in our society and as people have been more willing to question institutions, parents have become more vocal about textbooks. Now that these people are taking seriously their role in parenting, we as educators do a real disservice when we fail to listen. Day after day we put into kids so much

See the introduction for a description of the conversationalists.

Curriculum, Religion, and Public Education: Conversations for an Enlarging Public Square. Copyright © 1998 by Teachers College, Columbia University. All rights reserved. ISBN 0-8077-3706-2 (pbk.), ISBN 0-8077-3707-0 (cloth). Prior to photocopying items for classroom use, please contact the Copyright Clearance Center, Customer Service, 222 Rosewood Dr., Danvers, MA 01923, USA, tel. (508) 750-8400.

of our values, our ideas, our goals. Is it so awful for parents to want some sort of say in this?

Burgess: People who are employed at my school are religious and, regardless of the curriculum, one's values inevitably come across in the delivery of the curriculum through textbooks.

Pigford: One parent filed a lawsuit against our school system for providing her child the *option* of reading a Newberry Award book. We convened a committee whose job it is to look at texts whenever a complaint occurs and invited her to join. The committee then explained to the parent why the book in question was appropriate. The final decision was that the book would remain on our fourth-grade optional reading list of 120 books. In this situation we sought to listen to the parent's view and, to the extent possible, develop greater sensitivity and create appropriate choices. But we were not willing to remove this book as an option for the other 26,000 students.

Lindsey: Too many times we have rejected parental overtures for involvement in the schools. Out of their frustration, they then listen to others and come back more confrontative but no more knowledgeable about what schools are really doing.

Burgess: I was reading some writing by Robert Simmonds, who said: "School has become a psychological brainwashing organization headed by socialistic-oriented, atheistic philosophy." Perhaps this is the kind of attack Sewall refers to as coming from "the Bible-based vision articulated by politicized Christian activists." As a public school principal, this does *not* describe me.

Pritchett: I have worked with people who simply are misinformed about what is being done at the state level.

Lindsey: I had a mother come to me—she sits on a school district textbook committee and is a fundamentalist Christian—asking what she should know about the *Impressions* reading series. "What is wrong with it?" I was amazed that no one took the time simply to explain what the state meant; they simply wanted to get parents to do something because they didn't want trouble. So, when she looked at this textbook series, is it any wonder that she would throw it out as "dangerous" if it had anything to do with "self-esteem"? Now here is a person who legitimately wanted to help put a good textbook into the curriculum who became needlessly combative.

Sears: Should there be a standard set of textbooks for all students? Should textbook selection occur at the community level?

Lindsey: Public educators have not always been very clear about why they chose certain textbooks and what were the processes they used. So when a group of concerned parents come in and say "We don't like *Impressions*," our first reaction is that this is an "attack" and to stand our ground. Educators don't respond: "Is there some text that is equally as good that will not violate your beliefs?" When public school educators do not do this, then the parents become defensive and a confrontation ensues.

Pritchett: We should give parents and teachers more choices. While there are some practical limitations, technology affords us more opportunities.

Pigford: But right now we do not seem willing to listen or respect the right of others to believe what they believe. People have taken positions which they now must defend. I don't see it so much as the concern for text options as it is an attitude of distrust of public schools.

Sears: Should a particular child be compelled to read a specific text or complete a particular assignment if the parent objects?

Pigford: What is the purpose of schooling? Some persons who have the most concern about the curriculum view schools as places where children go to find truth rather than to seek truth. Now, if schools are places where children seek truth, then educators will give many text options. But many people only want *their* truth to be taught and for their children simply to receive this truth.

Pritchett: Many religions create uncertainty and then fill the gap with their doctrine. Are you suggesting that the purpose of public education is to help people evaluate these doctrines? If so, the fear among some parents is that the religion that they communicate to their children is now open for question.

Murphy: It is a false premise to assume that one can stop uncertainty.

Carper: You can think of religion in two broad ways. First religion as set of well-defined theological beliefs associated with religions such as Protestant Christianity, Judaism, or Catholicism. On a more anthropological level, we might think of religion as that set of beliefs that function as a religion for a particular people or culture such as a civil religion or secular humanism.

Sears: Shouldn't the texts (including supplementary instructional materials) first establish some certainties? Can you base our entire educational system on uncertainty? Shouldn't our textbooks—particularly at the grade school level—establish a foundation of basic beliefs even if they will be challenged later?

Murphy: People sometimes believe that children are too young to think, to engage in dialogue, to hear opposing views—to make up their own minds. But in a democratic society you cannot wait until these children enter high school or college. There is not a "magic age" to treat children like intelligent human beings.

Carper: Using texts—in its broadest sense—in a compulsory government-operated school to instill any particular way of seeing is questionable.

Sears: Doesn't the choice of the text itself send a message? Certainly if we choose to focus on the Druids, the Cherokees, or the Zen masters rather than the Christians, the Anglo-Saxons, or the Renaissance masters—or even give them equal weight—we are sending a message.

Murphy: It is not the text but how the text is approached that is the key. It is the questioning of the text, not its selection, that is most important. That is what I found so useful in the Marshall–Kincheloe essay; we don't want to silence dialogue, we want to foster it. Education must be structured in order that children come away with all sorts of answers, not just one.

Carper: That is my precise point! You are articulating a particular way of seeing the world—relativism.

Murphy: Well, one thing that I have learned is that many conservative Christians are not particularly interested in diversity of ideas or cultures. This influences texts, curriculum, and teaching. In their view, if we are heading rapidly toward Armageddon, then there is little reason to learn about the Druids.

Pritchett: So one's philosophical point of view influences the type of text and materials you might bring into the classroom as a teacher or want to have in the classroom as a parent?

Murphy: Absolutely.

Pritchett: Then how do we resolve your and Professor Carper's views?

Murphy: If people don't want to buy into public schools educating for "intelligent belief or unbelief," as Noddings has detailed, then they should go their own way. I have had the opportunity to read Christian textbooks that clearly articulate fundamentalist views which I would have a hard time bringing into my classroom. The Bob Jones biology text, for example, presents false information as scientific truth: Noah's Flood created mountain ranges including the Alps and the Rockies; dinosaurs lived on the earth simulatenously with humans. T-Rex on the Ark!

Pigford: How texts are presented is probably more important than *what* they are.

Murphy: But when we remove a book or consider its removal, we are sending a message to teachers who become scared of repercussions and will think twice the next time.

Pigford: I think you are probably right that a teacher would think twice before entering another controversy. But the teacher really has to assume responsibility for what she does in the classroom.

Pritchett: But when teachers won't assume that responsibility or take risks, we have a problem.

Pigford: Then much of what we need to do does not have to do with the textbook but with teacher training. Teachers must become informed decision makers.

Murphy: If so, we need to educate teachers to think about educating for intelligent belief or unbelief, not to train them to administer standardized tests or dutifully follow the textbook. Fear and anger are too often the underlying gestalt among teachers.

Pigford: Sometimes people who are in those positions do not yet have the strength, fortitude, conviction, maturity, or support to educate for intelligent belief or unbelief.

Sears: The role that you advocate for the teacher seems to be at variance with what many, if not a majority of, parents see as the role of public schools, teachers, and textbooks: Reinforce those beliefs embraced in the home and shared by the community.

Murphy: I am not advocating that teachers use texts and other materials to manipulate kids to not believe what they are taught at home or at school. The decision to believe or not believe must come from the individual. Schools do not exist simply to impose a narrow set of beliefs because that is what their culture, community, or parents wish. Texts must open up the world to students.

Burgess: In looking at textbook selection, I don't see how I can go against the values and beliefs of my community. I need to inform the community of what we are doing at my school, and my teachers cannot proselytize children. Teachers must present information and expose them to ideas but not challenge family or church beliefs.

Murphy: I used to teach eighth-grade reading and we had this really terrible, insulting textbook with selected excerpts from individuals like

Martin Luther King that included his flowery oratory but ignored its angry substance. I told my class, "This is really a terrible book. What do you want to read?" They told me they wanted to study civil rights. It was wonderful! We developed a six-week course. They read "Letter from Birmingham Jail"; they viewed "Eyes on the Prize"; they wrote essays.

Burgess: In our texts, are we trying to get them to believe in something or simply understand something? It was interesting that you gave as the example Dr. King, because there are not many parents who will object to him. He's "safe" for Caucasians. He's been canonized; we like him; he feels good.

Carper: What is so attractive about Dr. King for people?

Burgess: I don't think it was so much that he was attractive but that there were other contemporaries, such as Malcolm X, who were not attractive. It's not so much that he is liked, revered, or love—he is simply less objectionable.

Sears: What if a black parent came in and asked that her child not study Dr. King but instead learn more about Malcolm X, H. Rap Brown, or Louis Farrakhan?

Burgess: I would tell that parent that there is certain subject matter that we deal with in the curriculum and that she should seek out that teacher and ask that her child do an independent study. Interestingly, one of the students in my middle school is a convert to the Nation of Islam. I met with the student and told him I would bring him some books I had at home on Malcolm X and the Nation of Islam. In the past few weeks, we have had an interesting dialogue as he begins to understand some of the larger issues.

Pigford: Carolyn, what would have happened had you received a letter from a parent who objected to your spending so much time on African American culture and history? It stated, "This is not the prescribed curriculum or text. I want it ceased immediately." I got a letter like that last year.

Murphy: I would have gone to my principal, who would have supported me. I should mention that down the hall another teacher's class was reading *To Kill a Mockingbird* and one of the white parents did object. They pulled the student out of that class. Guess where they put him? In my class!

Sears: What you describe tends to support the evangelicals' suspicion: "Yes, you'll put us on the committees. Yes, you'll listen to our complaints. But the secular humanistic engine that drives public education is still running in high gear."

Murphy: It was the children deciding what they wanted to learn.

Sears: But you chose to deviate from the standard curriculum.

Murphy: Children must be brought into the dialogue and into the decision-making process. They have minds, they have wills, they have interests, they have needs.

Pritchett: What if they chose to study the New Testament texts of John or Matthew?

Murphy: That would be great!

Sears: It sounds as though people around this table are willing to make accommodation for persons who share different philosophical beliefs, but the train of public education is still going to speed down its tracks toward it final destination. The school curriculum will include Martin Luther King but not Malcolm X. The school curriculum will have its list of 120 "optional" books without deleting any of the objectionable texts.

Burgess: Those who prescribe the texts and curriculum are people generally who have the political and economic clout to hire and fire. The train will *not* go off the track; and *you* may just get tossed off the train!

Pigford: What will derail the train is when large numbers of persons want to take the train toward a different destination. But given the diversity of communities, you will have people who want to go to different destinations. The metaphor of the train implies that public schools are insensitive, but in actuality we are trying to bend over backwards. A few years ago, I'm not sure that we would even have accommodated the Nation of Islam student or the parent who objected to the optional book reading. If we keep making these small accommodations to a host of movements, our curriculum will look dramatically different.

Sears: Who makes text and curriculum decisions?

Pigford: The train is driven by legislators, not educators. During the past 10 years everything was legislated: the tests, the objectives, the texts. Clearly these drove our curriculum.

Sears: What is the role of the parents and what is the role of educators in text and curriculum decisions?

Pigford: Clearly from the time I was in public schools, it has changed dramatically in terms of who and what is presented in the text. These changes are the result of people placing pressure on the system.

Lindsey: I believe that many parents think public schools ought to teach and reflect our values in the texts. They do not believe, as Carolyn does, that schools should expose children to many values. Now, either the parents need to be educated, if this is the role of public schools, or the schools need to ask themselves whether they should provide texts, required or optional, that do not reflect this community's beliefs. Public schools would not be in existence if there were not children and tax-payers. Unfortunately, many parents with whom I speak simply do not trust public schools. They may like and trust the individual teacher; they distrust the bureaucracy.

Burgess: Most of our community—99%—share common beliefs and values. If our school would oppose those, we would have rebellion. I had to make a tough decision when the state adopted a black history text-book. A parent wrote our superintendent saying "I dare you to use this book in our middle school." The text states that, regarding slavery, Christianity was "a double-edge sword." On the one side it freed the spirit; on the other side it was used to enslave and justify slavery. This was a middle-class, respected member of the community who did not want his child exposed to that belief. My response to the superintendent was that the statement was true and well documented.

Carper: Were they reacting to the statement "Christianity justified slavery" or "Christianity was used to justify slavery."

Burgess: The second statement.

Carper: Well, then I agree with you.

Sears: At what point should that community and parents within that community determine texts or instructional material and at what point should educators?

Carper: Let me, first, stipulate two definitions of community. One, a functional community where persons know one another and there are close intergenerational connections. Two, a value community where people, though they may not know one another well, share a set of common beliefs.

Pigford: I think we are talking about a third community: persons who may not share a set of common beliefs and who do not know one another.

Carper: If communities are an extension of a common culture and culture rests on a set of moral commitments and understandings, then there are communities that transcend boundaries. The Christian community is one example.

Pigford: If the texts or materials in question lend themselves to an interpretation of a value issue, then I would be more inclined to listen. If the concern is with something factual and they simply don't want it included, then my responsibility is different.

Carper: The Holocaust, for example.

Sears: Okay, but what about the inclusion of homosexuals as Holocaust victims? There may be some in the community who would object, saying, "Well, although it may be factual, we don't believe that classroom time should be spent in acknowledging, legitimizing, or glorifying this group." Or what about the health textbooks? In this state there are perforated pages that permit those communities objecting to specific factual information simply to rip them out!

Carper: So, who has veto power over those stories that are told?

Murphy: Why are we talking about veto power in education? That's nuts!

Lindsey: I *want* to think that I, as an educator, have the responsibility. But, ultimately, I believe the parent has the right. They are the consumers; they are the parents; they are the taxpayers.

Pritchett: If I were a parent, I think I should have the right to decide for my child or with my child what text or instructional materials will be used. I don't have the right to decide for others.

Pigford: I think all of us would agree that if a student comes upon a topic and wants to pursue it, we could, within the current system, encourage that. The issue is can we now take that information, put it in the textbook or instructional materials, and make it a part of what we teach everyone?

Murphy: Sure.

Sears: So we've gone beyond the point of distinguishing between including material on the basis of whether it's factual or subject to interpretation to asking whose stories are going to be told?

Pigford: That is a political decision.

Pritchett: As a society, we have not come to an agreement on the purpose of public education. We haven't taken the time in our communities, aside from when a conflict occurs, to quietly and thoughtfully engage in dialogue.

Sears: Let's assume that such a dialogue has occurred in a school/ community. Wouldn't the predilection be to choose those materials that would generate little or no controversy and exclude stories some might find offensive?

Carper: Well, whose stories are told does depend, in part, on how we choose to order our lives together.

Pigford: But have we made a conscious decision as a community that we want to order our lives together?

Pritchett: We haven't decided we want to do that, and this is evidenced by *our* lack of common agreement. We haven't found common ground!

Murphy: We are a world community. Everyone's stories must be told.

Sears: Aren't some stories better told than others? Don't some stories, such as the *Iliad, Heart of Darkness,* or the Pilgrims' landing better reflect "universal themes" than others?

Pigford: It depends on the community as to which stories have the greatest meaning. The stories of African Americans should have greater emphasis in black communities. That is not to say that in another community such stories would not be told, but you probably wouldn't spend six weeks on Martin Luther King.

Pritchett: Then what gets left out for those African American students?

Pigford: As long as their stories are not the only stories told and that their curriculum reflects diversity, even though a larger proportion of their stories would reflect their own experiences.

Carper: Consciously or unconsciously we assume some vision of the nature of man, the world of the cosmos, the state of right or wrong, and the ideal society. Our stories, often articulated in textbooks, simply are a manifestation of that religious vision.

Pritchett: If we can agree that "unbelief" as well as "belief" is an aspect of religiosity, then I would agree.

Lindsey: Maybe our whole dialogue this evening is at the wrong level, just as the battle over textbooks may be just a reference for an underlying disagreement in values.

Suggested Additional Readings on Textbooks

Elaine Lindsey, with James T. Sears

Adler, L., & Tellez, K. (1992). Curriculum challenge from the religious Right: The *Impressions* reading series. *Urban Education, 27*(2), 152–173.
    A case study analysis of 22 school districts that lends insight into responses of conservative parents, community members, and educators.

Apple, M. (1986). *Teachers and texts.* New York: Routledge & Kegan Paul.
    An exploration of the ideological issues underlying textbook controversies and the centrality of the text in classroom instruction by a noted curriculum scholar.

Jenkinson, E. B. (1992). *The schoolbook protest movement: 40 questions and answers.* Bloomington, IN: Phi Delta Kappan Educational Foundation.
    Directed toward both educators and parents, the topics covered include legal issues, rights of parents and students, background of the protest movement, and guides for school districts.

Jenkinson, E. B. (1992). The search for alien religions in school textbooks. *Educational Horizons, 70*(4), 181–188.
    Examines some of the protests that have arisen over textbooks and some of the court cases that have resulted from them. The author looks at various definitions and interpretations of "secular humanism" and "New Age."

Napier, M. (1992, November). *Teachers making decisions when we know the censors are looking.* Paper presented at the annual meeting of the National Council of Teachers of English, Louisville, KY. (ERIC Document Reproduction Services, No. ED 355 540)
    Details the various activist groups and some of the legal cases they have instigated. Paper concludes by outlining methods schools can use to avoid such controversies.

Yaffe, E. (1994). Not just cupcakes anymore: A study of community involvement. *Phi Delta Kappan, 75*(5), 697–705.
    In these days of diversity and pluralism, it is hard for the public schools to service all its population. Yaffe examines how one school system avoided major textbook controversies by developing a community-based textbook selection committee.

PART III

Values in the Public Schools: What and Whose Values Should Be Taught?

It is difficult to imagine any human endeavor, particularly one involving a community of persons, that is value-free. Students and teachers, as a community of learners residing within a larger community, are engaged in a moral enterprise. The questions, however, are whose conception of moral education should be adopted and how those values attendant in such a curriculum should be fostered.

Here, both Richard A. Baer, Jr., and Nel Noddings consider the philosophical and political issues raised by these questions. While each holds a differing opinion regarding the process and, perhaps, content of moral education, both stress the critical role that schools and educators must play in the moral and character development of youth.

Baer cogently argues that the teaching of secular humanist beliefs and values in government-operated schools silences those holding theistic beliefs and values. He asks, "Does the state have the right to take a captive group of students and indoctrinate them in beliefs and values that will lead them to defect from the teachings of their church and parents?"

Noting problems associated with both cognitive and character-based moral education programs, Noddings calls upon educators not to surrender their ethical and professional responsibilities as moral educators: "Youth cannot develop sound character unless they associate with adults of sound character who are willing to share themselves as persons." She maintains, however, that this does not require religious instruction or disclosure of teachers' religious views. Rather she advocates that educators engage in "ordinary" conversations with pupils that are stimulating and relevant to them.

The community dialogue following these essays dramatizes the difficulties of moving beyond either a cognitive or character-based orientation. While participants find little consensus as to whether schools can teach values and, if so, which ones, Baer's call for the "disestablishment" of public schools animates the conversation.

CHAPTER 7

Why a Functional Definition of Religion Is Necessary If Justice Is to Be Achieved in Public Education

Richard A. Baer, Jr.

Is it possible to teach morality and character education effectively in our present system of public schools in America?[1] Is public education—from kindergarten to Ph.D.—fair to religious and cognitive minorities? Indeed, is it even possible for government actually to operate schools in a manner that is consistent with the demands of our Constitution and the American political compact? What does justice require regarding the funding of education in a democratic and pluralistic society? Questions such as these have troubled educators ever since the founding of the common school in the 1830s and 1840s and the establishment of state universities during the latter part of the nineteenth century.

Horace Mann, one of the guiding spirits in the founding of the common school, believed that his Unitarian/liberal Protestant understanding of Christianity was "nonsectarian" and thus appropriate for all students in what was even in his own day a reasonably pluralistic society, but Calvinists and Roman Catholics understandably did not concur. Catholic bishop John Hughes argued that the common school could not possibly be neutral or nonsectarian for Catholics when teachers routinely read from the Protestant King James Bible and pressed Protestant/Unitarian religious teachings on Catholic students. On the other hand, if religion were omitted altogether from the common school curriculum, then, Bishop Hughes argued, students would simply be left "to the advantage of infidelity" (quoted in McCarthy, Oppewal, Peterson, & Spykman, 1981, p. 90).

Americans have never satisfactorily resolved this question of religion and public education. During the post–World War II period, Bible readings, religious instruction, and prayers were gradually eliminated from government public schools, and the curriculum became progressively secular.[2] The courts assumed secular school curricula to be religiously neutral and thus not in conflict with the religion clause of the First Amendment.[3]

But is it really possible for a secular curriculum to be genuinely neutral with respect to religion? I think not. Any genuine education (as opposed to simple instruction in, say, how to type or how to operate a snowblower) inevitably rests on particular religious or metaphysical views regarding the nature of the good life and the good society. Quite apart from whether a school sponsors specific instruction in morality and religion, its curriculum, including decisions about which courses are to be taught and how they are to be taught, will inevitably presuppose particular metaphysical and religious views about who we are and about the world in which we live. Kenneth Strike (1982) states flatly: "In a liberal state publicly controlled schools cannot educate their students" (p. 87). He explains this strong statement by adding: "I do not mean that schools cannot succeed in teaching basic skills such as reading, writing, and arithmetic. Instead, I hold that liberal public schools cannot coherently transmit private values, and I hold that the transmission of private values is necessary for genuine education to occur."[4]

A FUNCTIONAL VIEW OF RELIGION

In trying to sort out questions about teaching religion and values or promoting good character in public education, we will make little progress unless we rethink the meaning of the term "religion" as it has to do with public education. My basic thesis is this: Public justice in education and respect for the First Amendment's religion clause demand that we adopt a functional definition of religion—at least for political and constitutional purposes. That is, in reflecting on the role of religion in education we should not focus primarily on the substantive content of religion or on some hallmark of religion such as belief in a supernatural power, but rather on what role religion plays culturally. This move is necessary precisely because neither religious nor secular answers to the Big Questions are religiously or metaphysically neutral. By "Big Questions" I refer to questions about the meaning and purpose of life, how we ought to live, and the nature of the good life and the good society.

My argument rests on the assumption that human beings are creatures that do not live simply by instinct but rather regularly inquire about the meaning and purpose of their existence. We create symbols and myths, tell stories, and constantly talk with each other about what reality is like and about how we ought to live. Paul Tillich described religion in terms of the category of "ultimate concern." Émile Durkheim argued that secular stories and myths can provide ultimate meaning for a society just as well as those that are supernatural. Secular descriptions of reality, in other words, can function just like supernatural descriptions.

Despite impassioned denial, even ridicule, from many academics and the liberal media, the evidence for the claim that our public schools are dominated by secular humanistic values and beliefs is overwhelming (Baer, 1982). My claim, of course, is not that some comprehensive system of thinking called "secular humanism" is being taught in our public schools and universities. Even less credible is the view that there exists an organized conspiracy, with secular humanists across America collaborating to indoctrinate public school children in their particular beliefs. My argument is much more specific, namely, that a detailed examination of curricula in America's government public schools demonstrates clearly that humanistic ideas and values dominate public education in America. Our schools are pervasively secular in an ideological sense. In virtually all government public schools humanistic values and beliefs are taught about the nature of the good life and the good society, and many of these values and beliefs directly compete with and undermine traditional Christian and Jewish beliefs. In sharp contrast, the latter are routinely excluded from school curricula. Unfortunately, the public school education establishment has for the most part either ignored or caricatured the claim that secular humanist beliefs and values are prominent in public school curricula, even though evidence in support of the claim is both clear and abundant (Baer, 1989; Vitz, 1977, 1986).

It is by no means necessary to adopt the claim of an organized conspiracy in order to make a strong case against the teaching of secular humanist beliefs and values in government public schools. Our courts routinely hold that public schools violate the Constitution's establishment clause if they recommend even fragments of Christian doctrine. For instance, no public school would be permitted to teach students that the meaning and purpose of life is to be found in obedience to Jesus Christ, or even that students ought to follow Jesus' example of self-giving, sacrificial love. By contrast, overwhelming evidence exists that our public schools are teaching many elements of secular humanist belief, often in very sensitive and controversial areas such as morality and sex education. The denial that secular humanist beliefs and values play a major role in public school curricula is little more than an ignorant and unthinking reflex for most liberal academics. But the claim is a strong one (Baer, 1977, 1980, 1981/82, 1982).

Now, if these secular humanist beliefs and values function like religion, then if we are to achieve justice in public education we must treat them like religion. Moreover, it is important to remember that the assertion that secular humanism is a religion was not originally made by conservative Catholics or Protestant fundamentalist critics of humanism but by humanists themselves. Writing as a nontheistic or secular humanist, John Dewey (1934) concludes his book *A Common Faith* with the words: "Here are all the elements for a religious faith that shall not be confined to sect, class, or race. Such a faith has always implicitly been the common faith of mankind. It remains to make it explicit and militant" (p. 87). Although Dewey's claim that his humanistic faith was always "implicitly the common faith of mankind" is simply mistaken, his statement about making it "explicit and militant" was prophetic, and it is no wonder that thoughtful religious leaders reacted with alarm. Their concern was only heightened when Dewey (1929) proclaimed that by advancing a common culture America's public schools "are performing an infinitely significant religious work" (p. 514).

One of the strongest reasons for insisting on a functional definition of religion when dealing with public education is that not to do so results in a *reductio ad absurdum* of monumental proportions. If we demand that our definition of religion must include some kind of belief in the supernatural, then the way is left open for atheists and secular humanists to promulgate their particular beliefs and worldviews in government public schools, for these views are considered nonreligious and thus cannot be excluded from public schools on the grounds of constituting a religious establishment or violating the free exercise of religion. In sharp contrast, Christians, religious Jews, and other religionists must remain silent in the public schools, for their views are religious, and thus the state is constitutionally prohibited from recommending them to children as true and worthy of acceptance.

Within such a framework, government schools are free to press on children humanistic beliefs such as the doctrine that the meaning and purpose of life is found in satisfying one's own needs and desires (the term "self-fulfillment" is often used). Under the banner of secular neutrality, sex education curricula and home economics texts simply assume and implicitly teach that rational behavior is self-interested behavior. Public schools routinely indoctrinate schoolchildren with humanistic beliefs like those found in values clarification, including the meta-ethical view that moral claims are subjective and relative (Bennett & Delattre, 1978; Lockwood, 1977; Stewart, 1975). Christians, on the other hand, who believe that life's meaning is found in learning to love God and serve one's neighbor, that committing one's life to Jesus Christ is the essence of rational behavior, and that morality consists of more than one's personal preferences, must remain silent in our government public schools. To believe that the founders of our republic could have had anything remotely like this arrangement in mind strikes me as bizarre and truly absurd. I can find no convincing historical evidence that would support such a position.

To be sure, as Americans we have developed practical ways of limiting religious influence on a broad range of "secular" activities, including many of those carried on by government. In part, this is because we have held so much of our religious and moral tradition in common that it has been relatively easy in many of our "secular" endeavors to presuppose this commonality and not get bogged down in endless controversy over those religious and moral beliefs on which we disagree. In particular, we have been able to develop something like what John Rawls (1993) refers to as an "overlapping consensus" about the structure of a liberal democracy. We are able to guarantee a high degree of "justice as fairness" to citizens without relying on metaphysical or theological argumentation that is grounded in a single comprehensive worldview.

However, when it comes to the Big Questions—those that deal with the meaning and purpose of life, who we are, and how we ought to live in light of our deepest religious and metaphysical commitments—Americans today hold highly divergent views about the nature of reality and about what is appropriate belief and behavior. Thus, although we do not ordinarily think of a Jewish position on harbor dredging or a distinctively Presbyterian view of managing the Post Office (although for Jews and Presbyterians these activities by no means remain outside the realm of God's concern and sovereignty), it is not at all difficult to envision a normative Catholic position on abortion, an orthodox Jewish view of the family, or an evangelical Christian understanding of marriage and child nurture. And these religious views often directly compete with secular views, for instance, those of groups such as Planned Parenthood or of individuals such as psychologists Carl Rogers and Sidney Simon (one of the founders of values clarification).

When nontheistic and humanistic beliefs serve as the philosophical basis for important parts of the curriculum in government public schools—courses in values clarification, decision making, and sex education are notable examples—citizens who take their religion seriously face a difficult problem. As noted above, many of these "secular" courses teach (implicitly, if not always explicitly) that self-fulfillment and satisfying one's personal needs are the goals of human existence. They insist that all value judgments are subjective and matters of personal opinion. They view tradition and traditional wisdom as a hindrance to achieving the good life. But each of these particular secular views, rather than being religiously neutral, directly competes with orthodox Christian teaching on these issues. Their promulgation in government schools constitutes an establishment of religion and also hinders the free exercise of religion by believing Christians and other traditional religionists. Secular instruction can be (and often is) just as "sectarian" (in the sense of narrow-minded, bigoted, one-sided, and parochial) as religious instruction can be. And if this is the case, then we must ask: Does the state have the right to take a captive group of students and indoctrinate them in beliefs and values that will lead them to defect from the teachings of their church and their parents?

Whether or not political philosopher John Rawls (1971, 1993) is right in his claims about justice as fairness, his views are basically relevant to how we govern ourselves, not to how we educate our children. Rawls himself concedes that, as a comprehensive doctrine, liberalism (and, of course, the same would apply to secular humanist beliefs and values) deserves to occupy no special place in our public life.

Nonetheless, the belief that the secular is the realm of the nonsectarian, although not defensible philosophically, continues to have great influence on how most Americans think about education. For instance, it seems to me quite remarkable that we permit secular philosophers in state universities actually to do metaphysics and normative ethics (and to recommend their results to their students), but scholars who deal with religion and religious ethics must confine their efforts to description and analysis. In many respects theological ethicists are far more open-minded than most secular ethicists; virtually all theological ethicists, for instance, have studied the most important writers in philosophical ethics, but the reverse is seldom true. In the field of animal rights/welfare, as an example, deontologist Tom Regan (Regan & Singer, 1989) uses the term "rationally defective" to describe the arguments of those who disagree with his conclusion that what he calls "the rights view" includes animals as well as humans (p. 111). Similarly, Peter Singer (1990) considers his views regarding animals to be rationally compelling, all the while overlooking the highly controversial character of his initial assumptions about the nature of human beings and animals. Explaining why he does not deal with the biblical concept of humans being created in the image of God or the theological concept of humans possessing immortal souls, he writes: "Logically, however, these religious views are unsatisfactory, since they do not offer a reasoned explanation of why it should be that all humans and no nonhumans have immortal souls" (pp. 270–271, note 14).

Most theological ethicists (e.g., Hauerwas, 1981a, 1981b), on the other hand, recognize that their viewpoints involve an element of faith and commitment. They may believe their positions to be both rational and true, but at the same time they recognize that technical reason as such usually does not compel acceptance.

There simply are no good reasons to believe that secular thinking about morality, character development, and the nature of the good life is inherently more universal, reasonable, or nonsectarian than is religious thinking. Just as was the case with Jefferson's conviction that his own religious views were "nonsectarian," the conviction of many educators today that the secular is more rational or universal than the religious is not warranted empirically or philosophically; it is a belief that is far sooner self-serving than self-evident! (Baer, 1990).

It seems clear that all human thought enterprises rest on certain initial assumptions and convictions about the nature of reality. All are limited, operate within a particular time and place, and entail risk of error. I find little justification for the widely accepted position that liberal, secular, humanistic reasoning of the sort that is prominent in public education in America today—from kindergarten to Ph.D.—is rational and scientific, whereas religious thinking about morality and the nature of reality rests on dogma and faith.

But even if secular thinking was inherently more rational than religious thinking, within the framework of the Constitution and the American political compact—assuming a functional view of religion—government would still not be justified in preferring secular answers to the Big Questions over religious answers. And insofar as school curricula always rest on one set of answers to the Big Questions or another, government's role in actually operating schools and universities must be seen as highly problematic.

A QUESTION OF CHOICE

If my arguments regarding the necessity of adopting a functional view of religion are basically correct, then choice is not just an option to be employed in the name of efficiency and better access to quality education. It is a political necessity for those who wish to be faithful to the American political compact and the spirit of the Constitution.

The argument is often made by those who oppose school choice that the requirements of liberal neutrality can be satisfied by exposing students to a multiplicity of values and ideas from which they are encouraged to make their own choices. This cafeteria approach permits the school, so it is argued, to remain neutral among various visions of the good life, while at the same time inculcating specific democratic values such as justice, tolerance, and rational deliberation.

But there are a number of telling objections to such an approach. First, taking a cafeteria-like approach to values and ultimate beliefs inevitably carries with it relativistic implications. We do not teach science in such a manner; instead we present students with the best science we have. We want them to come to believe and accept what is true. To be sure, good science teaching will help students see that scientists have proposed many theories that eventually failed and have taken many wrong turns along the way, but this is part of the normal course of science. It is not the same as presenting astrology, phrenology, or Lysenko's genetics and suggesting to students that they make their own choices about what they want to believe.

Second, the idea that students in grades K–12 are mature enough or know enough to make rational choices among different views of morality and the good life strikes me as just plain silly. That children in grades K–12 possess sufficient maturity and understanding to make intelligent choices among the great moral, religious, metaphysical, and political traditions of the world in which we live is wishful thinking. What actually happens in grades K–12—to put the matter bluntly—is that students become the patients of whichever social engineers have the power to push their own values and beliefs on them. The way schools have employed such fads as values clarification and most sex education curricula, or even their use of such an impressive intellectual achievement as Kohlberg's system of moral development, strongly supports this claim. And even a cursory look at today's fashionable commitment to diversity and multiculturalism in K–12 education makes clear that the range of diversity permitted seldom extends beyond the boundaries of the politically correct.

Attempts to deal with morality in government public schools in terms of specific courses have generally been either ineffective or problematic on constitutional grounds. Most such courses focus on trying to teach students how to improve their moral reasoning. Amy Gutmann (1987) argues that we should help students enhance "rational deliberation" (p. 51). But she largely ignores the telling arguments presented by Alasdair MacIntyre (1988) and others that there is little agreement today about precisely what we mean by rationality.

The structure of the public school is even less hospitable to the more traditional approach of focusing on character formation. Effective character formation requires the freedom to deal with symbols, myths, and stories, and it also demands opportunities to engage in ritual actions (worship, celebration, and so forth) that reinforce the lessons being taught. Furthermore, teachers must be permitted to function as role models—not at the level of the lowest common denominator, but in precise and specific ways. The public school is far too thin and fragile a moral community for effective character development, and in our society it is also severely limited by demands for religious neutrality.

At the time of the nation's founding, Americans agreed that the federal government should not establish a single national church. And over the following half century those states that had established churches gradually cut them off from public support. But McCarthy, Skillen, and Harper (1982) correctly argue in *Disestablishment a Second Time* that this move toward freedom of religion and conscience will not be completed until we end the religious establishment constituted by our government public schools. Such a move will require drastic changes in how we think about the relation between government and education, and it will also require that we begin to think of religion—for educational, political, and constitutional purposes—in functional terms.

Perhaps more than any other current social issue, school choice will challenge us as Americans to make clear whether or not we believe in religious tolerance. Will we, in the tradition of Horace Mann, side with the National Education Association in supporting a monopoly system of government schools that are fundamentally vehicles for one or another cultural elite to exercise social control, or will we, in the spirit of the First Amendment's religion clause, endorse school disestablishment and view the state's role in education as that of guarantor of just access to education rather than that of religious mentor and moral tutor?

Disestablishment will bring about wrenching changes in our educational structures and will not come about easily. But to reject such a move could very well contribute to a period of intense culture wars and widespread loss of confidence in the ability of government to guarantee justice to cognitive and religious minorities.

NOTES

1. An earlier version of this paper was presented at a conference on Religion, Politics, and Cultural Dynamics, Cornell University, April 9–10, 1994.

2. Here and elsewhere in this chapter I deliberately use the term "government public school" rather than simply "public school." This is because private or independent schools, as well as public schools, serve important public purposes. Also, because poor people typically cannot afford housing in neighborhoods with the best public schools, many public schools are not really open to the general public. Overall, social, economic, and racial integration in independent schools compares favorably with that in government public schools (Coleman, Hoffer, & Kilgore, 1982).

3. Here and elsewhere in this chapter I refer to the religion "clause" rather than "clauses" to underscore my belief that the framers understood nonestablishment to be in the service of free exercise: "Congress shall make no law respecting an establishment of religion, or (otherwise) prohibiting the free exercise thereof."

4. Although I concur with Strike's judgment about the inability of the state to educate (because it cannot coherently transmit what Strike calls "private values"), I find neither his distinction between private and public values nor his emphasis on schools stressing the development of rationality altogether convincing. Mediating structures in society—including schools, churches, business and labor groups, and

not-for-profit public interest groups—typically espouse values that are neither private in the sense of purely personal nor public in the sense of state-sponsored. The realm of the public is broader than the realm of the state. It is appropriate to use the term "public" in relation to the values and activities of these mediating groups, for they clearly serve public purposes, even though they are not owned and operated by the state.

Defining the term "public" as coextensive with the realm of the state begs important social and political questions. And when Strike emphasizes the development of rationality in government public schools, it is important to understand that rationality is not an altogether objective or morally neutral concept (Berger & Neuhaus, 1977; MacIntyre, 1988).

REFERENCES

Baer, R., Jr. (1977). Values clarification as indoctrination. *Educational Forum, 56*(2),155–165.

Baer, R., Jr. (1980). A critique of the use of values clarification in environmental education. *Journal of Environmental Education, 12*(1), 13–16.

Baer, R., Jr. (1981/82). Clarifying my objections to values clarification. *Journal of Environmental Education, 13*(2), 5–11.

Baer, R., Jr. (1982). Teaching values in the schools. *Principal, 61*(3), 17–21, 36.

Baer, R., Jr. (1989). The myth of neutrality. In K. Sidey (Ed.), *The blackboard fumble* (pp. 49–61). Wheaton, IL: Victor Books.

Baer, R., Jr. (1990). The Supreme Court's discriminatory use. *Journal of Law and Politics, 6*(3), 449–468.

Bennett, W., & Delattre, E. (1978, Winter). Moral education in the schools. *Public Interest, 50*, 81–98.

Berger, P., & Neuhaus, R. (1977). *To empower people: The role of mediating structures in public policy.* Washington, DC: American Institute for Public Policy Research.

Coleman, J., Hoffer, T., & Kilgore, S. (1982). *High school achievement: Public, Catholic, and private schools compared.* New York: Basic Books.

Dewey, J. (1929). Religion and our schools. In J. Ratner (Ed.), *Characters and events* (Vol. II, pp. 504–516). New York: Holt.

Dewey, J. (1934). *A common faith.* New Haven, CT: Yale University Press.

Gutmann, A. (1987). *Democratic education.* Princeton, NJ: Princeton University Press.

Hauerwas, S. (1981a). *A community of character.* Notre Dame, IN: University of Notre Dame Press.

Hauerwas, S. (1981b). *Vision and virtue.* Notre Dame, IN: University of Notre Dame Press.

Lockwood, A. (1977). Values education and the right to privacy. *Journal of Moral Education, 7*(1), 9–26.

MacIntyre, A. (1988). *Whose justice, which rationality?* Notre Dame, IN: University of Notre Dame Press.

McCarthy, R., Oppewal, D., Peterson, P., & Spykman, G. (1981). *Society, state, and schools*. Grand Rapids, MI: Eerdmans.

McCarthy, R., Skillen, J., & Harper, W. (1982). *Disestablishment a second time*. Grand Rapids, MI: Christian University Press.

Rawls, J. (1971). *A theory of justice*. Cambridge, MA: Belknap.

Rawls, J. (1993). *Political liberalism*. New York: Columbia University Press.

Regan, T., & Singer, P. (Eds.). (1989). *Animal rights and human obligations* (2nd ed.). Englewood Cliffs, NJ: Prentice-Hall.

Singer, P. (1990). *Animal liberation* (2nd ed.). New York: New York Review.

Stewart, J. (1975). Clarifying values clarification. *Phi Delta Kappan, 56*(10), 684–688.

Strike, K. (1982). *Education policy and the just society*. Urbana: University of Illinois Press.

Vitz, P. (1977). *Psychology as religion: The cult of self-worship*. Ann Arbor, MI: Eerdmans.

Vitz, P. (1986). *Censorship: Evidence of bias in our children's textbooks*. Ann Arbor, MI: Servant.

CHAPTER 8

Moral Education as a Form of Life

Nel Noddings

Philosophers and moral theorists have long debated questions about morality and moral education. The debate has, for the most part, centered on two conflicting positions: One holds that moral life begins with the recognition of certain a priori principles and proceeds through their faithful application; the other holds that a moral attitude and moral practices are learned by growing up in a moral community. Some thinkers have drawn a powerful analogy between language learning and the learning of morality. Just as Paul Ziff says of language that "one is not taught one's native language, one learns it" (1960, p. 35), Michael Oakeschott describes one view of moral life as a "habit of affection and behavior . . . an unreflective following of a tradition of conduct" (1962, p. 61).

The main point of this chapter is that either view, if it is pushed as the way to moral life, is mistaken. In both language and morality, much is learned by immersion, but many things must be taught, and neither approach prepares the young for problematic situations—moral crises—if it does not encourage regular dialogue, reflection, and practice. Moral education as a form of life must be closely connected to other forms of life.

TWO BASIC APPROACHES

The two basic approaches to morality do not, in practice, exist in pure forms. In theory, we can produce a purely deductive, cognitive morality, and we can give a pure description of an inductive morality; but in practice, moral life is necessarily more eclectic. In parallel to the two positions mentioned in the introduction, there are two general approaches to moral education—

one basically cognitive, the other more focused on behavior. However, cognitive programs rarely take a deductive form. They may assume that children will develop in the direction of principled thinking and, even, that there is some overriding principle at the apex of moral development (Kohlberg, 1981), but the principles are not explicitly taught. Similarly, and paradoxically, character education programs (in the second category) often teach explicit principles, attempt to inculcate definite values, and work to develop prescribed virtues.

Reflecting on the domain of morality, we should not expect or desire to find a pure, closed, systematic approach to moral education. Moral education, as a form of life, is intimately connected to other forms of life. The philosopher Ludwig Wittgenstein (1953) described forms of life in terms of patterns and regularities discernible in various human activities. The regularities include language as well as nonlinguistic behaviors. In looking at moral education as a form of life that has a characteristic set of aims, a recognizable language, and certain patterns of interaction among adults and children, we see also that it is connected to other forms of life: parenting, teaching, preaching, and governing, for example. These connections are obvious, and yet educators often overlook them and try to teach moral education in isolation from other forms of life.

The connection is frankly recognized and discussed by Sara Ruddick (1980) in her analysis of maternal thinking. She identifies three interests central to maternal thinking: preserving the child's life, fostering its individual growth, and shaping an acceptable child. Although different parents may have very different conceptions of acceptability, virtually all parents want their children to be acceptable by some definition. For example, even if we place a very high value on the intellectual growth of our children, most of us want our children to be not just smart and clever in reasoning but decent and compassionate. The three interests are intertwined. As Ruddick warns, "the interests in preservation, growth, and the acceptability of the child are frequently and unavoidably in conflict" (p. 349). Sometimes, for example, in the interest of growth, we must allow children to take some risks; other times, in the interest of acceptability, we have to forbid activities that might lead to growth. These conflicts represent just one way in which forms of life overlap.

Cognitive programs of moral education have the great strength that they resemble other subjects in the school curriculum; that is, because they emphasize reasoning and critical thinking, their processes reflect similar emphases in mathematics, science, and other academic subjects. By concentrating on reasoning they also avoid the overt inculcation of specific values—except for critical thinking itself, and that particular value is usually defended as inherent in any program of genuine education. However, that defense is coming under increasing attack from conservative parents who object to programs that encourage their children to doubt and to raise questions.

Another great strength of moral cognitivism, especially Kohlberg's cognitive developmentalism, is its connection to scholarly programs of research. First, it is clearly connected to earlier work by Piaget (1932/1965) and Perry (1970). Second, just as Noam Chomsky's work on transformational grammar induced a tremendous revival in psycholinguistics, Kohlberg's developmental theory has encouraged much psychological research on moral development (Garrod, 1993).

Kohlberg's work has stimulated research in another way. It has invited attack from feminists, who have challenged the universality of his description of moral development. Carol Gilligan (1982) contended that Kohlberg's work, because it was initiated in a study of young men, missed an alternative pattern of moral development that may be more characteristic of females. Gilligan's work has led to a great increase in gender studies and much debate about the adequacy of past studies (Larrabee, 1993). However, it may be more important to stress the alternative nature of the "different voice" identified by Gilligan. Not all people grow morally by moving toward a principle of universal justice; some (perhaps more women than men) become more sophisticated in their capacity to discern needs and to respond in ways that support not only immediate relationships but whole networks of care.

The care ethic, to which I will return in the last section, is more closely connected to forms of everyday life than its Kohlbergian predecessor. Indeed, a major defect in Kohlberg's program is its dependence on the Socratic equation of knowing and doing: To know the right is to do the right. Clearly, many people capable of exquisite and meticulous reasoning nevertheless behave immorally. The failure of cognitive developmentalism to connect with the usual patterns of parenting, with the forms of everyday life, is a major weakness.

Defenders of cognitivism often claim that such objections are baseless, that Kohlbergian dilemmas and the stories typically included in other cognitive programs—for example, Philosophy for Children (see any issue of *Thinking*)—make effective attempts to deal with real problems. Although this is true, the programs are still separated from the actual, ongoing moral life of the child. The stories are philosophical fictions; they do not originate in the actual incidents and problems of the children themselves. The conversations tend toward the formal; indeed, one objective is to introduce children to the power of philosophical thought. The fundamental objection to cognitive approaches, then, is this: They tend to identify moral life with the life of the mind; they make connections with academic life but not with the full-bodied life of everyday experience.

In contrast, character education programs concentrate frankly on behavior. The roots of character education are found in Aristotle's ethics and his recommendations for moral education. Aristotle's primary contention was that people learn to be virtuous by behaving virtuously; that is, children must be taught to behave virtuously, and moral reasoning should not be encouraged until a mature and dependable character has been established.

Today, in contrast to a period just two decades earlier, there are many advocates of character education (Lickona, 1991; Sichel, 1988). The movement has gained strength for several reasons: First, the alarming increase in youth crime and socially unacceptable behavior has led many critics to demand some form of direct instruction in moral behavior. Second, the growing strength of conservative religious groups is often exercised in behalf of traditional methods of childrearing, which have always been more or less Aristotelian. Third, character education more naturally connects to the everyday forms of life in which moral decisions are made; it aligns moral education not with academic studies but with the everyday behavior of the child in all domains.

So far I have emphasized differences between the two basic approaches, but there are also similarities. For example, in attempts at relevance, both cognitive and character education programs may use literature extensively, but they use it differently. Cognitive programs use stories as a means to launch critical thinking; character education programs use literature to exemplify virtues and to inspire virtuous behavior. The former rely heavily on stories as philosophical fictions, whereas the latter use a full range of literature—fictional stories and novels, biography, poetry, and drama. Some of the best character education programs put great emphasis on the quality of the literature. The Heartwood curriculum (n.d.), for example, has selected fine literature from many times and cultures to illustrate seven virtues. Discussion follows the readings, but emphasis is on helping children to see the world "covered in virtues" and to consider the role of virtues in their own lives. In general, character education programs aim explicitly at the development of virtues; cognitive programs aim at the development of reasoning.

Although the two kinds of program share some common features (Nucci, 1989), for example, the use of stories, they differ not only in their aims but also in the political difficulties they encounter. Cognitive programs run into objections from those who identify such programs with secular humanism and even nihilism. Character education programs often suffer objections from two directions. First, there are those who prefer more emphasis on critical thinking; these people are likely to dismiss character education as Kohlberg did—calling it "the bag of virtues" approach. Second, paradoxically, character education programs are sometimes assailed by the Christian Right (who espouse the same virtues) because they do not explicitly connect virtues to God and religious commandments. For example, the Heartwood curriculum has been vehemently attacked because it does not root the virtues as absolutes in some authority—God or parents, preferably God. In discussing recent political disputes, one writer noted that some critics contend:

> Character education programs tear children away from their faith and traditions, invade the family's privacy, promote moral relativism and "indifferentism" (the notion that all religions lead to salvation), endorse homosexuality and nontraditional family structures and further a left-wing political agenda. (Bates, 1995, p. 19).

Such attitudes, if they are allowed to prevail, would effectively prevent the public schools from engaging in any explicit form of moral education. However, we also see in these extreme attitudes a weakness in character education itself. It has always been rooted in particular traditions and depends heavily on community solidarity. When it tries to transcend particularity by recognizing a host of different particularities, it is condemned as relativistic. When it frankly embraces one particular tradition, it can become exclusive, oppressive, intolerant, and even fanatical. Is there a way of escaping these difficulties?

BEYOND SPECIFIC PROGRAMS

Moral education as a form of life—one with a pattern of linguistic regularities, characteristic aims, and so on—cannot be isolated from other forms of life, nor should it be confined to use between adults and children. It is, perhaps, the central form of human life, and its language reaches out to make connections with all forms in which people interact. We continue to learn from one another—even into old age—what it means to be hurt, to need, to respond with care, and to fail in response.

At the present time, many thinkers and critics deplore the moral condition of our society. Conservatives express deep concern about the decline in youth character and provide plenty of evidence to back up their contention. However, this kind of direct attack on the symptoms may be too simplistic. Why has youth character declined? Is the morality of mature Americans intact? What is missing in the lives of American youth? Have social conditions changed so dramatically that old measures no longer work? All of these questions should be probed in considerable depth.

I do not mean to suggest that we should do nothing until careful studies are completed. Kids are dying—physically and morally—right now, and as responsible adults we must do something to increase their chances of healthy survival—to preserve their lives, nurture their growth, and shape them as acceptable persons. But perhaps the most responsible suggestion that can be made at the general or universal level is one that calls upon individual adults to get involved and includes provision for the legitimation of such involvement.

Legitimation is a particularly important issue in education. Consider the contrast in attitudes between most public schools and some independent schools. In recent conversations with Quaker educators, I learned that teachers in Quaker schools are expected to spend time talking with their students about moral and social issues (see Hays, 1994). Teachers in these schools are considered remiss if they do not put aside regular instruction in favor of such issues when they arise. In contrast, teachers in most public schools (especially secondary schools) are castigated for allowing their students to deflect attention from academic instruction to conversation of any sort.

Indeed, because of the almost irrational emphasis on academic instruction, many public school teachers deny any obligation to engage in moral education. When urged to do so, many respond by saying that moral education is not their "field of expertise" and that they are untrained to do such work. Whereas most Quaker educators (and, very likely, the majority of teachers in other religious schools) accept the obligation as part of their vocation—indeed, as part of their obligation as adults, not solely as teachers— public school teachers have accepted the myth of bureaucratized knowledge. Every scrap of knowledge must be in its own box, clearly labeled, and only those duly authorized may address the contents of any given box. Ironically, this sharp separation of responsibilities makes the assigned work of academic instruction more, not less, difficult. Time spent in developing relations of care and trust, in discussing problems of adolescence, in acknowledging the world's political and social ills, and in getting to know one another as persons is not time wasted. Such conversations provide the web of trust and affection in which academic instruction can thrive.

This example, the startling contrast between public and religious school legitimation of "off-task" conversation, yields some support for the endorsement of religion for young people. But the support is limited. It is not religion or religious instruction per se that makes the difference. Students in classes where careful, stimulating, and relevant conversations occur need not even be aware that their teachers are motivated by commitments to a religion. Rather, what comes across is what John Dewey (1934) described as a religious attitude—one inspired not by doctrine or dogma but by an energetic and faithful dedication to the worthy tasks at hand. Surely this attitude can be legitimized in public schools.

When moral education is considered a form of life that intersects every other human form of life, we see that ordinary conversation can play a powerful role. Such conversation can be about almost any topic, and there need not be a moral learning objective. However, its tone or attitude is moral, and the adult partner remains sensitive throughout to moral issues. Elsewhere (Noddings, 1994) I have suggested that such conversations have at least three important characteristics:

1. That the adults are people who try to be good, even if they do not always bring it off.
2. That the adults have loving regard and respect for their child-partners.
3. That, for both parties, in the conversation under consideration, the partner is more important than the topic, the conclusion, or the argument. (p. 116).

In such conversations, I noted:

> Children learn all sorts of things—facts, the rules of polite conversation, manner and style, trust and confidence, how to listen, how to respond without hurting, and a host of other factors in human interaction. Because parents are so harried today and because so many do not fit the criteria I have suggested, teachers simply must engage their students in ordinary conversation. The kind of people we are turning out is far more important than national supremacy in mathematics and science. Teachers must be free to "jump all the fences" and explore matters of great and small importance with their students. (p. 117)

Superbly educated and artistically gifted teachers can also get lots of academic mileage out of these ordinary conversations. Almost any topic can be relinked to regular academic instruction through history, biography, fiction, or a host of other media. Suppose, for example, that a mathematics teacher takes time from regular instruction to discuss racial or religious discrimination. As a transition to academic instruction, she might tell a story about the great mathematician James Sylvester. When Sylvester studied at Cambridge, Jews could not receive degrees because they were unable to give the orthodox answers to questions posited by the Church of England (in its 39 Articles) for all degree recipients. As a Jew, Sylvester had to accept his degree from Trinity College in Dublin. Years later, as a much-admired mathematician, he received an honorary degree from Cambridge. His story is wonderful, too, in what it says about energy and dedication. Explaining his success, Sylvester said, "I really love my subject." He took a new professorial position at Oxford at age 70 and created new mathematics into his 80s. He said, "the mathematician lives long and lives young. The wings of the soul do not early drop off" (quoted in Bell, 1937/1965, p. 405). Now, the teacher might say, how is that for an incentive to do a bit more mathematics? At present, it is surprising how few mathematics teachers are prepared to tell such stories. Such storytelling is legitimated neither in their own classrooms nor in those where they, as students, learned to teach.

Policy makers, administrators, and parents often worry that legitimation of stories and ordinary conversation will give teachers license to indoctrinate, to engage in a quest for personal affection, or just to goof off. These worries reflect a deep and pervasive distrust of teachers, a distrust extended today to almost all professional and public workers. Such distrust is part of the general moral malaise that underlies the decline in youth character, but youth cannot develop sound character unless they associate with adults of sound character who are willing to share themselves as persons.

Teachers are in a unique position to do this. They should be able to induce and guide the critical thinking espoused by cognitivists; they should be ready to discuss the specific virtues admired by character educators; and they should be prepared to offer a host of stories that contribute to both great tasks: to stimulate or initiate critical thinking and to inspire virtuous action. Further, they should be able to connect their stories and conversations to standard academic instruction.

David Hansen (1995) describes Mr. James, a special education teacher in an inner-city secondary school, who regularly engages his students in ordinary conversation. Unfailingly composed and reasonable, he urges his students to be considerate, attentive, and reasonable. He models a way of being for his students, and it is clear that he wants them to think of him as "there for them." However, Hansen remarks:

> He concentrates so intently on his personal rapport with students that he sometimes treats that as an end in itself, rather than as an aspect of helping his students grow intellectually and succeed scholastically. (p. 68)

I have not observed Mr. James, and I am not in a position to evaluate Hansen's judgment. Mr. James may indeed miss many opportunities for academic engagement. However, to make personal rapport an end in itself with students whose main difficulty is that they have no such rapport with any adult does not seem to be a mistaken aim. In the incredibly trying circumstances Mr. James faces every day, I would rather have him there working steadily to coax and support "his kids" toward lives of decency and reasonableness than another teacher who might succeed merely in getting them to add fractions.

Can't we have both? As I remarked earlier, well-educated and artistically gifted teachers can certainly do both. I should have added, "if they have adequate resources and official legitimation." When either conditions or teachers' limitations make it impossible to do both, we should go with Mr. James. Unless we reorder our priorities, the decline in youth character is likely to continue and even spread more widely. We cannot responsibly treat moral education as a separate subject in the curriculum, whether its aim be moral reasoning or virtue. To recognize moral education as a form of life suggests living with our kids, talking to them, listening to them, and showing them by our example that moral considerations arise in every form of human life. If this requires setting aside academic goals for a while, we must have the courage to do so. New and more important academic goals may emerge from the ensuing conversations.

REFERENCES

Bates, S. (1995, January 8). A textbook of virtues. *The New York Times*, Education Life, pp. 16–49.

Bell, E. T. (1965). *Men of mathematics*. New York: Simon & Schuster. (Original work published 1937)

Dewey, J. (1934). *A common faith*. New Haven, CT: Yale University Press.

Garrod, A. (Ed.). (1993). *Approaches to moral development*. New York: Teachers College Press.

Gilligan, C. (1982). *In a different voice*. Cambridge, MA: Harvard University Press.

Hansen, D. (1995). *The call to teach*. New York: Teachers College Press.

Hays, K. (1994). *Practicing virtues: Moral traditions at Quaker and military boarding schools*. Berkeley: University of California Press.

Heartwood curriculum for elementary school children. (n.d.). Wexford, PA: Heartwood Institute.

Kohlberg, L. (1981). *The philosophy of moral development*. San Francisco: Harper & Row.

Larrabee, M. J. (Ed.). (1983). *An ethic of care*. New York: Routledge.

Lickona, T. (1991). *Educating for character: How our schools can teach respect and responsibility*. New York: Bantam.

Noddings, N. (1994). Conversation as moral education. *Journal of Moral Education, 23*(2), 107–118.

Nucci, L. (Ed.). (1989). *Moral development and character education*. Berkeley, CA: McCutchan.

Oakeschott, M. (1962). *Rationalism in politics*. New York: Basic Books.

Perry, W. (1970). *Forms of intellectual and ethical development in the college years*. New York: Holt, Rinehart & Winston.

Piaget, J. (1965). *The moral judgment of the child*. New York: Free Press. (Original work published 1932)

Ruddick, S. (1980). Maternal thinking. *Feminist Studies, 6*(2), 342–367.

Sichel, B. A. (1988). *Moral education*. Philadelphia: Temple University Press.

Thinking: The Journal of Philosophy of Children. Upper Montclair, NJ: Montclair State University.

Wittgenstein, L. (1953). *Philosophical investigations* (G. E. M. Anscombe, R. Rhees, & G. H. Von Wright, Eds.). Oxford, England: Oxford University Press.

Ziff, P. (1960). *Semantic analysis*. Ithaca, NY: Cornell University Press.

COMMUNITY DIALOGUE

Is There a Common Moral Framework That Schools Can Embrace?

Lindsey: It's not we, as conservative Christians, who do not want schools to teach values like tolerance, respect for individual difference, and self-reliance or it's not that we do not value those qualities in our children. We object to the methods. It's not a simple matter of bringing the children into the classroom and posing correct questions. Many parents feel that the children must have a framework before they can make their judgment. Parents whom I have spoken with who have objected to the Pumsy program, for example, feel that it fails to provide a values framework. Why does a child say "no" to drugs if they are offered to him? Why does a child be courteous to someone else? Why do we tell the child not to lie? Frequently, such guidance counseling programs fail to provide a moral framework before they ask students to engage in decision making. In a Christian school children first understand that their bodies are temples of God and they have to keep them strong and healthy. In a Christian school children show respect and courtesy to their elders because God teaches you to honor your parents and those who are over you. You learn not to lie because you value truth, which is from God. The problem is that the public school lacks this common framework of values. There is too much diversity. Parents do not trust that teachers share their moral framework.

Pigford: Are these values based upon the context or are they universal?

Lindsey: From my perspective, there are absolutes.

Sears: Is there—or ought there be—either a cognitive or character-based moral framework in public schools?

See the introduction for a description of the conversationalists.

Curriculum, Religion, and Public Education: Conversations for an Enlarging Public Square. Copyright © 1998 by Teachers College, Columbia University. All rights reserved. ISBN 0-8077-3706-2 (pbk.), ISBN 0-8077-3707-0 (cloth). Prior to photocopying items for classroom use, please contact the Copyright Clearance Center, Customer Service, 222 Rosewood Dr., Danvers, MA 01923, USA, tel. (508) 750-8400.

Pritchett: I think the problem for some parents is not the use of a particular framework but the denial of *any* framework within the public school system.

Sears: Would you advise the state superintendent to propose such a standard?

Pritchett: No, that discussion should occur at the community level. In our dialogue meetings, we ask what are those common values that a particular community wishes to see reinforced in their schools. If there is a common framework that can be agreed to within the community, then that should be used to guide curriculum and instruction. The state's responsibility, however, is to establish a framework that guides community discussions, not to establish a particular set of values to be stressed in all schools.

Sears: But the state of South Carolina has already proposed a set of academic frameworks in science, mathematics, social sciences, and the arts. Why should the state abdicate its responsibility when it comes to establishing a moral framework?

Shearer: Right! If you can establish curriculum review frameworks, why can't you establish value frameworks and strategies?

Lindsey: Perhaps a lot of the other curriculum conflicts over textbook selection and the teaching of evolution could be avoided if we establish some common values.

Sears: It is one matter to promote honesty, truthfulness, and respect for authority; it is another matter, however, to argue that those "right behaviors" must be embedded within a larger set of moral beliefs such a conservative Christian framework.

Carper: This gets back to the question of the sources of moral authority that Hunter raised in *Culture Wars*. As he pointed out, while both the progressive and the orthodox agree that justice is a moral value worthy of transmission, they understand "justice" quite differently. This concept is rooted in two very different sources of moral authority. While the secular humanists' source may be the Constitution or the individual, for the practicing Christian or Jew it is the Bible or the Torah.

Murphy: I cannot say that the Bible is the source of moral authority in my classroom. But, as a public school teacher, the number of times the word *God* has come up in my class this week must have been over 25. In my science class I use the phrase "Nature or God." But the students must choose which one to use. These children are not blank slates, and it is not my job to inculcate a particular set of values. I do reinforce the values of the school like honesty, integrity, and respect—most teachers do. What I don't say, though, is that you must have the value that the Bible is the Word of God! Telling the child not to use drugs because her body is a "temple of the Holy Spirit" is something she should receive at home. Teachers are not ministers.

Lindsey: I would not expect you to say that in a public school.

Shearer: I can go along with that. The problem, however, is that within public schools there is a militant need among some teachers to teach children to "think for themselves" and include terms like *self-empowerment, tolerance,* and *inner-directiveness.* These teachers, operating from a cognitive development framework described by Noddings, are not interested in reinforcing what children are taught in conservative Christian homes.

Burgess: I hear the phrase "conservative Christians" all the time. At one point I thought it was simply enough to be a Christian.

Murphy: The goal of teachers is to help students become "self-empowered" in that they need to know what they believe in, why they believe in it, and to intelligently stand up for their beliefs—whatever those beliefs are.

Pigford: Students must arrive at their position as a result of reflection rather than someone simply telling them what to believe.

Lindsey: At what grade level are we talking about "self-empowerment" and "thinking for self"? At the elementary school, children often see their teachers as more important than their parents. We are afraid that if the teacher says, "You decide this; don't worry about what others say," then they will ignore their parents.

Pigford: I think the issue is one of problem solving as opposed to simply saying to the child this is what should happen. For example, a first-grade child might be presented with a situation that demands a decision. You ask the child what he or she thinks would be the appropriate action given our value of honesty. The child will choose the action that supports the value and in the process the child develops the thought process.

Pritchett: The child needs to understand the *why,* not just the *what.*

Lindsey: If parents felt that the first-grade teacher was going to teach honesty and hold that as a value, there wouldn't be such struggle going on.

Sears: Now let's push ourselves a bit. No responsible educator advocates dishonesty or disrespect.

Shearer: Of course, those are easy. But values like "tolerance," "diversity," and "self-reliance" come down to definition. For example, I know what "don't steal" means and I know what it means to be truthful even though we may want to debate some of its situational ethics. Now, how the secularist will define "self-reliance" and the way I define it as a parent will be different. What I am concerned with is that the school will encourage my children to be reliant in areas of their lives where I don't want them to be reliant.

Pigford: What would be such an area?

Shearer: Condoms! Condom distribution without parental permission isn't just prudish Christians who don't think their kids ought to know anything about sex. I know my children know about sex. What I don't want them to think is that they are reliant enough to make sexual decisions on their own. The issue, here, is the attitude of the school that students ought to be "safe" because they are going to make certain sexual decisions. Now, if schools and families are not on the same wavelength on *this* issue, how many other issues are there on which home and school are sending mixed messages? How then can we trust the schools with harder-to-define values such as "tolerance" or "diversity"?

Burgess: It's not enough to talk about religious tolerance—what about racial and economic tolerance? I am intrigued by some conservatives who pinpoint to the early 1960s [as the beginning of] our moral decline—right at the height of racial integration.

Murphy: I teach sex education as well as drug education, and one of the statements we don't make is "Condoms make safe sex; just go and buy them at the 7–11 and you're fine." Eighty percent of what we say is don't have sex until you are ready to have a loving, committed, and monogamous relationship.

Sears: But that is different from saying "Don't have sex until you are married."

Shearer: Now you are at the heart of this debate. Elaine mentioned, "say 'no' to drugs." For me as a conservative Christian, if public schools are going to teach values, then they need to say more than "don't do drugs, don't get pregnant." The problem is that parents want the schools to say "do something": protect your body because God gave it to you; abstain.

Murphy: In our sex education class we pose moral dilemmas. But I can't stand there and say "God doesn't want you to have sex; don't have sex until you are married." In a public school setting, that's not my role; that is the parents' role!

Pigford: I wish educators had that kind of power! We are talking as if schools exist in a social vacuum and that teachers can change the reality from which many of their children come. Now we can say—and I am sure that it is said—"You should abstain." But the reality is that there will be children who do not adhere to that value. Now, do we then have another responsibility to give those children the information that they need to have in order to deal with the fact that they choose not to adhere to that value?

Pritchett: There may also be parents in the school who hold values different from Pastor Bob or who hold no values at all. How do the public schools and teachers cope with such parental diversity?

Shearer: I realize the dilemma, and I agonize with you about it. Perhaps our discussion should be to what degree the public school is responsible for solving these problems. You are making the assumption that schools have been tasked with the responsibility of protecting children. There was a time when teachers shouldered that responsibility and they had the common value framework to do it. Now, as Baer points out, the framework has been lost but they still carry on the task. If we don't have the value framework, the moral truths, and the positive messages, then schools shouldn't engage in these moral tasks.

Burgess: Now, as a principal I think we have a very moral school whether we judge it on Christian principles or the mores of our community. The people who teach classes in my school are good people. They are not trying to bend the mind but to expand it. But today, if you are an advocate for public schools, it is almost like saying that you are willing to be hung at the gallows.

Sears: Can you teach morals and instill character in public schools that is separate from religious education? Or, as Professor Baer argues, must we rethink the term "religion" has come to mean within public education?

Murphy: I have a 28-year-old daughter who has wonderful values. I hope the foundation of who she is came because she saw me as her parent *doing* what I said. The essential moral teaching must come from the home. My job as a teacher is to facilitate critical thinking and discussion in the classroom. However, ultimately you have to allow the child to decide. Hopefully, he or she will make right decisions.

Carper: What goes on in your classroom, Carolyn, I think is rare and commendable. You reinforce that moral structure out of which that particular child comes. However, there are those who would see what you do as a kind of veiled moral relativism: There is no absolute right or wrong except for the individual. For example, it's wrong for you to take drugs because Christians don't violate the temple of God; it's wrong for you to take drugs because you are breaking the law; it's wrong for you to take drugs because it is unhealthy.

Sears: Can Christian conservatives accept the role of public schools within a democratic society serving as a facilitator for a variety of ideas and values but not the endorser of any particular set? Or must public schools return to the McGuffey Readers or simply shut down? Is there an area for agreement among this group on the values public school teaches and the character traits it instills?

Burgess: My concern is that there are people out there who are arrogant enough to think that is it their way or no way.

Carper: But isn't it the very nature of moral commitment that it is not compromisable?

Murphy: But that is for *you.* I am committed to a moral framework that does *not* allow me to impose my moral commitment on you.

Carper: Can you compromise that? There are certain issues that I consider closed because they are true.

Pigford: For example?

Carper: The Bible is the infallible word of God.

Pigford: How would that translate into a school setting that would affect me as a teacher?

Carper: A commitment to a pluralistic classroom. As a conservative Christian, how do I relate to a morally inclusive classroom when I do not believe in such inclusiveness? You see, institutions embody a particular moral framework. Whose is it going to be?

Lindsey: I agree. Teachers do not teach in a moral vacuum. Values must be instilled, but when values are so divergent parents come to a point of saying that they don't want their children influenced by this teacher who has a contrary value.

Burgess: My children attend public schools, but it is up to my church and our family to teach them religious values. They may hear some of that in the public school, but it is not the responsibility of the schools to endorse it or promote it.

Lindsey: Public schools, as Baer so ably details, have not been free of religion! Many of the conflicts in our school system have arisen from what people felt were religious beliefs being forced on them or particular values not being allowed to be taught.

Shearer: Let's simply admit that public schools are no longer equipped to teach values. Schools should simply teach what they are crafted to teach—academics—and let the churches teach values.

Murphy: I have to differ. The curriculum in my class touches on all types of values and moral issues: Galileo, evolution, civil rights. The curriculum is an arena for discussion of ideas which insist upon moral perspectives.

Shearer: This is not where I would like to be; it is here where I find myself as a conservative Christian on the outside looking in.

Pritchett: I want the school to stick to its academic role and not teach a particular set of values. I can teach about nutrition in the health curriculum, but schools should not teach my child to be a vegetarian.

Sears: Could we agree that schools ought to reinforce values brought by the children from different homes, perhaps engaging in the types of conversations advocated by Noddings, but not to endorse or enforce one set of values on all children? Or should we accept Bob's proposition that schools simply get out of the value business if we cannot agree on a common set?

Murphy: I would not reinforce those values with which I disagreed. For instance, I would not condone drug use, racial prejudice, or the inequality of women in my classroom.

Pigford: But you can respect those beliefs even though you may say that you personally don't accept them. This, in turn, enlarges the whole conversation as we learn about others' values and beliefs.

Sears: What about moral education, character development, and the teaching of values linked to a democratic society? How can we respect the values of Elaine's children as well as those of Carolyn's within a public school?

Carper: That is precisely the problem! Perhaps the best solution today is to move toward a true voucher system. Ironically, this is where my forefathers screwed up in that they said "Catholics should become Protestants and think like we do."

Shearer: And, if they don't, they ought to pay their educational way.

Sears: This is a paradox! Following the civil rights movement the tables have turned. Those who were once on the governing boards of education no longer exercise hegemony. Now "on the outs," as Pastor Bob noted, you want the money and resources for those very options that your forefathers were unwilling to provide a century ago.

Shearer: Public schools are at the point where they don't have any credibility among conservative Christians. We are accused of not being tolerant because our particular view of morality does not jibe with the view of others. We don't have *any* role to play.

Pigford: I am a Christian, but I have no problem with presenting options to students or presenting varying moral reasons for choosing right behavior, such as not taking drugs. I do not believe that we should send one particular moral message. There is a danger in seeking or claiming a single voice represents an entire group or should represent the public school curriculum.

Burgess: I was raised in a church in which it was not proper for one to "think for oneself." As a result certain abuses occurred in misguiding people. I have a son and I am a preacher. I want my son to be able to think but also to be able to understand that there are some things we believe are right and others that we believe are wrong.

Sears: But if we teach our children to think but their thinking is not built upon a moral foundation or doesn't flow from spiritual fountainhead, then right-thinking people, as Noddings observed, can choose immoral acts. Rational thought divorced from moral reasoning has caused enormous human suffering over millennia.

Shearer: I certainly want my sons to think critically. But what do critical thinking skills have to do with what has to be accomplished in public schools today? Why do we have to debate values or critical thinking in order to teach reading, writing, and arithmetic? What does critical thinking have to do with moral education?

Pritchett: You can reinforce values in the public schools, but you cannot impose a moral curriculum.

Pigford: We are trying to teach kids something in school that may not be a part of their lives. We suspend children because they make certain decisions that are in opposition to certain values that we want them to have. We have all kinds of punishment that we mete out to children because they violate some value. The level at which you have to teach depends on the child. For some children, if you say "don't do this" because there is some external punishment, that behavior stops. But what we are trying to do is to create an internal value framework. So we don't simply say, "don't do drugs because the police will lock you up." Because when the police are not around, they would feel perfectly comfortable taking the drugs.

Shearer: That's exactly right.

Pigford: So, then we go to the next level with that child and say, "You don't take it because it will harm your body. If you have a body that is not working, you will ultimately suffer for it."

Shearer: I would like to think it is possible for us to operate as moral people in public schools, but I don't think public schools can equip people to act morally. Perhaps they can reinforce values, but we don't have the ability to teach morals.

Burgess: We need to decide at what point we want to make the public school system work, or if we are going to continue to be on opposing corners. I'm not worried if the system does fail. In that case I will get my voucher, open my church school, and teach those poor and black children what I may not have been able to teach them in the public school system.

Pigford: Each of us around this table is privileged. None of us represents other voices within the public school system. We can intellectualize without having to deal with the realities of many of these families. We don't know their experiences. Sometimes we assume an air of arrogance when we talk about the public schools.

Pritchett: We have all been silenced, we have all withdrawn, we have all taken it personally and therefore it is hard for us enter into dialogue and share our voices.

Sears: Is a common school with a diverse population that encourages those values which you prize possible?

Pigford: It not only is possible but it is the type of school I want my grandchildren to attend: one that respects diverse values. If we can't do this in the schools, is our next step to eliminate diversity in our society?

Lindsey: I would like to believe that it is possible, but having observed human nature, I would say no.

Burgess: It can be achieved if we truly want to work toward that end. But there must be sincere efforts like we are engaged in around this table.

Pritchett: It may be possible, but I'm not sure it will happen in individual classrooms.

Murphy: I saw it this morning in my school! It is not hypothetical; it is happening in public schools where a diverse group of students are learning how to get along.

Suggested Additional Readings on Values

Elaine Lindsey, with James T. Sears

Belanger, W. A. (1993). Imparting values—A multidimensional perspective. *Journal of Moral Education, 22,* 111–124.

    The author maintains that there are nine ways in which values are imparted throughout the curriculum; an understanding of these will help the schools to be more proactive in teaching values.

Haynes, C. C. (Ed.). (1994). *Finding common ground.* Nashville, TN: Freedom Forum First Amendment Center.

    Distinguishing between "teaching religion" and "teaching about religion," Haynes argues that the First Amendment provides the "common ground" on which people can negotiate their differences. Includes historical court cases, strategies for finding "common ground," and resources for teaching about values and religion in U.S. history and world history.

Hare, R. M. (1992). *Essays on religion and education.* Oxford, England: Clarendon.

    The author develops a rationale for values education in schools, claiming the way to live in a pluralistic society is to use the "language of morality." Thought-provoking philosophical essays include: "Are There Moral Authorities?", "Value Education in a Pluralistic Society," and "Language and Moral Education."

Leming, J. S. (1993). In search of effective character education. *Educational Leadership, 51*(3), 63–71 (entire issue devoted to character education).

    A summary of the extensive research on character education wherein the author describes practices in public schools from the beginning of this century.

Lickona, T. (1991). *Educating for character: How our schools can teach respect and responsibility.* New York: Bantam.

    Asserting the need for values education in the school, Lickona develops his arguments with examples from schools in the United States and Canada. Two umbrella values that he promotes are respect and responsibility. Respect takes three forms: "respect for oneself, respect for other people, and respect for all forms of life and the environment." Responsibility is defined as "orienting toward others, paying attention to them, actively responding to their needs." A practical resource guide for school administrators and teachers is included.

Lickona, T., & Skillen, J. W. (1993). Is character education a responsibility of the public school? Yes, no. *Momentum, 24*(4), 48–54.

In this debate, Lickona takes the position that it is the responsibility of the public schools to teach children core ethical values. Skillen asserts that there are no core values that the schools should teach, leaving this responsibility to the parents and advocating parental choice.

Mitias, M. (Ed.). (1992). *Moral education and the liberal arts*. New York: Greenwood.

Explores the role of the liberal arts college in the moral education of its students, featuring contributions by Robert Ginsberg, Edwin Giventer, and Thomas Alexander.

Page, L. (1995, September). A conservative Christian view on values. *The School Administrator*, pp. 20–22.

Spokesperson for Focus on the Family provides summary of a curriculum based on "transcendent values and moral absolutes." The essay is followed by four reactions from educational leaders and authorities on character education.

Power, F. C., & Lapsley, D. K. (Eds.). (1992). *The challenge of pluralism*. Notre Dame, IN: University of Notre Dame Press.

Based on a symposium on moral education held at Notre Dame, each chapter author shares the editors' belief that, "As members of democratic society, we must undertake an open and sustained analysis of the kind of moral education necessary for a responsible engagement with pluralism." The first three chapters provide a context in which pluralism must be addressed. Nicgorski and Apple emphasize the affect of religious groups on the framework of moral education. The next two chapters explore pluralism from the framework of liberal moral theory. The last three chapters develop methods that can be used in schools to teach moral education.

Starratt, R. (1991). Building an ethical school: A theory for practice in educational leadership. *Educational Administration Quarterly*, *27*(2), 185–202.

Describes the building of a school upon three foundational themes of critique, justice, and caring. Using this "multidimensional ethic," the author describes implications for school administrators.

PART IV

Sexuality Education:
What Does Teaching
Sexual Responsibility Mean?

The debate raging over the teaching of sexuality in public schools has extended across generations. The current controversy, however, has taken on greater importance as advocates for comprehensive health education point to the rising cases of HIV-infected adolescents while those on the right, championing an abstinence-only message, see no reason to compromise moral beliefs for sexually suspect practices.

Rekers and Hohn provide extensive documentation to support their contention that sexuality educators must implement abstinence-only programs. Citing failures of safer-sex programs, they discuss several unscientific assumptions underlying such programs. Arguing for risk elimination, not merely risk reduction, they cite data supporting the comparative effectiveness of abstinence-only sexuality curricula. Thus they conclude this is "the only logical and truly compassionate health goal for sex education and counseling."

In my essay, I place the debate about sexuality education within a larger cultural and political context wherein assumptions about cultural universalism, sexual essentialism, positivistic empiricism, and managerial behaviorism blind us to the "black box" of adolescent sexual behavior. Arguing that we need to begin with "new basics," I challenge both those who advocate distribution of contraceptives and those who urge moral instruction to revise the teaching and researching of sexualities.

The community dialogue reflects the diverse views held in many communities as the participants discuss how cultural differences, parental voice, and moral beliefs can be accommodated within the public schools. Given the lack of consensus on such issues, some conclude that teaching about sexualities in today's schools may not be possible.

CHAPTER 9

Sex Education Should Exclusively Endorse Abstinence as the Only Effective Prevention of the Unacceptable Risks of Nonmarital Sexual Relations

George A. Rekers and Richard C. Hohn

During psychotherapy, 13-year-old Tracy claimed her sexual partner, Tom, "loves me." The next week, she discovered Tom's sexual relationship with another girl. The third week, Tracy "loved" Chad, sharing intercourse. Two weeks later, she described sexual relations with 20-year-old Mike, "because I'm his now." Tracy's emotional need for affection from males was related to neglect by her father. These sexual relationships were motivated by desire for affection more than sexual stimulation.

NONMARITAL SEXUAL RELATIONS
CAUSE MASSIVE PROBLEMS

Tracy's parents had divorced when she was 6 years old, and her father had not made any effort to contact her since she was 7. Tracy understandably felt rejected by her father (Heatherington, 1972; Rekers, 1981). But not only had her father tragically failed her, Tracy's school sex education also failed her, pretending that no recommendation regarding "right" or "wrong" could be made, even though it should have been "concerned with moral as well as health-related issues" (Post & Botkin, 1995, p. 41). Tracy's contraceptive education could not protect her from her immaturity and the emptiness she felt when losing a sexual partner (Bagley, 1995). Psychological risks (Schumm, 1995; Seidman & Rieder, 1994) are associated with premature sexual involvement (Fagan, 1988; Kilpatrick, 1993; Petty, 1995; Rekers, 1978, 1992, 1995; Schumm & Rekers, 1984). Sexualized dating gives a false sense of emotional intimacy, short-cuts communication (Lickona, 1992; Schumm & Rekers, 1984), and results in pregnancy and sexually transmitted diseases (STDs) (Mellanby, Phelps, & Tripp, 1993; Seidman & Rieder, 1994), as Tracy also experienced. Adolescent motherhood is associated with increased medical complications, lower occupational and educational attainment, greater eventual marital instability, higher rates of child abuse, and generally poorer mothering (Kilpatrick, 1993; Schumm, 1995). As was the case for Tracy's pregnancy, national studies indicate that about two-thirds of fathers of children born to adolescent mothers are "postschool adult men" (Males, 1992; Males & Chew, 1996). By contrast, abstinence frees a couple to invest more time to relate at deeper emotional levels (Schumm & Rekers, 1984) and provides the only genuine protection from pregnancy and STDs.

DECADES OF "SAFER-SEX" EDUCATION APPROACHES HAVE NOT ADEQUATELY PREVENTED PROBLEMATIC SEXUAL BEHAVIOR

"The failure of sex education," was the conclusion of the lead article of *The Atlantic Monthly* in October 1994 (Whitehead, 1994).

Inadequacies of Older "Safer Sex"/Contraception Education

Stanford University professor Larry Cuban's (1986) earlier review similarly had concluded that from the time sex education courses were initiated in the 1930s up until 1986, statistics found them to be ineffective in reducing sexual relations, unwanted pregnancy, and STDs among adolescents. A Centers for Disease Control study of 14 separate sex education programs concluded that none of them had a measurable influence on whether or not the students experienced subsequent sexual intercourse or on their frequency of sexual intercourse (Kirby, 1984). A review by Visser and van Blisen (1994) concluded that safer-sex contraceptive education courses seemed to have no impact on sexual behavior; instead, the adolescent students exposed to them acquired more liberal attitudes toward sexuality.

The review by Marsiglio and Mott (1986) concluded that a greater percentage of adolescent females exposed to the older contraceptive sex education courses initiate sexual activity at ages 15 and 16 than those not receiving sex education. Even when scientifically controlling for factors that might be associated with both the likelihood of taking a course and the outcome variable, taking a contraception sex education course has been found to be positively associated with the initiation of sexual activity at these ages (Marsiglio & Mott, 1986). A review by Dawson (1986) similarly concluded that while "safer-sex" education (without the newer abstinence emphasis with a clear goal to postpone sexual activity) was not found to contribute to an increase in sexual activity for older teens, it actually increased sexual activity by 50% in 14-year-olds (see also Stout, 1989).

Disappointing Effectiveness of Abstinence-or-Contraception Approaches

A more recent form of public school sex education combines the older contraception education approach with a strong abstinence message that specifically sets the curricular goal as being to encourage the delay of onset of intercourse by the adolescent students. Some recent studies of sexuality curricula have not found an increase in sexual activity following this newer type of sex education, which combines an abstinence message with contraception education (Kirby et al., 1994). Kirby and colleagues (1994) concluded that while some of these recent sex education programs have been reported to be effective, "there has been considerable disappointment, partly because programs have not been nearly as effective as many people had hoped, and partly because program evaluations have been incapable of measuring small effects" (p. 358). This review of the effectiveness of such school-based programs designed to reduce sexual risk behavior, which described the various methodological limitations of various types of studies evaluating sex education, concluded that "results are mixed" (p. 342); studies based upon national surveys found sex education to be associated with greater probability of subsequent initiation of intercourse for some populations, associated with lowered probability for initiation of intercourse with other populations, and not significantly related to subsequent intercourse for other groups. Kirby and colleagues (1994) also reviewed the greatly varied pretest/posttest studies of specific sex education programs, noting their methodological limitations, and concluded that contraception education in combination with abstinence or topics such as resistance skills were not associated with earlier onset of intercourse; further, some recent studies of curricula that combine contraception education with the clear goal of delaying onset of intercourse "successfully reduced the proportion of sexually inexperienced students who initiated sex during the following 12 to 18 months" (p. 352), and some of these curricula increased contraceptive use among those who initiated intercourse after the program.

UNSCIENTIFIC ASSUMPTIONS PERVADING
FAILED SEX EDUCATION

Proponents of "safer-sex" education often assume that adolescents are normally "sexually active" and thus require "preventive" intervention.

Unscientific Assumptions About Adolescent Sexual Behavior

However, in spite of great shifts in the number of *episodic* sexual relationships among a *minority* of secondary school students, the best data indicate that abstinence is the norm for that group (Kokotailo & Stephenson, 1993). A study of seventh and eighth graders in Washington, Oregon, California, and Idaho, revealed that only 16% had had sexual intercourse more than once, only 9% had had sex in the past four weeks, only 6% had had sex five or more times, and only 2% had had sex ten or more times (Jensen, deGaston, & Weed, 1994). The Lou Harris/Planned Parenthood poll found that 72% of 12- to 17-year-old girls had not engaged in intercourse (cited by Kilpatrick, 1993, p. 59). The National Center for Health Statistics (1988) found that 65% of all high school females under 18 are virgins. The mean age at which adolescents experience their first sexual contact is 16 for males and 16.5 for females, and these teens and society would be better served if sexual activity could be further postponed to even later ages through school sex education.

Unscientific Assumptions Regarding Epidemiology

This being the case, Lundy and Rekers (1995b) pointed to a major risk in delivering "safe-sex" contraceptive education to the entire school population:

> "Preventive" intervention, if applied to one not actually at high risk for the outcome for which the intervention is designed, will not only fail to help the recipient, but may cause overt harm. . . . Since almost *all* interventions, whether medical, surgical, or psychosocial, carry some inherent risk in and of themselves, it is essential to focus interventions where they are both necessary and likely to be efficacious (Lundy & Pumariega, 1993). By inadvertently encouraging the very activity that one wishes to prevent (Aldrich, 1974), "preventive" efforts can have an effect precisely opposite of that intended. The application of so-called preventive interventions across the board without an actual assessment of risk (Boyle & Offord, 1990; Lundy, Pfohl, & Kuperman, 1993) is irresponsible, and betrays a fundamental misunderstanding of epidemiology (Kelsey, Thompson, & Evans, 1986; Schlesselman, 1982). (pp. 333–334)

Unscientific Assumptions About "Protection" of Contraceptives

With a false sense of "protection" acquired from unrealistic contraception curricula, increasing numbers of adolescents have engaged in risky sexual relations, mistakenly at ease, thinking that they are having essentially "safe" sex (Kilpatrick, 1993; Pollner, 1988). Empirical evidence indicates that "safer-sex" education likely caused overt harm by increasing sexual intercourse among unmarried youth by endorsing the underprotected practice of condom use and other contraception strategies that expose otherwise abstinent adolescents to vulnerability to pregnancy, AIDS, and other STDs. Ravenel (1988, 1989) observed that the dangerous effects also include various complications caused by early use of oral contraceptives and the increased risk of cervical cancer with early onset of sexual activity. "It is unfortunate that an approach that is both effective and possible to maintain, abstinence, has been challenged in favor of one that is both much more difficult to achieve and to maintain in adolescence, sexual moderation" (Lundy & Rekers, 1995c, p. 352).

Unscientific Assumptions About Disclosure by Sexual Partners

An unrealistic prescription for "safe sex" is "Know your partner." But research indicates that many are untruthful; Kilpatrick (1993) asked, "But how well can you know your partner if he or she lies?" (p. 63) A study of 400 college students revealed that 34% of the males and 10% of the females admitted they had told another person a lie in order to have sex with them; 47% of the males said they would deliberately underestimate the number of previous sexual partners if asked; and 20% of the men said they would lie about the result of their HIV test (Cochran & Mays, 1990; see also Desiderato & Crawford, 1995, on high rates of failure to disclose prior risky sexual behavior).

Furthermore, recent studies indicate that in the initial weeks after a person contracts HIV, he or she may be up to 1,000 times more infectious than in the following symptom-free years. Unfortunately, this early period of "primary infection" occurs before antibodies, as measured by widespread cheaper HIV testing methods, appear. This means that a person at this stage would receive negative test results. So even a partner who honestly reveals a negative result could, in fact, be in the early most infections stage ("AIDS Update," 1995).

Unrealistic Assumptions of the Decision-Making Approach

Surprisingly (in view of AIDS), some sex educators still endorse a moral relativism. Mosher (1991) contended that respect for human autonomy implies that individuals should be free to practice sexual abstinence, lifelong monogamy, safer sex, and even less-safe sex. Kilpatrick (1993) pointed out that such relativism means anything is permissible. Teachers following this approach try to lend support to everyone's value system.

Imagine having a 4-year-old daughter who was abducted, raped, mutilated, and then murdered. How would you react to the perpetrator? Would you say, "You've violated a rule of society that we just shouldn't do that." Not likely. One would think that something outrageously immoral had taken place, not simply some transgression of a social convention. Virtually all honest, sane people think that child rape, child sexual abuse, and child murder are always wrong—intrinsically evil, unfair, and unjust.

Because of the existence of such absolute moral values, it logically follows that many world religions would also recognize and teach that murder, rape, torture, and so forth are moral evils, but one does not need to endorse any particular creed to arrive at the truth of absolute moral values. In fact, the review by Kirby and colleagues (1994) concluded that the methods of sex education curricula that are effective in postponing intercourse are those that took a "clear stand and emphasized clear behavioral values and norms" (p. 355), whereas the ineffective sex education programs tended to use a decision-making model in which students were "instructed to make their own decisions" (p. 355).

Unscientific Assumptions Regarding Parents and Religion

Religious variables are strong predictors of sexual attitudes and behavior (e.g., Dawson, 1986; Marsigilo & Mott, 1986; Miller & Olson, 1988; Struder & Thornton, 1989; White & DeBlassie, 1992). Adolescents who value their spiritual life and who frequently attend church have significantly less-permissive sexual attitudes and engage in less sexual activity (Thornton & Camburn, 1989). Behavioral motivation is highly correlated with personal beliefs, and behavioral change typically follows a change in values, which is itself commonly induced by a religious conversion (Pattison & Pattison, 1980). A conservative Protestant childrearing has stronger demonstrated effects upon adolescent sexual activity than prior exposure to a school course in sex education (Marsiglio & Mott, 1986). Weekly church attendance reduces the likelihood of first intercourse at all ages (Dawson, 1986).

But rather than build on such powerful supports for sexual self-restraint, a widely used textbook for sex education, *Changing Bodies, Changing Lives*, tells the student:

> If you feel your parents are overprotective . . . or if they don't want you to be sexual *at all* until some distant time, you may feel you have to tune out their voice entirely.

Many Catholics, Protestants, Jews, and Muslims believe sex outside marriage is sinful. You will have to decide for yourself how important these messages are for you. (quoted in Kilpatrick, 1993, p. 53)

In a society where religious faith is a constitutionally protected right and where the major religions teach that sexuality is to be reserved for marriage, the public schools have taught the relativistic values of "safer sex" in opposition to the common values of the majority of parents. This has been widely perceived by parents as an infringement of the right to free exercise of religion without interference by the state. Thus "safer-sex" contraceptive education has proven to be very controversial in American society.

Public school teachers and textbooks should convey respect, rather than skepticism and disdain, for the values of religious students and parents (Bennett, 1987). Teachers should encourage children to talk to their parents about sexual values.

For a university course on sexuality, the first author invited several clergy to class. One clergyman conveyed permissiveness regarding premarital sex. A curious student inquired, "Do you give your own teenagers this same advice that it is OK to have 'protected' heterosexual or homosexual relations before marriage, and that unmarried cohabitation is merely the decision of the couple involved?" This clergyman, now speaking as a parent, retorted: "Of course not! My kids know I would never tolerate that. I expect them to wait for sex until they are married with a faithful member of (his religion)."[1]

LOGIC AND SCIENTIFIC FACTS INDICATE THAT ONLY EXCLUSIVE ABSTINENCE EDUCATION WILL ACHIEVE GENUINE PREVENTION

For the two decades since 1970, when the U.S. government began to spend billions of dollars for contraception programs, unwed pregnancies increased 87% among 15- to 19-year olds (Family Research Council, 1992),[2] and although abortions among adolescents rose 67% (Crouse, 1992), unwed births increased 83.8% (National Center for Health Statistics, 1993). (These trends have moderated recently in that the unwed teen pregnancy rates for the most recent two years have declined slightly, but the decade effects still show huge increases over rates prior to 1970.) Three million adolescents are infected by STDs annually (U.S. Department of Health and Human Services, 1991). Many STDs are incurable (e.g., genital herpes and AIDS), certain STD strains are antibiotic-resistant (Goldstein & Garabedian-Ruffalo, 1991), and AIDS leads to premature death (Rekers, 1989). Genital cancers associated with the human papilloma virus cause more deaths in women than AIDS (McIlhaney, 1990). With such risks, it is significant that condoms cannot provide 100% protection from STDs and AIDS.

Most Minors Lack Competence to Avoid Risks with Sex

Minors are rarely competent to make decisions to engage in sexual relationships, which involve such potential lifetime consequences (Lundy & Rekers, 1995a, 1995b, 1995c). It is easier for minors to delay the onset of sexual behavior than to later modify sexual patterns (Rotheram-Borus & Gwadz, 1993). A Yankelovich poll found that two-thirds of all adult Americans believe that schools should urge teenagers not to have sexual intercourse ("National poll," 1986); 86% of sex education teachers endorse abstinence as the best way to prevent pregnancy and STDs (Forrest & Silverman, 1989). Because the primary reason adolescents engage in intercourse is peer pressure (*American Teens Speak*, 1986), it is not surprising that 87% of adolescent girls want to learn how to decline sex without hurting the boy's feelings (U.S. Department of Education, 1988). Thus there is an overlapping consensus that abstinence is best for minor children. Furthermore, abstinence does work for the majority of adolescents, and minors need to be taught that *abstinence is normal* for their age (L. K. Brown, DiClemente, & Beausoleil, 1992; Kokotailo & Stephenson, 1993).

High-risk behavior, such as having multiple sexual partners, is related to young age of first intercourse (Koyle, Jensen, Olsen, & Cundick, 1989; Mellanby et al., 1993; Seidman & Rieder, 1994). Sexually active adolescents are less knowledgeable about HIV and have a greater history of other risk behavior (L. K. Brown et al., 1992).

Adolescents are inconsistent users of condoms, even after contraceptive education (Kilpatrick, 1993). Although contraception education has been widespread, many sexually active teenagers have multiple, serial sexual relationships, and the vast majority of them do not use condoms consistently (Seidman & Rieder, 1994). Fifty-eight percent of adolescent girls under 18 do not use contraception during their first intercourse (Mosher & McNally, 1991). Adolescents continue unprotected intercourse for a full year, on the average, before initiating any form of contraception (Hayes, 1987). Fifty-three percent of homosexual/bisexual adolescents aged 14 to 19 do not consistently use condoms during risky homosexual activity (Rotheram-Borus, Reid, Rosario, & Kasen, 1995). It is more demanding for the average teenager to always use condoms than to achieve complete abstinence (Hayes, 1987; Kilpatrick, 1993).

Unacceptable Risk for AIDS and STDs Exist with Condom Use

Even with condom use, the failure rate is unacceptable; condoms fail 36.3% of the time annually in preventing pregnancy among young, unmarried minority women (Jones & Forrest, 1989). The annual unplanned pregnancy rate with condom use is 10% for women and 18% for adolescents under age 18, but these figures increase for women who use them additional years (Kilpatrick, 1993).

Condoms are even less effective in protecting against the AIDS virus, which is 410 times smaller than sperm; 30% of males who use condoms during anal sex report one or more episodes of condom breakage in the previous six months (Kilpatrick, 1993). Weller's (1993) meta-analysis of 11 independent studies concluded that condoms are 69% effective in preventing HIV transmission in heterosexual couples (that means 31% transmitted HIV to their partner). Thus, if an adolescent developed a sexual relationship with a partner unknowingly infected with HIV, using a condom would reduce the chances of contracting AIDS from nearly 100% down to 31%, but total abstinence would reduce HIV transmission to 0%. So recommending condom use by unmarried teens is like advocating "safer" Russian roulette by recommending reducing the number of pulls of the gun's trigger.

The Only Totally Effective Prevention Strategy Is Mutual Abstinence Until Monogamy

The Food and Drug Administration, the Center for Prevention Services, and the Centers for Disease Control (CDC) jointly concluded:

> Abstinence and sexual intercourse with one mutually faithful uninfected partner are the only totally effective prevention strategies. Proper use of condoms with each act of sexual intercourse can reduce, but not eliminate, risk of STD. Individuals likely to become infected or known to be infected with HIV should be aware that condom use cannot completely eliminate the risk of transmission to themselves or to others. (quoted in American Medical Association, 1988, p. 1926)

We should be able to reach the "overlapping consensus" that this research-based health fact should be taught in the public school. In light of this established scientific fact and life-threatening STDs, the worst thing public sex education could do would be to advocate—directly or indirectly—that adolescents become involved in sexual relationships outside a mutually faithful, monogamous marriage. The United States Department of Education similarly concluded:

> In particular, young people must know that the use of condoms can reduce, but by no means eliminate, the risk of contracting AIDS. Condoms can and do fail. The use of condoms can reduce the risk of infection when engaging in sexual activity, but they must be used from start to finish and in a manner that prevents any exchange of bodily fluids. Even then there is no guarantee of safety.

. . . The Surgeon General has also warned that condoms have "extraordinarily high" failure rates among homosexuals. (p. 16)

THE ONLY TRULY COMPASSIONATE
TYPE OF SEX EDUCATION ENDORSES
RISK ELIMINATION, NOT RISK REDUCTION

Schools should consistently and exclusively endorse self-restraint from all behaviors that needlessly place one at risk for illness or death. Just as with drug education, teaching sexual abstinence should not be compromised just because some rebelliously have sexual intercourse. Just as physicians may ethically refuse to offer second-rate treatment if the patient refuses safer, available, and more cost-effective treatment of first choice, those educating children should resist pressures to prescribe less than the best available (Lundy & Rekers, 1995b). Resumption of abstinence by drug-abusing or sexually active teenagers often occurs when they hear an uncompromising abstinence endorsement (Ravenel, 1989). Therefore sex education should unequivocally and exclusively endorse the postponement of sexual relations by minors until marriage. The promotion of the deferment of decisions best reserved for maturity is much more ethical and compassionate than taking a supposedly "'neutral' approach to matters of life and death" (Lundy & Rekers, 1995b, p. 326). Students should be taught the moral, emotional, and health advantages of such prevention (Petty, 1995; Rekers, 1984, 1989, 1991b).

One faulty argument for the failed "safer-sex," "value-free" sex education was that it was necessary to promote cultural diversity; supposedly, the school's promotion of the cross-cultural truth of the health benefits of abstinence until marriage would denigrate individuals whose behavior is sexually different, such as those who perform nonmarital heterosexual or homosexual behavior, bestiality, or prostitution. However, there is no empirical reason why sex education promoting abstinence cannot successfully teach compassion toward individuals who take real health, emotional, legal, or moral risks by nonmarital sexual patterns. A national poll found that the vast majority of Americans do not support teaching public school students "that homosexuality is just an alternate sexual activity" (Leo, 1986). Adolescent homosexual behavior is associated with significant disadvantages, life-threatening health risks, and sharp cultural controversy regarding its morality (Barna, 1992; Lundy & Rekers, 1995a, 1995b; Rekers, 1981, 1982a, 1982b, 1989, 1991a; U.S. Department of Education, 1988). However, research shows that individuals who engage in homosexual behavior can be warmly accepted and helped although their sexual behavior is simultaneously disapproved of (Pattison & Pattison, 1980).

Some sex educators try to graft an abstinence message onto nondirective contraceptive education in a relativistic decision-making curriculum, but this risk-reduction (instead of the risk-elimination) approach conveys a compromised message (Kilpatrick, 1993). Many teens report that teaching contraception along with sexual abstinence is problematic for them (D. L. Brown, 1993). An unnecessary credibility problem occurs when schools educate students to abstain from sex while simultaneously teaching that condom use acceptably reduces the risks of sexual activity (Lickona, 1992), even though such mixed-message programs at the university level increase abstinence among males (Turner, Garrison, Korpita, & Waller, 1994). Former U.S. education secretary William Bennett (1988) convincingly argued that moral realism cannot be sacrificed in sex education. He contended that it is irresponsible for adults to give up by telling teenagers that we expect them to have sex but to limit the damage by using condoms. It is more responsible to tell the adolescent how we expect him or her to behave, as we do in other important areas of life (Bennett, 1988).

Recent Sex Education Exclusively Endorsing Abstinence

It was not until 1981 that the Adolescent Family Life Act made several million federal dollars available for programs that would unequivocally promote sexual abstinence (Title XX of the Public Health Service Act, Section 2001[a][1][A]). Because "abstinence-only" sex education is a recent innovation in the history of American public schools, there has not been the same opportunity for extensive outcome research as has been conducted on the contraceptive sex education approach. There remains the need for more extensive research on the effectiveness of abstinence-only sex education, but preliminary findings tentatively suggest a significant decrease in pregnancies among adolescents as a function of exclusively teaching abstinence. Significant reductions in pregnancy rates have been reported with abstinence education that excludes contraception education, although the available studies are currently few in number and have some design limitations; even 10 years ago, Ravenel (1988) noted that empirical data suggested that an abstinence-only message was associated with stable declines in unwed teen pregnancy in populations with previous high pregnancy rates. Participants in the *Project Taking Charge* abstinence-based program were significantly "less likely than comparison subjects to report the initiation of sexual intercourse within the six months following the program" (Jorgensen, Potts, & Camp, 1993, p. 401). The *Sexuality, Commitment and Family* curriculum's endorsement of abstinence was evaluated in a school district with one of the highest pregnancy rates in California in 1984: A preliminary study reported that the adolescent pregnancy rate of nearly 20% was reduced to 2.5% in 1986 and then to 1.5% in 1988, suggesting that positive effects may be produced by abstinence-only education, although further research is indicated because the empirical investigation had some design limitations.[3] Similarly, a recent federal study of girls who had taken the *Sex Respect* program over a five-year period in 26 schools found the pregnancy rate to be 5%, which was 44% less than for girls who had not participated; this finding also tentatively suggests the potential benefits of an abstinence-only message and further lends support to the pursuit of more extensive, follow-up research on the long-term effects of this newer abstinence-only sex education for the general population of public school students (U.S. Office of Pregnancy Programs, 1990).[4]

A review of studies on the effectiveness of new abstinence-based education (Lickona, 1992) found positive outcomes for: *Community of Caring* programs, sponsored by the Joseph P. Kennedy, Jr., Foundation; *Decision-Making: Keys to Total Success*, by the San Marcos, California, school system; *Postponing Sexual Involvement*, by Atlanta's Grady Memorial Hospital (Howard & McCabe, 1990); *Project Respect*, federally funded; *Sex Respect*, by Colleen Kelly Mast, federally funded; *Sexuality, Commitment, and Family*, by Teen-Aid. Other successful curricula include *AANCHOR, Responsible Sexual Values Program (RSVP)*, and *Me, My World, My Future* (Kilpatrick, 1993). Positive outcomes in acquisition of abstinence values have been empirically demonstrated with pre- and postmeasures for abstinence programs (Eisenman, 1994; Olsen, Weed, Daly, & Jensen, 1992a), including *Values and Choices, Teen Aid*, and *Sex Respect* (Olsen, Weed, Nielsen, & Jensen, 1992b; Olsen, Weed, Ritz, & Jensen, 1991; Weed & Jensen, 1993). Further, all three programs are rated positively by both teachers and students (Olsen et al., 1992b). A study of an abstinence sex education implemented in 24 Washington, Oregon, California, and Idaho public schools reported: "The program was effective across all student groups studied. However, more change took place when the teachers were supportive of the program objectives" (deGaston, Jensen, Weed, & Tanas, 1994).

The Empirical Rationale for Parental Involvement

"Liberal" parents and "conservative" parents alike share the same desires regarding abstinence from sexual conduct by *their own* children. Parents overwhelmingly prefer that their own children postpone sexual relations until marriage. Even most homosexual parents prefer that their own children become married heterosexuals (Javaid, 1993; Kirkpatrick, 1987; Lundy & Rekers, 1995a; Wolfson, 1987). Across various cultures and subcultures, adolescents with the lowest rates of risk-taking behavior (substance abuse or sexual behavior) have close communication and involvement with their parents that promotes shared religious and nonreligious values (Baumeister, Flores, &

Marin, 1995; Flores-Ortiz, 1994; Marchi & Guendelman, 1994–1995; Regier, 1986; Rekers, 1984, 1988; Uhlenberg & Eggebeen, 1986). Thus parental protectiveness is normally a good ally in promoting the kind of adolescent risk elimination endorsed by the CDC.

Many sex educators cite the failure of many parents to provide sex education to their own children as a rationale for sex education in the schools. However, this fact combined with the empirically observed relationship between close parent–child communication and lower adolescent pregnancy rates (Baumeister et al., 1995; Flores-Ortiz, 1994; Marchi & Guendelman, 1994–1995; see Rekers, 1984, 1985) more logically forms the rationale for those public schools serving diverse cultural groups that now actively collaborate with parents by providing them training on *how* to teach their own children about sexuality (King de Arias, 1989)—a task that has been successfully accomplished where attempted (Bundy & White, 1990; Caron, Knox, Rhoades, & Aho, 1993; Huston, Martin, & Foulds, 1990).

One public school designed a sex education process in which all parents were invited to submit names of willing professionals from their faith community to be the sex education instructor for their child. Groups of students with their parents were formed such that Roman Catholic parents agreed on a Catholic nurse to be the sex educator for their children; Jewish parents agreed on a Jewish physician; some Baptist parents agreed on a Baptist counselor; and so forth. No parents were denied the opportunity to select the sex educator for their own children. For parents who did not designate a person to be the sex educator, the instructors selected by other parents were offered as options. Parents were invited to participate in the classes with their children.

This approach (1) accomplished the task of sex education, (2) led to parental satisfaction, (3) eliminated contentious controversy, and (4) resulted in effective promotion of postponement of sexual behavior until marriage (Denton, 1984). The newer *Family Honor* program commendably goes a further step in promoting a commitment to chastity by *mandating* that one or both parents be present with their child in order to empower the parents to be the primary sex educators of their own children (Hucks, 1995).

COUNSELING FOR THE SEXUALLY INVOLVED MINORITY

There is a delinquent-prone minority of adolescents who rebel against the abstinence message, whether applied to illicit drugs and/or sexual intercourse (Arndt, 1995; Elliott & Morse, 1989). And many teenagers have "unprotected" sexual intercourse even after receiving contraceptive education in school; a study in Denmark, for example, found high rates of intercourse without contraception in spite of early and extensive contraceptive sex education (Arnett & Balle-Jensen, 1993). While some risk reduction for sexually involved adolescents is afforded by condoms, the benefit/risk ratio for an individual having sex with condoms is so deadly that it is fraudulent for schools to recommend condoms, because that endorses behavior with significant risk of death in exchange for brief pleasure (Lundy & Rekers, 1995c).

So, how should public schools deal with the minority of adolescents who are sexually involved? The only responsible answer is

1. *Educate* them (collaboratively with their parents, if possible) with these truths: They have not followed the best moral course. Their nonmarital sexual interaction risks their health and life even if they use condoms to somewhat reduce that risk. Contraceptive devices cannot make premarital sex emotionally or physically safe. One can return to abstinence (Bennett, 1987, 1994).
2. *Provide individual counselling* to compassionately motivate and equip them to return to abstinence (Lundy & Rekers, 1995c; Petty, 1995). "Physicians should not be value-neutral, with respect to sexual activity, nor resigned to defeat against cultural forces that promote intercourse as the gateway to maturity" (Post & Botkin, 1995, p. 41). Refusal skills technology from addiction research has been successfully applied to sexually active adolescents (St. Lawrence, Brasfield, Jefferson, & Alleyne, 1995; Warzak, Grow, Poler, & Walburn, 1995; Warzak, Kuhn, & Nolten, 1995).

CONCLUSION: UNIVERSAL CROSS-CULTURAL, COMPASSIONATE EDUCATION

Culture is, and should be, foundationally transmitted to a child by the child's family of origin. Various cultures and subcultures contain different meanings and different ethical, moral, and/or religious standards regarding sexuality and sexual behavior, and we observe that this fact is at the core of the sex education debate. A central point of overlapping consensus is the recognition that in American society, these differences in parent-transmitted culture and subculture should be *freely held* without a "solution" of one cultural value system imposed by political dominance or public educational coercion (as Kenneth Strike observed). Thus in our free society, parents should be free to perpetuate the pluralistic society by transmitting their own culture, religion, and values to their own children. For this reason, public school teachers should encourage children to talk to their parents about sexual values.

Because nonmarital sexual relations in adolescents cause premature death and other massive health and social problems, and because human life and health are greater goods than premature illness and death, sexual relations by minors should and can be prevented by parent-involved public school education and counseling. This premise regarding the superior value of life is a self-evident, universal, absolute moral value; it applies to all our diverse subcultures; it has a clear consensus in American society; and it can and should be legally taught in public schools. No public school sex education should contradict each student's family religious values, for constitutional and empirical reasons.

The "safer-sex"/contraception education approach fails to reliably reduce adolescent rates of sexual intercourse, conception, and abortion because of (1) relativistic ethics, (2) a neglect of potent parental and religiosity variables, (3) unrealistic assumptions about adolescent behavior, and (4) a fundamental misunderstanding of epidemiology. In contrast, preliminary research studies tentatively demonstrate that teaching the value of abstinence contributes to the prevention of premarital sexual relations and related problems of pregnancies and STDs.

All students must be taught the medical facts that also apply to all subcultures, namely that only mutual abstinence until monogamous marriage is genuinely safe and that unacceptable, life-threatening risks for AIDS and other STDs exist with all other sexual relations whether with or without condom use. Risk elimination, not risk reduction, is the only logical and truly compassionate health goal for sex education and counseling. There is an overlapping consensus among parents and teachers, who overwhelmingly agree with the sex education goal of encouraging and equipping adolescents to abide by the scientifically established recommendation of the CDC to abstain from sexual intercourse until they can attain a mutually faithful monogamous relationship in adulthood.[5]

NOTES

1. A "neo-conservative" is said to be defined as a liberal whose daughter is approaching puberty.

2. Although part of this increase was due to an increase in the population size of this adolescent age group, population size does not account for all of the increase; shifts in societal factors, shifts in moral values, and the presence of contraceptive sex education could account for the remainder of the increase. See Family Research Council (1992), p. 2.

3. A nonrefereed study cited by Kilpatrick, 1993, p. 73.

4. Not published in a refereed academic journal, but by the U.S. government.

5. At this point, it is important for the reader to be informed that Chapter 9 was written to describe and present a case for teaching abstinence in sex education. In writing Chapter 9, we had no prior knowledge of the content or references of Chapter 10, nor did we ever have any access to peer reviewers' comments on Chapter 10; however, the author of Chapter 10 not only had full access to the content and references of our chapter but also to all the peer reviewers' comments on our chapter and our responses to those reviewers. We do not believe that the process originally proposed by the book editors to us and as originally agreed to by all parties was fairly carried out, because we were not afforded the same parallel opportunity for access to Chapter 10, its references, and its reviewers' comments as afforded to the author of Chapter 10.

We were given the limited and brief opportunity at the last minute (and at an inopportune time for our academic and travel schedules) to respond to Chapter 10 with the restriction of not being allowed to cite any additional research references. But we have chosen not to do so, not only because of time constraints but also because we believe that the logical case we stated *for* abstinence education is a strong one and will stand up to the scrutiny of the discerning reader who realizes that reason, values, and available empirical evidence must be considered and that because public school abstinence education is a more recent innovation about which there has not been time to develop a more comprehensive body of evidence, it therefore has been afforded only initial research efforts at empirical evaluation. Let the reader decide which sex education approach and which presented case is the strongest—and which viewpoint is ultimately the best for our children and for society at large.

REFERENCES

AIDS update. (1995, May). *Men's Health, 10*(4), 42.

Aldrich, C. K. (1974). Youth's fulfillment of adult prophecies. *Australian New Zealand Journal of Psychiatry, 8,* 127–129.

American Medical Association. (1988). Condoms for prevention of sexually transmitted diseases. *Journal of the American Medical Association, 259*(13), 1925–1927.

American teens speak: Sex myths, TV and birth control. (1986). New York: Louis Harris & Associates.

Arndt, W. B. (1995). Deviant sexual behavior in children and adolescents. In G. A. Rekers (Ed.), *Handbook of child and adolescent sexual problems* (pp. 414–435). New York: Lexington Books.

Arnett, J., & Balle-Jensen, L. (1993). Cultural bases of risk behavior: Danish adolescents. *Child Development, 64*(6), 1842–1855.

Bagley, C. (1995). Early sexual experience and sexual victimization of children and adolescents. In G. A. Rekers (Ed.), *Handbook of child and adolescent sexual problems* (pp. 135–163). New York: Lexington Books.

Barna, G. (1992). *The invisible generation: Baby busters.* Glendale, CA: Barna Research Group.

Baumeister, L. M., Flores, E., & Marin, B. V. (1995). Sex information given to Latina adolescents by parents. *Health Education Research, 10*(2), 233–239.

Bennett, W. J. (1987, January 14). Sex and the education of our children. *America*, p. 122.

Bennett, W. J. (1988). AIDS education. In G. P. Regier (Ed.), *Values and public policy* (pp. 15–23). Washington, DC: Family Research Council of America.

Bennett, W. J. (1994). *The de-valuing of America*. Colorado Springs, CO: Focus on the Family Publishing.

Boyle, M. H., & Offord, D. R. (1990). Primary prevention of conduct disorder. *Journal of the American Academy of Child and Adolescent Psychiatry, 29*(2), 227–233.

Brown, D. L. (1993, November 21). Virginity is new counterculture among teens. *The Washington Post*, p. 3.

Brown, L. K., DiClemente, R. J., & Beausoleil, N. I. (1992). Comparison of human immunodeficiency virus related knowledge, attitudes, intentions, and behaviors among sexually active and abstinent young adults. *Journal of Adolescent Health, 13*(2), 140–145.

Bundy, M. L., & White, P. N. (1990). Parents as sexuality educators: A parent training program. *Journal of Counseling and Development, 68*(3), 321–323.

Caron, S. L., Knox, C. B., Rhoades, C., & Aho, J. (1993). Sexuality education in the workplace: Seminars for parents. *Journal of Sex Education and Therapy, 19*(3), 200–211.

Cochran, S., & Mays, V. (1990, March 15). Correspondence. *New England Journal of Medicine*, p. 774.

Crouse, G. L. (1992, March 12). *Report based on data from Planned Parenthood's Alan Guttmacher Institute since 1973*. Office of Planning and Evaluation, U.S. Department of Health and Human Services, Washington, DC.

Cuban, L. (1986, December). Sex and school reform. *Phi Delta Kappan*, p. 321.

Dawson, D. A. (1986). The effects of sex education on adolescent behavior. *Family Planning Perspectives, 18*(4), 162–169.

deGaston, J. F., Jensen, L., Weed, S. E., & Tanas, R. (1994). Teacher philosophy and program implementation and the impact on sex education outcomes. *Journal of Research and Development in Education, 27*(4), 265–270.

Denton, Senator J. (subcommittee chair). (1984). Commentary on parental involvement in a school sex education program. In Hearings before the Subcommittee on Family and Human Services, Committee on Labor and Human Resources, United States Senate, *Parental involvement with their adolescents in crisis*. Washington, DC: U. S. Government Printing Office.

Desiderato, L. L., & Crawford, H. J. (1995). Risky sexual behavior in college students. *Journal of Youth and Adolescence, 24*(1), 55–68.

Eisenman, R. (1994). Conservative sexual values: Effects of an abstinence program on student attitudes. *Journal of Sex Education and Therapy, 20*(2), 75–78.

Elliott, D. S., & Morse, B. J. (1989). Delinquency and drug use as risk factors in teenage sexual activity. *Youth and Society, 21*(1), 32–57.

Fagan, P. F. (Ed.). (1988). *Hope for homosexuality*. Washington, DC: Center for Child and Family Policy of the Free Congress Research and Education Foundation.

Family Research Council. (1992, February). Condom roulette. *In Focus*, p. 2.

Flores-Ortiz, Y. G. (1994). The role of cultural and gender values in alcohol use patterns among Chicana/Latina high school and university students: Implications for AIDS prevention. *International Journal of the Addictions, 29*(9), 1149–1171.

Forrest, J. D., & Silverman, J. (1989, March–April). What public school teachers teach about preventing pregnancy, AIDS, and sexually transmitted disease. *Family Planning Perspectives*, pp. 56–72.

Goldstein, A. M. B., & Garabedian-Ruffalo, S. M. (1991, August). A treatment update to resistant gonorrhea. *Medical Aspects of Human Sexuality*, p. 39.

Hayes, C. D. (Ed.). (1987). *Risking the future: Adolescent sexuality, pregnancy and childbearing*. Washington, DC: National Academy Press.

Heatherington, E. M. (1972). The effects of father absence on personality development in adolescent daughters. *Developmental Psychology, 7*, 313–326.

Howard, M., & McCabe, J. (1990). Helping teenagers postpone sexual involvement. *Family Planning Perspective, 22*, 21–26.

Hucks, B. (1995, February). Bringing families closer together through chastity education. *Palmetto Family Council Citizen*, pp. 1–2.

Huston, R. L., Martin, L. J., & Foulds, D. M. (1990). Effect of a program to facilitate parent–child communication about sex. *Clinical Pediatrics, 29*(11), 626–633.

Javaid, G. A. (1993). The children of homosexual and heterosexual single mothers. *Child Psychiatry and Human Development, 23*(4), 235–248.

Jensen, L. C., deGaston, J. F., & Weed, S. E. (1994). Societal and parental influences on adolescent sexual behavior. *Psychological Reports, 75*(2), 928–930.

Jones, E. F., & Forrest, J. D. (1989). Contraceptive failure in the United States. *Family Planning Perspectives, 21*, 105.

Jorgensen, S. R., Potts, V., & Camp, B. (1993). Project taking charge: Six-month follow-up of a pregnancy prevention program for early adolescents. *Family Relations, 42*, 401–406.

Kelsey, J. L., Thompson, W. D., & Evans, A. S. (1986). *Methods in observational epidemiology*. New York: Oxford University Press.

Kilpatrick, W. (1993). *Why Johnny can't tell right from wrong*. New York: Touchstone.

King de Arias, A. (1989). La comunicacion sexual y las actitudes y valores de los adolescentes [Sexual communication and the attitudes and values of adolescents]. *Revista Mexicana de Psicologia, 6*(2), 179–187.

Kirby, D. (1984). *Sexuality education: An evaluation of programs and their effects*. Santa Cruz, CA: Network Publications.

Kirby, D., Short, L., Collins, J., Rugg, D., Kolbe, L., Howard, M., Miller, B., Sonenstein, F., & Zabin, L. S. (1994). School-based programs to reduce sexual risk behaviors: A review of effectiveness. *Public Health Reports, 109*(3), 339–360.

Kirkpatrick, M. (1987). Clinical implications of lesbian mothers studies. *Journal of Homosexuality, 14*, 201–211.

Kokotailo, P. K., & Stephenson, J. N. (1993). Sexuality and reproductive health behavior. In M. I. Singer, L. T. Singer, & T. M. Anglin (Eds.), *Handbook for screening adolescents at psychosocial risk* (pp. 249–292). New York: Lexington Books.

Koyle, P., Jensen, L., Olsen, J., & Cundick, B. (1989). Comparison of sexual behaviors among adolescents having an early, middle, and late first intercourse experience. *Youth and Society, 20*(4), 461–475.

Leo, J. (1986, November 24). Sex and schools, *Time,* p. 59.

Lickona, T. (1992). *Educating for character: How our schools can teach respect and responsibility.* New York: Bantam.

Lundy, M. S., Pfohl, B. M., & Kuperman, S. (1993). Adult criminality among formerly hospitalized child psychiatric patients. *Journal of the American Academy of Child and Adolescent Psychiatry, 32*(3), 568–576.

Lundy, M. S., & Pumariega, A. J. (1993). Psychiatric hospitalization of children and adolescents. *Journal of Child and Family Studies, 2*(1), 1–4.

Lundy, M. S., & Rekers, G. A. (1995a). Homosexuality: Development, risks, parental values, and controversies. In G. A. Rekers (Ed.), *Handbook of child and adolescent sexual problems* (pp. 290–312). New York: Lexington Books.

Lundy, M. S., & Rekers, G. A. (1995b). Homosexuality: Presentation, evaluation, and clinical decision making. In G. A. Rekers (Ed.), *Handbook of child and adolescent sexual problems* (pp. 313–340). New York: Lexington Books.

Lundy, M. S., & Rekers, G. A. (1995c). Homosexuality in adolescence: Interventions and ethical considerations. In G. A. Rekers (Ed.), *Handbook of child and adolescent sexual problems* (pp. 341–377). New York: Lexington Books.

Males, M. (1992). Adult liaison in the "epidemic" of "teenage" birth, pregnancy, and venereal disease. *Journal of Sex Research, 29*(4), 525–545.

Males, M., & Chew, K. S. Y. (1996). The ages of fathers in California adolescent births, 1993. *American Journal of Public Health, 86*(4), 565–568.

Marchi, K. S., & Guendelman, S. (1994–1995). Gender differences in the sexual behavior of Latino adolescents. *International Quarterly of Community Health Education, 15*(2), 209–226.

Marsiglio, W., & Mott, F. L. (1986). The impact of sex education on sexual activity, contraceptive use and premarital pregnancy among American teenagers. *Family Planning Perspectives, 18*(4), 151–160.

McIlhaney, J. S., Jr. (1990). *Sexuality and sexually transmitted diseases.* Grand Rapids, MI: Baker Book House.

Mellanby, A., Phelps, F., & Tripp, J. H. (1993). Teenagers, sex, and risk taking. *British Medical Journal, 307,* 25.

Miller, B. C., & Olson, T. D. (1988). Sexual attitudes and behavior of high school students in relation to background and contextual factors. *Journal of Sex Research, 24,* 194–200.

Mosher, D. L. (1991). Ideological presuppositions: Rhetoric in sexual science, sexual politics and sexual morality. *Journal of Psychology and Human Sexuality, 4*(4), 7–29.

Mosher, W. D., & McNally, J. W. (1991). Contraceptive use at first premarital intercourse. *Family Planning Perspectives, 23,* 111.

National Center for Health Statistics. (1988). Percent of women 15–19 years of age who are sexually experienced, by race, age and marital status. *National survey of family growth.* Washington, DC: Centers for Disease Control, U.S. Department of Health and Human Services.

National Center for Health Statistics. (1993, February 25). *Monthly Vital Statistics Report, 41*(9), supplement.

National poll on sex. (1986, November 24). *Time,* pp. 58–59.

Olsen, J., Weed, S., Daly, D., & Jensen, L. (1992a). The effects of abstinence sex education programs on virgin versus nonvirgin students. *Journal of Research and Development in Education, 25*(2), 69–75.

Olsen, J., Weed, S., Nielsen, A., & Jensen, L. (1992b). Student evaluations of sex education programs advocating abstinence. *Adolescence, 27*(106), 369–380.

Olsen, J., Weed, S., Ritz, G., & Jensen, L. (1991). The effects of three abstinence sex education programs on student attitudes toward sexual activity. *Adolescence, 26*(103), 631–641.

Pattison, E. M., & Pattison, M. L. (1980). "Ex-gays": Religiously mediated change in homosexuals. *American Journal of Psychiatry, 137*(12), 1553–1562.

Petty, D. L. (1995). Sex education toward the prevention of sexual problems. In G. A. Rekers (Ed.), *Handbook of child and adolescent sexual problems* (pp. 31–51). New York: Lexington Books.

Pollner, F. (1988, August 28). Experts hedge on condom value, *Medical World News,* p. 60.

Post, S. G., & Botkin, J. R. (1995). Adolescents and AIDS prevention: The pediatrician's role. *Clinical Pediatrics, 34*, 41–45.

Ravenel, S. D. (1988). On the other hand. *North Carolina Medical Journal, 49*(7), 397.

Ravenel, S. D. (1989, June 28). Birth control doesn't curb teen pregnancies. *The News and Observer* (Raleigh, NC), p. 15A.

Regier, G. P. (Ed.). (1986). *Cultural trends and the American family.* Washington, DC: Family Research Council.

Rekers, G. A. (1978). Sexual problems. In B. B. Wolman (Ed.), *Handbook of treatment of mental disorders in childhood and adolescence* (pp. 268–296). Englewood Cliffs, NJ: Prentice-Hall.

Rekers, G. A. (1981). Psychosexual and gender problems. In E. J. Mash & L. G. Terdal (Eds.), *Behavioral assessment of childhood disorders* (pp. 483–526). New York: Guilford.

Rekers, G. A. (1982a). *Growing up straight.* Chicago: Moody Press.

Rekers, G. A. (1982b). *Shaping your child's sexual identity.* Grand Rapids, MI: Baker Book House.

Rekers, G. A. (1984). Parental involvement with agencies serving adolescents in crisis: Adolescent sexuality and family well-being. In Hearings before the Subcommittee on Family and Human Services, Committee on Labor and Human Resources, United States Senate, *Parental involvement with their adolescents in crisis.* Washington, DC: U.S. Government Printing Office.

Rekers, G. A. (Ed.). (1985). *Family building: Six qualities of a strong family.* Ventura, CA: Regal Books.

Rekers, G. A. (1988). *Counseling families.* Waco, TX: Word Books.

Rekers, G. A. (1989). AIDS: Behavioral dimension of medical care. *USC School of Medicine Report, 65*, 1272–1274.

Rekers, G. A. (1991a). Cross-sex behavior problems. In R. A. Hoekelman, S. Blatman, S. B. Friedman, N. M. Nelson, & H. M. Seidel (Eds.), *Primary pediatric care* (2nd ed.; pp. 691–693). St. Louis, MO: Mosby.

Rekers, G. A. (1991b). The need for a primary emphasis on prevention and for intervention research in community-based mental health services for children. In Hearings before the Select Committee for Children, Youth and Families, United States House of Representatives, on *Close to home: Community-based mental health services for children* (pp. 138–180). Washington, DC: U.S. Government Printing Office.

Rekers, G. A. (1992). Development of problems in puberty and sex roles in adolescence. In C. E. Walker & M. C. Roberts (Eds.), *Handbook of clinical child psychology* (2nd ed.; pp. 606–622). New York: Wiley.

Rekers, G. A. (Ed.). (1995). *Handbook of child and adolescent sexual problems.* New York: Lexington Books.

Rotheram-Borus, M. J., & Gwadz, M. (1993). Sexuality among youths at high risk. *Child and Adolescent Psychiatric Clinic of North America, 2*(3), 415–430.

Rotheram-Borus, M. J., Reid, H., Rosario, M., & Kasen, S. (1995). Determinants of safer sex patterns among gay/bisexual male adolescents. *Journal of Adolescence, 18*(1), 3–15.

Schlesselman, J. J. (1982). *Case-control studies: Design, conduct, analysis.* New York: Oxford University Press.

Schumm, W. R. (1995). Nonmarital heterosexual behavior. In G. A. Rekers (Ed.), *Handbook of child and adolescent sexual problems* (pp. 381–424). New York: Lexington Books.

Schumm, W. R., & Rekers, G. A. (1984). Sex should occur only within marriage. In H. Feldman & A. Parrot (Eds.), *Human sexuality: Contemporary controversies* (pp. 105–124). Beverly Hills, CA: Sage Publications.

Seidman, S. N., & Rieder, R. O. (1994). A review of sexual behavior in the United States. *American Journal of Psychiatry, 151,* 330–341.

St. Lawrence, J. S., Brasfield, T. L., Jefferson, K. W., & Alleyne, E. (1995). Cognitive-behavioral intervention to reduce African American adolescents' risk for HIV infection. *Journal of Consulting and Clinical Psychology, 63*(2), 221–237.

Stout, J. W. (1989). Schools and sex education: Does it work? *Pediatrics, 83*(3), 375.

Struder, M., & Thornton, A. (1989). The multifaceted impact of religiosity on adolescent sexual experience and contraceptive usage. *Journal of Marriage and the Family, 51,* 1085–1088.

Thornton, A., & Camburn, D. (1989). Religious participation and adolescent sexual behavior and attitudes. *Journal of Marriage and the Family, 51,* 641–652.

Turner, J. C., Garrison, C. Z., Korpita, E., & Waller, J. L. (1994). Promoting responsible sexual behavior through a college freshman seminar. *AIDS Education and Prevention, 6*(3), 266–277.

Uhlenberg, P., & Eggebeen, D. (1986, Winter). The declining well-being of American adolescents. *The Public Interest, 82,* 25–38.

U.S. Department of Education. (1988). *AIDS and the education of our children: A guide for parents and teachers.* Washington, DC: Office of Public Affairs, U.S. Department of Education.

U.S. Department of Health and Human Services. (1991). *1991 division of STD/HIV prevention annual report.* Washington, DC: U.S. Public Health Service, Centers for Disease Control.

U.S. Office of Pregnancy Programs. (1990). *A five-year pilot study: Project Respect performance summary* (Final Report #000816, Title XX, 1985–1990). Washington, DC: U.S. Department of Health and Human Services.

Visser, A. P., & van Blisen, P. (1994). Effectiveness of sex education provided to adolescents. *Patient Education and Counseling, 23*(3), 147–160.

Warzak, W. J., Grow, C. R., Poler, M. M., & Walburn, J. N. (1995). Enhancing refusal skills: Identifying contexts that place adolescents at risk for unwanted sexual activity. *Journal of Developmental and Behavioral Pediatrics, 16*(2), 98–100.

Warzak, W. J., Kuhn, B. R., & Nolten, P. W. (1995). Obstacles to the sexual adjustment of children and adolescents with disabilities. In G. A. Rekers (Ed.), *Handbook of child and adolescent sexual problems* (pp. 81–100). New York: Lexington Books.

Weed, S., & Jensen, L. (1993). A second year evaluation of three abstinence sex education programs. *Journal of Research and Development in Education, 26*(2), 92–96.

Weller, S. C. (1993, June). A meta-analysis of condom effectiveness in reducing sexually transmitted HIV. *Social Science and Medicine, 36*(12), 1635–1644.

White, S. D., & DeBlassie, R. R. (1992). Adolescent sexual behavior. *Adolescence, 27*(105), 183–191.

Whitehead, B. D. (1994, October). The failure of sex education. *The Atlantic Monthly, 274*(4), 55–80.

Wolfson, A. (1987). Toward the further understanding of homosexual women. *Journal of the American Psychoanalytic Association, 35,* 165–173.

CHAPTER 10

Teaching and Researching Sexualities in a Socially Responsible Manner

James T. Sears

During the 1992 presidential election, Dan Quayle took on Murphy Brown, a fictional television character and unwed mother, in one skirmish between two competing elites over sexuality in America. Though they appealed to different audiences, their common goal was to sell the corporate line. This is hardly surprising. We live in a society where sex sells automobiles and newspapers, toothpaste and politicians, films and televangelists. Sex is a commodity.

Quayle and Brown represent privileged white America. Both walk in the corridors of power, not in the shadows of economic fear. Quayle visited riot-torn central Los Angeles and Brown reported on the struggles of the poor, but neither fully appreciated what "a baby of my own" means in the life of a 14-year-old child in the ghetto, the barrio, or the reservation. In a society where white elites prepare sex ed materials for students attending schools along the tree-lined streets of middle America, this failure to appreciate the impact of culture and class on adolescents' sexual behaviors is understandable. Sexuality education is EuroAmerican.

The debate between the politician and the television character was one of wit and passion absent compassion and knowledge. Neither Quayle's campaign speeches nor the scenes of the popular television show addressed sexuality substantively. Their focus was on the consequence of premarital intercourse, raising questions such as: Why can't an unmarried woman bear and raise a child? and How can we encourage teenagers to abstain from sexual intercourse until marriage? These issues, of course, were much too narrowly framed.

This is hardly surprising. We live in a society where there is greater concern over our children's scientific literacy than their sexual illiteracy, where the debate about teaching sex in our schools has been polarized between moral vigilantes on the right and contraceptive crusaders on the political left, and where the effectiveness of sex education has been determined by input–output measures for programs that link text and teaching to teen sexual knowledge and behaviors.

GETTING BACK TO BASICS

Teaching sexual responsibility poses tough questions: What are our sexual values and how do they relate to our sexual behaviors? How do we learn about sexuality? In what ways has culture influenced our sexual understandings, values, and behaviors? Teaching about sexuality in our public schools today is much more than lectures on sexually transmitted diseases and appeals for sexual abstinence. It involves competing understandings of culture and sexuality, and the often conflicting interests of state, community, school, and family. Teaching sex in America "effectively" means first a recognition that we don't share one culture; we live in a multicolored society—red, white, yellow, brown, and black—holding various cultural understandings about sexuality.

Being born male or female, identifying oneself as man or woman, exhibiting masculine or feminine traits, engaging in sexual behavior with the same or the other gender are commonly found across cultures (e.g., Benedict, 1934; Ford & Beach, 1951; Frayser, 1985). However, what traits are defined as feminine; the moral valuation placed on someone who engages in homosexual behavior, practices "date rape," or chooses abortion; the relationship of biological sex to social role; and the necessity to link identity with sexual behavior vary enormously across cultures (e.g., Cortese, 1989; Ezzard, Cates, Kramer, & Tietze, 1982; Fausto-Sterling, 1994; Fischer, 1987; Ortner & Whitehead, 1981; Sears, 1997). Yet conventional sexuality education as well as research largely ignore multicultural populations as well as culture (Nettles & Scott-Jones, 1992; Pallotta-Chiarolli, in press; Trudell, 1993; Ward & Taylor, 1992; Wiederman, Maynard, & Fretz, 1996); multicultural sexuality education programs are practically nonexistent.

Understanding that we construct different meanings about sexuality should be at the core of the sex education debate. But, instead, we are led to believe that the issue is a conflict of values between the progressive and orthodox, not a conflict of interests between privileged EuroAmericans and the "others." This debate between those demanding we teach sexual abstinence and those advocating we distribute contraceptives, however, is as unidimensional as that of the Quayle–Brown controversy. "Both sides" of the sex ed debate share an ideology that focuses on the consequences of sexual behavior while ignoring the meanings constructed about such behavior. Absent in this sexual cross-fire is the importance of viewing other cultures from the inside-out and looking beyond our narrow cultural frame.

During the past two generations, many Americans' view of culture has changed radically from the schoolbook image of America as a social melting pot; our view of sexuality has not. Most sex educators share a Norman Rockwell–like cultural view of sexuality. In the conservative *Sex Respect* (Mast, 1990) curriculum, for example, adolescents are taught to write bumperstickers with titles such as "Pet Your Dog Not Your Date" and "Control Your Urgin', Be a Virgin" and scan sketches like that of a group of middle-class youngsters with European features at a malt shop talking about renting a video camera as a way to idle away a Friday night. Meanwhile, the liberal focus has tragically failed to account for culturally different sexual understandings in early AIDS-prevention language and continues to pose a relativistic view of sexual values and behaviors. Acknowledging and understanding the complex interaction of gender, race, ethnicity, and social class on sexual attitudes and behaviors are critical if we are to effectively teach about sexuality in our public schools (e.g., Amaro, 1995; Carrier & Magana, 1991; Flaskerud, Uman, Lara, Romero, & Taka, 1996; Gomez & Marin, 1996; Marin, 1989; Morales, 1990; Pavich, 1986; Wingood & DiClemente, 1992; Wright, 1993).

If we are to teach effectively, then we must first invent new basics. In a multicultural society, teaching sex should mean more than counting the number of persons of color in sex ed materials or looking at teen pregnancy rates. There are more fundamental issues: How does culture frame sexual beliefs, values, and behaviors? (Is it a coincidence that photographic images of blacks in sex education texts often depict them as pimps and prostitutes while whites appear to have Ozzie & Harriet lifestyles?) In whose interest is sexuality education being taught? (Is it coincidence that Procter & Gamble produces booklets for teenage girls on sexuality, absent any positive emotions related to sexuality, emphasizing menstruation and stressing the need for constant "protection"?) What is the relationship between the sexual socialization and political socialization of adolescents? (Is it a coincidence that boys and girls still learn little about the "opposite sex" and that most teen pregnancy prevention efforts focus on the female?)

In a postmodern world inhabited by creatures of modernism, it is unremarkable that sex education is not judged more deeply than level-of-significance tests on pre/post questionnaires or the rate of increase in teen pregnancy rates and developed more thoughtfully than top-down curriculum models in which teacher and student are merely end-users. There are more fundamental issues: Can we construct and implement well-designed research studies to assess program effectiveness? (How valid and reliable are studies whose questionnaire wording avoids sexual slang or culturally based phrases, whose behavioral indicators rely on self-reporting, and whose instruments are administered within weeks of one another? How do effectiveness measures really relate to actual teen knowledge, attitudes, and behaviors?) What really does an increase or decrease of teen pregnancy rates tell us? (Is it surprising that urban nonwhite adolescent females—often with fewer economic resources and dimmer career horizons—have a higher rate of pregnancies than white suburban young women?) How have we and others defined "sex outside of the context of marriage"? (Is it acceptable to mutually masturbate one's partner as long as one does not "go all the way"? Can one really be a "secondary virgin"? Is it okay if you are a passive, perhaps drunken, partner in a homosexual experience?)

In the make-believe worlds of Murphy Brown and Dan Quayle, there is no need to explore these fundamental questions or to challenge our basic assumptions. But in the real world—where adolescents are the U.S. group with the fastest-rising rate of HIV infection, where sexual harassment is common, and where aberrant intersections of sexuality and culture are artfully portrayed in *Trainspotting* and *Natural Born Killers*, *Beverly Hills 90210* and *Married with Children*, as well as televised events such as the McMartin preschool trial and the Hill–Thomas hearings, we need to begin with new basics.

THE NEW BASICS OF SEXUALITIES EDUCATION AND RESEARCH: A CONFLICT PERSPECTIVE

Advocates of a particular sexuality program often assume that the state, the community, the school, and the family/church have a functional relationship to one another. In this idealized Cabot Cove community, state legislators vote to require an abstinence-only program based upon their constituent concerns. A school district, under the guidance of its locally elected board of education in unison with state education consultants and district staff, develops policies and selects materials to implement this legislation. Skilled and knowledgeable teachers, comfortable with the board's philosophy and their own sexuality, instruct students. This, in turn, is reinforced within the adolescents' families, who reside in a community of shared cultural beliefs and values.

This Norman Rockwell portrait of sexuality education reflects reality in precious few American communities. In fact, the state, the community, the school, and the family are more often *competing* vectors of power and ideology, exerting a differential impact on the form and substance of sexuality education, which itself is only marginally related to the cultural understandings and sexual realities of adolescents.

The State

The reemergence of Christian conservatism coupled with the abortion controversy and the twin crises of AIDS and teenage pregnancy have catapulted sex education once again into the center of public policy debate. Legislators have demonstrated an increasing willingness to mandate minutia, ranging from the minutes of school sexuality instruction to particular topics and grade levels.

In South Carolina, a legislatively mandated 750 minutes comprise the reproductive and comprehensive health curriculum at the high school level. Males and females are separated during instruction in pregnancy prevention, education in sexually transmitted diseases before the sixth grade is prohibited, and discussion of abortion and homosexuality are banned. Yet there are disjunctions between these mandates and classroom practice.

An informative case study of the South Carolina experience documents some of these disjunctions. For example, within the "arena" of the state educational agency charged with implementing these mandates, the authors reported a "conflict between the bureaucratic mind-set and machinery of the state agency . . . and the progressive sexuality ideology of health advocates, educators, and state employees, who were seeking to implement legislation in an emancipatory form" (Earls, Fraser, & Sumter, 1992, p. 313). In practice, this meant delays in forming state-mandated community councils, the splitting of curriculum development and program monitoring between divisions with dissimilar ideologies, the adoption of textbooks with perforated pages about contraception, and the development of a paper-audit trail for a pro forma check of local compliance. Resistance and subversion among state agency health educators as well as bureaucratic intransigence, technocratic mindedness, and interdivisional conflict contributed to the loose coupling between the statehouse and this state agency.

The Community

It is odd that in a society in which less than a third of its citizenry vote in local elections, community debate on sexuality education is viewed as an impediment to social change rather than as an opportunity to expand participation in the public square. Demagoguery, democracy's shadow, though, is often visible in sex ed battles where the "moral" and educational agendas of national organizations are fought out in local communities with disguised agendas, creating polarization and simplifying complexities.

Demagoguery triumphs and the public square shrinks when there is an absence of an informed and involved citizenry, a willingness to engage in dialogue, and respect for those who hold opposing positions. "Stealth" school board candidates who sanctify their crusades in houses of worship, local newspapers that fail to publish the spectrum of community voices and their proprietors who manufacture or escalate community discord, activists who reduce adolescent sexual decision making to either/or choices of heterosexual intercourse or contraceptive use, and researchers who veil their ideological views with scientism masked as science are the community front of America's culture wars. The controversy in Beaufort County, South Carolina, is an illustration.

The Comprehensive Health Act mandated that local school boards appoint a 13-member committee to recommend text and materials. Dutifully, the Beaufort County Board of Education appointed a diverse group, including students and physicians, to the advisory committee. The committee deliberated for almost a year before recommending the adoption of the state-approved text, *Education for Sexuality*—a 132-page book revised to meet state requirements that emphasized the role of parents as the primary sex educators of their children and reinforced the choice of abstinence for young people.

Within three weeks, the board voted 5–3 to reject it and adopt *Sex Respect*[1] and other supplementary materials for use with high school seniors. The board majority argued that sex was a "moral issue" as well as a biological one and that the committee's recommended book was "value-free."

Community reactions were immediate and swift. Newspaper editorials and cartoons condemned the decision. In the weeks that followed, residents from the Coalition of Responsible Education collected 2,500 signatures opposing the board's decision and held a town meeting spurned by the board majority, who attended an alternative community meeting to which they invited an out-of-state expert. Press conferences were held, calls to local radio talk shows were jammed, and letters to the editor poured into the local newspaper. Educators in the district were particularly incensed. One teacher confronted a conservative board member shouting "Your program will fail!"

In the midst of this community outrage, the school superintendent declared that any teacher who criticized the board's decision—including public discussion via letters to the editor or comments to reporters—was insubordinate. As a result, 152 signatures were collected on a petition signed by teachers decrying the board's decisions. By November, more than 2,500 signatures to reconsider the sex education text were presented to the board. The board accepted the petition without comment while *Sex Respect* was approved by the same vote as in August. Thus ended the experiment in local democracy.

The School

Sexuality education appears under various titles (most commonly, "family life education," "human growth and development," "sex education," and "health education") in about nine out of ten schools nationwide. Here, sexual abstinence and/or the use of contraceptives are the goals stressed by most programs, with most sexuality teachers promoting rational and informed decision making about sexuality and providing knowledge about reproduction (Forrest & Silverman, 1989). The assumption is that knowledge about sexuality (and particularly the consequences of heterosexual intercourse) will result in changes in behavior (sexual abstinence, the use of safer-sex techniques). But this association is "very weakly related to adolescent sexual behavior" (Kirby et al., 1994, p. 341), with a correlation of about .17 (Whitley & Schofield, 1985/86), or less than 4% of the total variance.[2]

Effectiveness of Abstinence-Only Programs to Reduce Sexual Activity. For those who believe in the logic of "scientific facts"—and who characterize those who disagree as "unscientific," the only acceptable form of research inquiry is experimental or quasi-experimental studies.[3] Here, there is *some* empirical data to suggest a relationship between adolescent exposure to sexuality education programs and changes in students' self-reported sexual behaviors, but *little* to support the claim that abstinence-only programs reduce such behaviors (Kirby et al., 1994). This is due in part to the inherent limitations of such forms of research and in part to the slippage or "loose couplings" from program development to implementation through evaluation.

A review of research studies of school-based programs that measured their behavioral impact and were published in peer review journals was commissioned by the Centers for Disease Control and Prevention (Kirby et al., 1994). Among the 11 experimental or quasi-experimental studies studying programs that were either abstinence-only or abstinence-based (i.e., abstinence and contraception), the three abstinence-only programs resulted in *no* significant reduction of the initiation of sexual intercourse. However, those studies measuring the impact on teen initiation of intercourse in the other program model found no hastening of the onset of sexual intercourse, and, for this same program model, those studies measuring the reduction of sexual activity found neither a significant increase or decrease in sexual intercourse among experienced teens and mixed results for increasing contraceptive use.

Unfortunately, much of what passes for "scientific research" and cited by proponents of abstinence curricula is little more than quick pre/post questionnaires administered by the teachers themselves absent any of the standard procedures (e.g., random assignment of the treatment and/or the subject, use of a control group) that would allow questions of casuality to be scientifically addressed. Further, several of these studies have problems relating to both validity and reliability (i.e., wording of the questions, the short interval between administration of the pre and post surveys, absence of standard reliability and validity measures [see Trudell & Whatley, 1991]).

Not surprisingly, such "research studies" are reported in non–peer reviewed publications ranging from reports to government funding agencies to those issued by the very groups that produce or support these programs. As an example, I would cite a federally reported study, prepared and submitted by Project Respect, of 26 schools over a five-year period to document the effectiveness of *Sex Respect* using a simple pre-/post-test format with poorly constructed questions lacking the conditions of random assignments and control groups (U.S. Office of Pregnancy Programs, 1990). Other studies sometimes cited by proponents of abstinence-only programs to document the "positive outcomes" (a nonscientific phrase that has nothing to do with the cause-and-effect relationship implied) of such programs include non-research-based books such as *Why Johnny Can't Tell Right from Wrong* (Kilpatrick, 1993) and *Educating for Character* (Lickona, 1992).

There, too, is the sometimes cited Ravenel (1988) publication—a letter to the editor—which appeared in the *North Carolina Medical Journal* as a response to letters Ravenel had received following an earlier editorial in the journal. In neither case were empirical data presented subject for independent review; some of those studies quickly summarized by Ravenel were themselves distorted.[4] One study cited by Ravenel is from one North Carolina school that had reported a substantial increase in student pregnancies only *the year before* the program was implemented. Following the program, in response to a reporter's inquiry, an unnamed source at the school volunteered that there had been a dramatic decrease in pregnancies and attributed it to the abstinence program.[5]

The studies that are reported in peer-reviewed journals are pre/post correlational studies that fail to examine sexual behaviors, focusing instead on acquisition of abstinence attitudes (Olsen, Weed, Daly, & Jensen, 1992; Weed & Jensen, 1993), favorable student evaluations (Olsen, Weed, Nielsen, & Jensen, 1992), and intentions to have sex (deGaston, Jensen, Weed, & Tanas, 1994). Of particular interest is that *all* of these studies excluded urban students, relying exclusively on those attending suburban or rural schools with the posttest administered at the end of the program by the teachers responsible for its implementation.

Such studies do not exclusively endorse abstinence but rather study the interactional relationships with one or more of the abstinence-only programs vis-à-vis student evaluation, teaching philosophy, student sexual attitudes, and the like. Even had a quasi-experimentally designed study been used to determine the causal link between these programs and such dependent variables, in the absence of including non-abstinence-only programs, the statement "exclusively endorse abstinence" is, by definition, the only possible result. None of these studies evidence a significant reduction in adolescence pregnancy that is related exclusively to using an abstinence-only approach. One of these studies found sexually active junior high school students moving toward a more "permissive attitude" or simply no significant change for any group (Olsen et al., 1992a), although a follow-up study a year later, using a larger sample size and more rigorous training and monitoring of teachers, reported more positive results (Weed & Jensen, 1993).

Loose Couplings in School. In addition to ignoring the less than direct relationship between sexuality programs designed by adults and sexual behaviors practiced by adolescents, the modernist approach to sexuality education fails to acknowledge the "loose couplings" existent in any school curriculum; that is, the one-to-one mis-translation of mandated sex education legislation and policies into curriculum objectives, instructional materials, and assessment tools. These materials are presumably used-as-designed by often poorly educated teachers who are sometimes uncomfortable with "the topic." Completing this rationalist design, adolescents then are expected to interpret the materials as taught and behave accordingly in other social and cultural contexts. But, in fact, this correspondence exists only in the minds of those who are naive about curriculum and instruction or whose political aspiration and ideological motivation override curriculum common sense.

Ethnographic and case studies are particularly useful in identifying these loose couplings as well as providing an understanding of how individuals make sense of sexuality and act upon it. In my case study of Chicago's Latino community of Little Village and the North Carolina Native American community of the Cherokee Boundary, I found many such examples (Sears, 1996; Sears, in press b). At one public school in Chicago's near west side, the seventh-grade physical education teacher articulated the importance of an abstinence-only message, explaining to me the advantages of using *Sex Respect*. As I observed his practice over the next several weeks, however, he routinely discussed contraceptive usage and responded to questions from sexually active teens. Nevertheless, each student dutifully completed the pre/post test judging the effectiveness of this abstinence-only curricula on student attitudes and behaviors. Later, school officials received data summarizing the effectiveness of their use of the *Sex Respect* unit.

Eight hundred miles south, in the rugged foothills of the Smokey Mountains, the tribal-operated high school offered counseling services for sexually active teens and distributed contraceptives at the nearby teen center. *Minimal* instruction about sexuality, however, occurred in the classrooms with cognitive-based materials that had little relationship to Cherokee culture or the adolescent reservation realities of high unemployment, drug and alcohol abuse, and government dependency. A local Indian Health Service staff member reported the formal school programs had little affect, noting that fewer than half of Cherokee teenagers who engaged in sex report using condoms. And an independent evaluation of the school program reported an absence of any "specific academic theory or body of literature" underlying the school's prevention programs, concluding the curriculum was so fragmented that any appreciable impact on students' sexual behavior was coincidental (Pelavian Associates, 1991).[6]

There are also loose couplings between classroom teachers and district programs. Many teachers, in fact, subvert the rationalistic plans and authoritarian directives of school officials (e.g., Beck & Marshall, 1992; Fine, 1988; Sears, in press b). For example, three years later, when I interviewed members of various factions in the Beaufort County controversy, there was a surprising degree of support for the program. This support, though, was based on a limited or wishful understanding. The director of the conservative-oriented Teen Crisis Center astutely observed: "They're keeping it quiet. They [the teachers] are supplementing it with what they wanted in the first place. They're subverting it!" An activist teacher commented, "The *Sex Respect* curriculum has been lost in the beast called public education. It has been bureaucratized. By default its working; it's not working by design."[7]

So, too, do students subvert the prescribed curriculum. In her excellent ethnographic study of one high school sexuality classroom, Bonnie Trudell (1993) focused on how minority adolescents made meaning of their watered-down sexuality program, posing fundamental questions such as:

> Do students "receive" the same messages the teacher "transmits"? Are these messages passively accepted, resisted or rejected by the students? How are student interpretations and reactions similar or different across gender, race, and class lines? To what degree are these messages congruent or contradictory to students' lived experience outside the classroom? (p. 8)

Following five months of classroom observations as well as interviews, she concluded:

> Students reinterpreted reified school knowledge about sexuality through their cultural experiences . . . to reach different understandings about appropriate sexual behavior. Furthermore, they actively weighted their own interests in acquiescing to or contesting course content and form. Most expressed satis-

faction with the class and conformed to classroom procedures; however, interviews revealed that they chose to do so largely for a good grade in the required course and to avoid embarrassment. (p. 172)

Similarly, a focus group study of how 27 African American males ages 15 through 19 understood their sexual lives found a series of complex scripts that differentiated their sexual conduct, such as the decision to engage in intercourse or to use a condom, as well as their choice of sexual partners or particular sexual behaviors. The researchers concluded:

[The] black male's sexual decision making reflects his representations or constructions of social "facts." . . . Some motivation to engage in unprotected sex may reflect perceived links between intercourse and what it means to be a man. (Gilmore, DeLamater, & Wagstaff, 1996, p. 364)

The Family/Church

It has become fashionable to talk about the importance of "the American family"; "family values" are convenient code words among pundits, preachers, and politicians. However, during adolescence the family is less often a haven from a heartless world and more often the site of conflicts revolving around the adolescent search for autonomy and self-identity. Not surprisingly, while a majority of adults cite the importance of parents as the primary source for a child's sexual education, fewer than one in ten adolescents note this to be the case (Sears, 1992). Admonishing teachers to work with parents who have little communication or credibility with their children, although emotionally appealing, ignores the everyday reality of those cultures or families in which sexual discussion is taboo, truncated, and unidirectional.

For Filipino Americans, for example, the family is at the center in a culture in which family size brings security, wealth, and social status. Here personal allegiance, respect for and dependence on authority, the value of affiliation, and the importance of harmony are most evident. Yet there is little reciprocal communication among family members, and the frank discussion of sexuality is discouraged by Catholicism and Asian civility (Andres & Andres, 1987; Medina, 1991; Sears, 1997, in press a). Here the needs and interests of the individual are subservient to those of the family—often extended to the *compadre* system of godparents and to the *barkada* (one's peer group).

The church, temple, mosque, or ashram may be the last refuge of cultural homogeneity in America, but there is hardly a uniformity of sexual views among different religious groups. Conservative Protestant denominations such as the Southern Baptists as well as orthodox Roman Catholicism—

borrowing from the commentaries of Paul, Augustine, and Aquinas—have focused on man's sinful nature and the procreative role of sexuality. The condemnation of sexuality education programs that promote condom use or omit moral judgments when discussing issues of homosexuality or abortion has been most forcefully launched by allied groups such as the Christian Coalition and the Knights of Columbus. In sharp contrast are religious denominations such as the Evangelical Lutheran Church in America and the Unitarian Universalist Fellowship. The former produced a 21-page report, "The Church and Human Sexuality," which characterized masturbation as healthy unless compulsive, recommended the use of condoms for sexually active teens (echoed by the quickly deposed Surgeon General Joycelyn Elders), and advocated tolerance or support for gays and lesbians. The latter routinely recognizes lesbian and gay unions as well as homosexual clergy and supports the woman's right to choose.

Conflict is also apparent within denominations and even within church congregations. The admonition of the Roman Catholic hierarchy against homosexual behavior, for instance, is ignored by many practicing Catholics, resulting in the formation of scores of informally affiliated Dignity chapters comprised of unrepentant Catholics who are homosexual. The dissension in the Episcopal Church regarding the ordination of women and gays or the insistence of one North Carolina Southern Baptist church on hiring an openly gay minister also reveal deep fissures within denominations and within particular congregations.

CONCLUSION

Given conflicts among and within the state, school, community, and church/family, acknowledging that we construct culturally different meanings about sexuality, admitting the limitations of input-output sex education programs and research, and accepting systemic loose couplings are the new basics of sex ed. If we truly wish to enlarge the public square, then we must enter into collaborative dialogue by bracketing these modernist understandings and begin with a new paradigm of basics.[8] Suffice to say that these new basics will please neither Dan Quayle nor Murphy Brown.

NOTES

1. Mast, 1990. For a thoughtful critique of this program, see Trudell & Whatley, 1991.

2. In one abstinence-only focused study (Olsen, Weed, Ritz, & Jensen, 1991, p. 639), a correlation of $-.548$ was reported between "attitude toward premarital

sex and actual sexual behavior." Here, sexual behavior (intercourse within the past month) was correlated with a 12-item Likert-type scale, Attitudes Toward Premarital Sex (e.g., "It is all right for teenagers to have sex before marriage if they are in love."). Though there is a commonsensical relationship between positive attitudes toward premarital sex and self-reported heterosexual intercourse, the authors then go on to speculate "if an abstinence program produces an attitude change [no such causal relationship was demonstrated in this study] and attitude is correlated with [self-reported] behavior, will the behavior also change?" (p. 640). While the authors clearly "hoped" for a decrease in sexual activity as a result of the abstinence-only program, the correlational design could not have provided such data.

3. Experimental studies, if properly designed, allow for questions of causality to be addressed. Distinguishing features of this research design include the random assignment of subjects and/or treatment, the use of a control group, and hypotheses and data analysis techniques specified prior to design implementation.

4. For example, Ravenel (1988, p. 398) cites Vincent, Clearie, and Schluchter's (1987) article as one of "two reports of a significant reduction in pregnancies following intervention in which premarital abstinence is the education focus, to the exclusion of birth control information and availability." However, as Vincent (1996) responded:

> [T]he author [Ravenel] failed to read or misinterpreted the context of the original article. . . . To attribute the reduction to the abstinence components in the intervention is not possible. The JAMA article also speaks directly to the family planning instruction component of the intervention. On page 3383 is stated, "The secondary behavioral objective is to promote, among never married teens and preteens who choose to become sexually active and who do not desire pregnancy to occur, the consistent use of effective contraception." In a broad-based community program involving numerous awareness, instruction and skills development interventions one cannot attribute outcome effect to any single cause.

5. A similarly misused California anecdotal account is cited in Trudell, 1993, p. 211.

6. A theoretically grounded program is one of the key components of more effective sexuality education programs (Kirby et al., 1994). Researchers studying another Indian community have documented this gap between sexual knowledge and sexual behavior. They found that although most were knowledgeable about the types of behaviors that placed one at risk for HIV infection and knew that condoms provided effective protection, nearly one-half of those who engaged in "high-risk" behavior never used condoms and another 40% only used this protection "sometimes" (Freeman, Hamilton, & Carney, 1992).

7. The problem of curriculum subversion is cited as a critical factor by researchers into the effectiveness of abstinence-only programs: "Negative or no program effects occur when nonsupportive teachers are used with the Teen-Aid program" (Weed & Jensen, 1993, p. 91); "The Teen-Aid and other sex education curricula are in many respects at the discretion of the teacher. As currently designed, this program does not require screening of teachers, special accreditation, or teacher accountability" (deGaston et al., 1994, p. 269).

8. Elsewhere (Sears, in press b), I have outlined four conceptual frameworks that would allow for such to occur.

REFERENCES

Amaro, H. (1995). Love, sex, and power. Considering women's realities in HIV prevention. *American Psychologist, 50,* 437–447.

Andres, T., & Andres, P. (1987). *Understanding the Filipino.* Quezon City, Philippines: New Day.

Beck, L., & Marshall, C. (1992). Policy into practice: A qualitative inquiry into the work of sexuality educators. *Educational Policy, 6*(3), 319–334.

Benedict, R. (1934). *Patterns of culture.* New York: Houghton Mifflin.

Carrier, J., & Magana, J. (1991). Use of ethnosexual data on men of Mexican origins for HIV/AIDS prevention programs. *Journal of Sex Research, 28,* 189–202.

Cortese, A. (1989). Subcultural differences in human sexuality: Race, ethnicity, and social class. In K. McKinney (Ed.), *Human sexuality: The societal and interpersonal context* (pp. 63–90). Norwood, NJ: Ablex.

deGaston, J., Jensen, L., Weed, S., & Tanas, R. (1994). Teacher philosophy and program implementation and the impact on sex education outcomes. *Journal of Research and Development in Education, 27*(4), 265–270.

Earls, R., Fraser, J., & Sumpter, B. (1992). Sexuality education—In whose interest? In J. Sears (Ed.), *Sexuality and the curriculum* (pp. 300–327). New York: Teachers College Press.

Ezzard, N., Cates, W., Kramer, D., & Tietze, C. (1982). Race-specific patterns of abortion use by American teenagers. *American Journal of Public Health, 72*(8), 809–814.

Fausto-Sterling, A. (1994). The five sexes: Why male and female are not enough. In O. Pocs (Ed.), *Human sexuality 94/95* (pp. 44–47). Guilford, CT: Dushkin.

Fine, M. (1988). Sexuality, schooling, and desire. *Harvard Educational Review, 58*(1), 29–53.

Fischer, G. (1987). Hispanic and majority student attitudes toward forcible date rape as a function of differences in attitudes toward women. *Sex Roles, 17* (1/2), 93–101.

Flaskerud, J., Uman, G., Lara, R., Romero, L., & Taka, K. (1996). Sexual practices, attitudes, and knowledge related to HIV transmission in low income Los Angeles Hispanic women. *Journal of Sex Research, 33*(4), 343–353.

Ford, C., & Beach, F. (1951). *Patterns of sexual behavior.* New York: Harper.

Forrest, J., & Silverman, J. (1989). What public school teachers teach about preventing pregnancy, AIDS and sexually transmitted diseases. *Family Planning Perspectives, 21*(2), 65–72.

Frayser, S. (1985). *Varieties of sexual experience: An anthropological perspective on human sexuality.* New Haven, CT: Human Relations Area Files Press.

Freeman, K., Hamilton, V., & Carney, C. (1992). Indian Community. Unpublished paper, Tacoma, WA.

Gilmore, S., DeLamater, J., & Wagstaff, D. (1996). Sexual decision making by inner city black adolescent males: A focus group study. *Journal of Sex Research, 33*(4), 363–371.

Gomez, C., & Marin, B. (1996). Gender, culture and power: Barriers to HIV-prevention strategies for women. *Journal of Sex Research, 33*(4), 355–362.

Kilpatrick, W. (1993). *Why Johnny can't tell right from wrong.* New York: Touchstone.

Kirby, D. et al. (1994). School-based programs to reduce sexual risk behaviors: A review of effectiveness. *Public Health Reports, 109*(2), 339–360.

Likona, T. (1992). *Educating for character.* New York: Bantam.

Marin, G. (1989). AIDS prevention among Hispanics: Needs, risk behaviors and cultural values. *Public Health Reports, 104,* 411–415.

Mast, S. (1990). *Sex respect: The option of true sexual freedom.* Bradley, IL: Respect, Inc.

Medina, B. (1991). *The Filipino family.* Diliman, Quezon City: University of Philippines Press.

Morales, E. (1990). HIV infection and Hispanic gay and bisexual men. *Hispanic Journal of Behavioral Sciences, 12,* 212–222.

Nettles, S., & Scott-Jones, D. (1992). The role of sexuality and sex equity in the education of minority adolescents. In S. Klein (Ed.), *Sex equity and sexuality education* (pp. 257–272). Albany: State University of New York Press.

Olsen, J., Weed, S., Daly, D., & Jensen, L. (1992a). Student evaluation of sex education programs advocating abstinence. *Journal of Research and Development in Education, 25*(2), 69–75.

Olsen, J., Weed, S., Nielsen, A., & Jensen, L. (1992b). Student evaluations of sex education programs advocating abstinence. *Adolescence, 27*(106), 369–380.

Olsen, J., Weed, S., Ritz, G., & Jensen, L. (1991). The effects of three abstinence sex education programs on student attitudes toward sexual activity. *Adolescence, 26*(103), 631–641.

Ortner, O., & Whitehead, H. (1981). (Eds.). *Sexual meanings: The cultural construction of gender and sexuality.* Cambridge, England: Cambridge University Press.

Pallotta-Chiarolli, M. (in press). "Multicultural does not mean multisexual": Social justice and the interweaving of ethnicity and sexuality in Australian schooling. In D. Epstein & J. Sears (Eds.), *A dangerous knowing: Sexual pedagogies and the master narrative.* London: Cassell.

Pavitch, E. (1986). A Chicano perspective on Mexican culture and sexuality. *Journal of Social Work and Human Sexuality, 4,* 47–65.

Pelavian & Associates. (1991). *Cherokee central schools.* Mimeograph. Cherokee, NC: Cherokee Central Schools.

Ravenel, S. (1988). Dr. Ravenel's response to a letter critiquing his editorial. *North Carolina Medical Journal, 49*(7), 397–398.

Sears, J. (1992). Developing a critical based sexuality curriculum. In J. Sears (Ed.), *Sexuality and the curriculum* (pp. 139–156). New York: Teachers College Press.

Sears, J. (1996, April). *The Keetoowah curriculum: Policies, politics, and possibilities in the teaching of sexuality on the Cherokee Boundary.* Paper presented at the annual meeting of the American Educational Research Association. New York.

Sears, J. (1997). Centering culture: Teaching for critical sexual literacy using the sexual diversity wheel. *Journal of Moral Education, 26*(3), 273–283.

Sears, J. (In press a). In(ter)ventions of sexualities and HIV education in the Philippines. In D. Epstein & J. Sears (Eds.), *A dangerous knowing: Sexual pedagogies and the master narrative.* London: Cassell.

Sears, J. (in press b). *Teaching sex in America: Case studies of culture and sexualities.* San Francisco: Jossey-Bass.

Trudell, B. (1993). *Doing sex education.* New York: Routledge.

Trudell, B., & Whatley, M. (1991). *Sex respect:* A problematic public school sexuality curriculum. *Journal of Sex Education and Therapy, 17*(2), 125–140.

U.S. Office of Pregnancy Programs. (1990). *A five-year pilot study: Project Respect performance summary,* Final Report #000816, Title XX, 1985–1990.

Vincent, M. (1996, June 13). Personal communication. Sears Papers (see Chapter 3, Note 1).

Vincent, M., Clearie, A., & Schluchter, M. (1987). Reducing adolescent pregnancy through school and community-based education. *JAMA, 257*(24), 3382–3386.

Ward, J., & Taylor, J. (1992). Sexuality education for immigrant and minority students. In J. Sears (Ed.), *Sexuality and the curriculum* (pp. 183–202). New York: Teachers College Press.

Weed, S., & Jensen, L. (1993). A second year evaluation of three abstinence sex education programs. *Journal of Research and Development in Education, 26*(2), 91–96.

Whitly, B., & Schofield, J. (1985/86). Meta-analysis of research on adolescent contraceptive use. *Population and Environment, 8,* pp. 173–203.

Wiederman, M., Maynard, C., & Fretz, A. (1996). Ethnicity in 25 years of published sexuality research. *Journal of Sex Research, 33*(4), 339–342.

Wingood, G., & DiClemente, R. (1992). Cultural, gender and psychosocial influences on HIV-related behavior of African female adolescents. *Ethnicity and Disease, 3,* 381–388.

Wright, J. (1993). African-American male sexual behavior and the risk for HIV infection. *Human Organization, 52,* 421–431.

COMMUNITY DIALOGUE

Sexual Behaviors and Sexual Cultures

Burgess: We are mandated through state law to teach comprehensive health education. But if we are going to teach sex ed, we can't teach it in a vacuum.

Murphy: Kids need to talk about sex in relationship to values and religion as well as economics and history rather than simply being told, "If you don't do this, you will be in trouble."

Burgess: As a supervisor of teachers, I have been in the classroom when sex ed is being taught. It has been a very sterile delivery of the subject matter for fear of causing an uproar in the community or the principal saying, "You shouldn't have done that!"

Shearer: If it is to be taught, do we include sexual responsibilities as part of the course material? This can involve the teaching of facts (e.g., consequences of sexual activity) but in teaching about responsibility, we also need to talk about the impact on a person's life: the mind, the emotions, the soul.

Lindsey: If we took sex ed out of the classroom altogether, what difference would it really make in kids' behavior?

Burgess: What do you mean by behavior?

Lindsey: Change in responses or attitudes toward sex. The school should seek change in attitudes and behaviors, not just "head knowledge."

Burgess: But we don't do this in any other curriculum area!

Murphy: My fear is that we are defining sexuality education only as "keeping them out of bed"!

See the introduction for a description of the conversationalists.

Curriculum, Religion, and Public Education: Conversations for an Enlarging Public Square. Copyright © 1998 by Teachers College, Columbia University. All rights reserved. ISBN 0-8077-3706-2 (pbk.), ISBN 0-8077-3707-0 (cloth). Prior to photocopying items for classroom use, please contact the Copyright Clearance Center, Customer Service, 222 Rosewood Dr., Danvers, MA 01923, USA, tel. (508) 750-8400.

Shearer: Teaching sexuality is more than a behavioral unit; it is moral.

Carper: What is the goal of sexuality education?

Murphy: When I teach sex ed, I often see these kids' thinking as very shallow. I try to open up the dialogue and discuss values.

Burgess: Do we want the students to "stay out of bed"? Yes! Do we want the child to answer value questions regarding sexuality? Of course!

Shearer: The whole question about whether we are teaching them or should teach them to "stay out of bed" shows what is at the heart of sex education. We really don't much care if our kids go to bed with one another; we are more concerned about whether they get sick, have babies, and are an inconvenience or embarrassment. We are offering sex ed and passing out condoms so that they don't cause a problem. Frankly, I don't think teaching sexuality in the public schools is a good idea. We don't have the right foundation and motivation.

Pigford: I disagree; we do care if our kids go to bed with one another for reasons other than our fear that the will get sick or have babies. We want our children to understand and appreciate the emotional commitment involved in intimate relationships.

Murphy: When we say, "just toss sex ed out," that says a lot about what we think about sexuality. Why are *we* so scared of it and why do *we* insist on defining sexuality education so narrowly?

Pritchett: I don't believe we define it narrowly; we haven't defined it at all. We don't have agreement, or even discussions, about what we mean by sexuality. We only talk about reproductive health.

Burgess: But how do you move from a sterile, clinical environment of teaching sex ed and actually deal with the subject in a manner that will make a difference?

Shearer: Rekers makes a distinction between some students who are probably more prone to be out there in dangerous sexual situations. These are the students who should be the school's focus. Someone must tell them the "facts of life"; if it is not done at home, then it needs to be done at school. But if we have to teach some of the students who are disadvantaged, must we teach all?

Burgess: As a sex ed teacher, how do I differentiate who needs to hear what?

Shearer: We have remedial classes and gifted education.

Burgess: As soon as we categorize a student as "at risk," the more likely he will become an "at-risk" kid; the same situation occurs with the "gifted student."

Murphy: What I hear is that we need to tell these "delinquents" not to do it, tell them the consequences, and scare the hell out of them. This assumes that *we* understand sexuality. I'm not sure that either of these are true. However good or true our cultural understanding of sexuality is, it still is limited unless we explore different views. Too often I hear echoes of white Calvinism.

Burgess: Minority groups have been defined by others. There seems to be a notion that minority groups may have a sexual standard that is not as high as other groups without recognizing that—to the degree this is true—it has evolved from situations created by others. Look at the master using African American women at his will and breaking up of intact families. It is a wonder the African American family has survived! The issue is much broader; it is economic and political, bounded by race. There is really no genuine effort by those in power to alter those situations. Until there is that commitment, what we do in sexuality education will have little impact.

Shearer: Sexuality education is probably not going to positively affect the lives of African American women because of the dynamic of economics and politics?

Pigford: I'm not sure what you're saying.

Burgess: With my nieces and nephews, regardless of what the school system teaches, it will *not* make a difference. As a culture, we have prolonged adolescence yet demanded sexual abstinence until marriage.

Shearer: If I buy into the fact that there is a cultural view of sexuality based on my heritage, I am not sure that I want my children encouraged to consider other views of sexuality.

Burgess: I had a young man in my office several days ago who is very bright and athletic. On his shirt he had one of his music idols—a person who committed suicide—who was bisexual. As we talked about his idol, I came to the conclusion he was having some identity problems and not feelings good about himself. I could not address these issues in my office, the counselors didn't address them, and I'm not sure the young man felt comfortable talking to his parents. Now, if someone does not talk with him soon, he will be lost and headed for trouble.

Murphy: We need to allow historical and cultural analyses into our sex education curriculum. What is the history of the treatment of women in different cultures? What is our vision for the treatment of women in this society? How does the positioning of male and female impact on cultural understanding of sexuality? What do we think of Paul's view of women? What about the role of Ruth or the depiction of Mary Magdalene?

Lindsey: I am not convinced that eighth-grade students can understand all of that while they are so involved with their own bodies. While we know we have to teach them about sexuality when they are young, if we want to give them a historical and cultural understanding about sexuality, they are simply too young to be able to step back and think about sex intellectually.

Burgess: While the poor white child maybe in a slightly better position than the poor black child, those kids are not going to critically reflect if they have just left a home where someone has shot up or mom is in bed with a strange man.

Murphy: But if we define education as critical reflection, not just information, then we can be successful.

Burgess: However, I am not sure how you get students, teachers, and community in a meaningful dialogue that will create such a classroom climate.

Lindsey: What particularly interested me is the sex ed curriculum in Denton, where the school contacted parents to identify who they would like to teach it and then formed groups around a common teacher who taught it from their cultural perspective. What about allowing parents to choose those teachers they would feel comfortable teaching about sexuality?

Murphy: The Catholics go to Room 102 and the evangelicals to Room 103?

Lindsey: My suspicion is that if this was done you would find the Jewish man teaching about the same thing as the Baptist man.

Burgess: If there was something in the schools that taught sexuality from an Afrocentric or Asian perspective, would people in the community who are not familiar with these cultures be supportive?

Murphy: You can step back and look at the culture in which we have immersed our children. We promote the most blatant kind of sexuality that deprecates women and hurts children. If you go to the streets of

Cairo, there are very few men pinching or whistling at women. Yet we talk about restraint and responsibility! Despite the influence of television, radio, and movies, are you saying these kids are too young to engage in thoughtful dialogue and critical reflection? The message is: Get stoned, get laid, and get AIDS—now!

Lindsey: We certainly have a social problem that no sex ed program can solve.

Shearer: We have created a moral vacuum. But I'm not sure that the blame should be put on the white Anglo-Saxon Protestant culture. Nor I am at all sure that "critical reflection" is the remedy. While we have been minimizing the Puritan and Victorian understandings of human sexuality, we have opened the door to the other European model: Canal Street in Amsterdam. The problems we are experiencing are due to our wrenching out of the school curriculum this very white Anglo-Saxon Protestant view that has become a convenient whipping boy.

Lindsey: Is the African American culture much different in its conceptualization of sexuality?

Burgess: I'm not sure. But, when we talk about culture monolithically, we do individuals within that group a great disservice.

Lindsey: I grew up in China, whose people rejected premarital sex for the woman. Even today, the Korean students who come to our school are forbidden by their parents to date until they have finished high school. I don't think there is that much difference across the cultures.

Murphy: Well, we can go to some countries in Africa and see them cutting the clitoris in order that the woman doesn't have an orgasm and stays faithful. Unless we engage students in these type of dialogues and really discuss other cultural practices and values, we are cheating them.

Shearer: You feel we are "cheating" the American child?

Murphy: Yes. I don't think kids can understand the sexuality portrayed in their culture unless they gain a perspective. When they get to our classrooms, we need to allow students freedom for critical reflection and then insist on it.

Pritchett: Even if that discussion involves values that individual families object to their child being exposed?

Burgess: Once the students "critically reflect" in your classroom, are they really going to use that skill when they go back into the same situation they left before they entered your classroom?

Murphy: That is part of the Afrocentric movement: Critically reflect on your history and then make different choices.

Burgess: But that is at a school level, not at the classroom level.

Shearer: A lot of people who are evangelical conservatives believe that what is called "critical reflection" in schools is not what I consider education. It is a lot of wheel-spinning and fluff. Maybe if we just spent time teaching reading, writing, and arithmetic. If we just taught them the way we used to teach them, they will be better off to live in this world victoriously. Education should be teaching absolutes. Let's get down to the business of education and teach those matters that we know are true. Why bring sexuality or critical reflection into the school?

Carper: It also presupposes that "truth" is an individual judgment. Using "critical reflection" I might come to one position and you another. Now if it is the same proposition, one of us is wrong!

Pritchett: Wrong if based on *your* moral framework.

Murphy: People must ultimately make their own moral choices. It's not that you are wrong, but I see it differently and make a different choice.

Carper: Underlying your position is a relativistic view of the world. As for me, I subscribe to position that there is an absolute, universal truth that is not subject to debate. Now, how do we handle these two epistemological traditions?

Lindsey: The students at our Christian school critically reflect—although Carolyn may disagree. In teaching older students, I feel very comfortable sharing with them the presuppositions upon which my life is based. These are revealed biblically. I also teach them other, non-biblical presuppositions and tell them that it is incumbent upon them to figure out their presuppositions before they make their choices about sexuality. Now, they must make their own free choice. I can't choose for them and neither can their parents. They must come to grip with God.

Shearer: While I am personally tolerant and understand these various models, my view is absolutist relating to the human body. Just as God is absolute about how he created the stars in the universe, so He is about how we should relate to one another as sexual beings.

Lindsey: I have a standard, which I believe is correct, but I want to teach these students to respect other persons as well as differing value system and to understand them. But I stress that there is a standard that is accepted and against which all of these other systems will be judged.

Suggested Additional Readings
on Sexuality Education

Elaine Lindsey, with James T. Sears

David, M. E. (1993). *Parents, gender and education reform policy*. Cambridge, England: Cambridge University Press.

Explores the relationships between education reform and the changes in family life. As families have changed, the role of the school has changed, particularly in the areas of social and emotional support provided. Emphasis is placed on the developing sex education and moral education curriculum.

Miller, P. F. (1993). Sexuality education—Forward or backward? *Momentum, 24*(1), 49–52.

Elaborates on the document produced in 1990 by the bishops titled "Human Sexuality: A Catholic Perspective for Education and Lifelong Learning," and explains the new Catholic position and what is being taught in Catholic schools.

Preventing HIV/AIDS in adolescents (Report by the National Commission on AIDS). (1994). *Journal of School Health, 64*(1), 39–50.

An examination, based on a four-year study, of HIV/AIDS among adolescents today, including the increasing occurrence among various groups, cultural attitudes, and the role of the school and parents in prevention. Recommendations for educational practice and references are given.

Sears, J. T. (Ed.). (1992). *Sexuality and the curriculum: The politics and practices of sexuality education*. New York: Teachers College Press.

Fifteen essays that challenge current practices and concepts in today's sexuality education. Essayists examine issues such as teen pregnancy, censorship, sexual scripting, sexual harassment, impact of culture, and HIV education using feminist theory, critical social theory, and existential phenomenology.

Spiecker, B. (1992). Sexual education and morality. *Journal of Moral Education, 21*(1), 67–75.

Spiecker states that today there are five different definitions of sexual education: giving information on procreation, teaching children to rule sexual drives, sex as a part of real love, education of the infantile sexual desire, and the teaching of the application of moral principles with reference to sexual conduct. The author advocates the last definition and develops it by comparing it to the others.

Spies, J. (1992, October 30–November 2). *Sex education: Issues of power and participation.* Paper presented at the annual meeting of the University Council for Educational Administration, Minneapolis. (ERIC Document Reproduction Service No. ED 354 628)

A look at how one school district avoided a serious controversy over sex education by forming a community committee and developing a common language. The emphasis is that language has power and that communication is the key to stemming conflict.

Tapia, A. (1993). Abstinence: The radical choice for sex ed. *Christianity Today, 37*(2), 24–29.

Details the debate in schools today over sex education curricula and advocates an abstinence approach.

PART V

Outcome-Based Education: Who Should Set the Standards?

From the beginning of the "common school," the state has had a vested interest in the "outcomes" of public education. With the increased role of the federal government following *Sputnik* and during the Great Society and the demand for educational accountability by governors a decade later, "local control" of public schools diminished. During the 1990s, as states imposed new outcome measures and the federal government toyed with national standards, an awakened citizenry reacted to the erosion of local control.

Both Professors Glenn and Carlson are troubled by the increased role of the state in local school governance. Glenn quotes William Bennett, who lambastes outcome-based education (OBE) as a "Trojan Horse for social engineering"; Carlson considers it no less than a "a larger struggle in American culture and public education . . . concerning which (and whose) vision of a new, postmodern America is to prevail."

Unlike Carlson, Glenn has no problem with setting national standards or the concept of accountability of results provided it is "modest, demonstrably necessary, and measurable." However, he prefers to leave issues of values and character to parents and those whom they specifically entrust to impart them. Carlson, though, views standards or outcomes—including content and skills—as inherently value-laden. He links the OBE controversy to the larger social-economic structural shift, creating uneasiness among the working poor and conservative Christians and making strange bedfellows of corporate elites, educational bureaucrats, and some progressives. OBE, for Carlson, affords an opportunity for democratic empowerment of local communities and the "rearticulation of democratic rights" fostering equity and caring. Glenn, clearly troubled by Carlson's analysis, counters, "On whose authority do you do these things?"

During the community dialogue, issues revolve around the desirability and possibility of measuring and teaching basic skills and civic values. This conversation reflects the diversity of opinion found along the OBE divide. For some, like Pastor Shearer, OBE is the "line in the sand" that forces school accountability for specific academic and behavioral standards while teachers prepare students to compete in a world economic system. Professor Carper, however, is more wary of the state's imposing instructional outcomes, particularly in schools that have largely lost community trust. Others, like the Reverend Burgess and Dr. Murphy, hold a more jaundiced view, decrying the cultural code embedded in many of these standards or challenging the teacher deskilling that results from such a top-down accountability system.

CHAPTER 11

The Fundamentalist Right, the "New Paradigm," and Outcome-Based Education

Dennis Carlson

Recently, while chatting with a teacher in an inner–city high school where I am involved in a school–university collaboration project, I was told that the state department of education had notified teachers and administrators in the district that it was moving away from specifying various "inputs" into the educational process—such as what textbooks to use, topics that had to be covered in courses, the sequencing of courses, and so forth. Instead, the state planned to establish "competencies" in various subject areas that all students had to "master" before graduation. When the system was fully operational in a few years, school districts were to be free to use a number of different methods, including portfolio assessment, to evaluate mastery of competencies, although students would also still need to pass the state's "basic skills" high school proficiency exam as well. I remarked to the teacher that this sounded an awful lot like "outcome-based education," or OBE as it is known. "Oh," he said, "it is OBE. It's just that the central office and the state no longer call it that. It's 'competencies' now, not 'outcomes.' No one around here uses the language of OBE anymore. You'd have the religious Right on your back right away if you did." In fact, while the school district had instituted staff development in OBE only a year before for principals and teacher leaders, OBE and "outcomes" were now forbidden words in the district and exorcised from major planning documents. It was also apparent, however, that the district and the state were going ahead with OBE—under a different name.

Why has OBE become the reform movement that dare not speak its name? In what follows I want to try to answer this question and by way of doing so say something about the current moment in public school reform and restructuring. Specifically, I want to examine the conflict over OBE as one manifestation of a broader struggle going on in public education that has its roots in shifts occurring in culture as we enter a "postmodern" historical era. The first of these shifts involves a restructuring of the economy in a high-tech, information age, with concurrent changes in organizational development and the structuring of work experiences. The "new paradigm" perspectives in organizational development and management are manifestations of this shift in thinking in the business world, and they have begun to have a significant impact on school reform as well—with OBE one example of this impact. A second major shift occurring in culture is the emergence of new social movements of identity and lifestyle that have begun to push for changes in the public schools and other sites of the state consistent with their particular sets of values and interests. The battle over OBE is, thus, partially about how much power new social movements operating outside of the state, such as those of the religious Right, are able to bring to bear on curriculum reform. Finally, and related to these developments, I mean to view the battle over OBE as an exemplar of a larger struggle in American culture and public education as we move into a new century concerning which (and whose) vision of a new, postmodern America is to prevail. In this regard, I want to point to some of the lessons democratic progressives might learn from the battle over OBE.

OBE, POST-FORDISM, AND THE "NEW PARADIGM" IN SCHOOL RESTRUCTURING

Let me begin by locating OBE a bit more specifically as a response by the state to transformations occurring in the way organizations are structured and work is defined in an era of what Stuart Hall (1990) and others have called "post-Fordism" capitalism. While post-Fordism is characterized by a number of interrelated shifts in organizational development, I want to focus on three major clusters of changes. The first of these is a shift to site-based management, involving the decentralization of technical decision-making power to local plants and offices in close touch with customers and rapidly changing market conditions. Since the computer allows the central office to monitor activities at local offices, centralized control can be maintained without mandating every procedure from the top. Second, the computer is not only allowing for the tailoring of products to meet individual customer needs, it is also freeing up communication in the firm, so that lateral communication and networking are replacing the traditional, hierarchical chain of command. Third, and closely related to this last point, post-Fordist firms place a strong emphasis on communication and "people skills." In high-tech companies, workers are increasingly working together in ad hoc teams to come up with new product ideas, market strategies, and other ways of staying ahead of the competition, and this necessitates knowing how to cooperate and communicate effectively in teams. In the new service industry jobs at the bottom of the labor hierarchy, interpersonal skills also receive emphasis since these jobs involve a good deal of interaction with customers and other workers. Fourth, in all job fields learning how to get along with various "others" in an increasingly diverse work force has become more important. Consequently, most corporations and larger businesses have begun to institute staff development in multiculturalism and respect for diversity (by race, religion, gender, sexual orientation, etc.).

While acknowledging that very significant and far-reaching changes are occurring in advanced capitalist economies, changes which are as significant for the organization of work as those changes that occurred early in this century with the shift to a mass industrial society, I do not want to imply that capitalism is "reinventing" itself in ways that involve a fundamental redistribution of power. The trend toward decentralization in firms is occurring within the context of the continuing concentration of economic power and wealth in a relatively few multinational corporations. In almost all firms, top CEOs and their staffs now hold more of the power over substantive decisions about what products and services to offer, where investments will be made in product development or marketing, and so forth. Furthermore, the emphasis on cooperation and other "people skills" may actually involve greater control by managerial elites over workers and work processes. In some ways the concern with "people skills" links this new management discourse with a long tradition of human relationism in industry, which has sought to better integrate the worker into the company family.

Over the past few years, the newer corporate models of management and organizational development have begun to influence the discourse of public school restructuring, and OBE is just one example of restructuring models that rather directly incorporate post-Fordist managerial perspectives. OBE represents itself as a comprehensive system of school restructuring that not only draws on corporate models of "effectiveness" but also prepares young people for the new world of work. William Spady, who developed OBE as a comprehensive system for school restructuring in the mid-1980s, previously had served as director of the Far West Laboratory for Educational Research and Development. That agency is funded by the federal government to engage in the development, testing, and national dissemination of outcome-based educational reform models; and it was while at the Far West

Lab that Spady first began assembling the basic components of what he later came to call OBE (Spady & Marx, 1984). The development of OBE thus also speaks to the close working relationship between the corporate world and the state in educational reform.

The core principle or theme of OBE is a shift from state or central office regulation of various inputs into the educative process (for example, how many "Carnegie units" are required for graduation, the specific sequencing of courses, the content of courses, textbooks) toward specifying a set of educational outcomes—the specific competencies *all* students are to have mastered by the time they graduate. According to Spady (1992), "OBE means: defining, organizing, focusing, and directing all aspects of an instructional . . . system in relation to the thing we want all learners to demonstrate successfully when they exit the system" (p. 3). While this clearly implies more standardized testing of students, Spady argues that more use should also be made of a mix of evaluation techniques including student portfolios and exhibitions. In its most fully developed form, OBE involves evaluating students on what Spady calls "transformational outcomes: complex role performance in authentic [i.e., "real-life"] contexts"(p. 35).

OBE also involves establishing outcomes in all major subject areas, including music, art, and physical education, and in some interdisciplinary and "values education" areas such as learning to respect diversity, work cooperatively with others, and think critically. As an example, one upstate New York school system currently switching to OBE breaks learning outcomes down into five major areas: "self-esteem as a learner and person, thinking and understanding in academics, problem solving and decision making, being self-directed as a learner and person, and concern for others" ("Religious Right," 1993, p. 10). In contrast to previous outcome-based models of education that emphasized individual achievement, OBE is based on the proposition that to produce "transformational outcomes," instruction must be reorganized consistent with principles of cooperative learning more than competition. Spady (1992) talks of a shift from seeing "students as isolated performers" to seeing "students as collaborative performers" engaged in "empowering learning experiences" (p. 22). The teacher is viewed as a coach rather than director of instruction, and interdisciplinary team teaching is supported. In its pure or idealized form, then, OBE advances an approach to restructuring that seeks to "reinvent" public education by casting it in the image of the new, post-Fordist business and workplace.

OBE AND THE FUNDAMENTALIST RIGHT

Because it had the support of major power brokers in business, the state, and the educational profession, along with social movements of the democratic left, the shift to OBE seemed unstoppable by the early 1990s. Yet, rather suddenly, OBE found itself in the middle of a well-orchestrated attack from groups of the religious Right in a number of states, including Pennsylvania, New Mexico, Colorado, Florida, Iowa, New York, Ohio, Virginia, Kansas, and Minnesota (Brockett, 1993; Jones, 1993). By religious Right I mean to refer to social movements organized around a belief in the Bible as the literal word of God and as containing absolute and thus timeless "truths" about how culture should be organized and according to what values. Culturally, the religious Right has been associated with the reassertion of puritan, traditionalist conception of morality and social order, based on erecting rigid boundaries between right and wrong, good and evil, and "normal" and "abnormal." This implies, in most cases, a reassertion of tradition gender roles and sexual norms.

The opposition to OBE among social movements of the religious Right has been grounded in several somewhat distinct, if interrelated, arguments. One of these arguments is that OBE provides a mechanism for the state to override a long tradition of local control of the schools. This certainly is a concern that democratic progressives share with those on the religious Right, and something that needs to be taken very seriously. In taking on OBE, the fundamentalist Right has not only opposed elite corporate and bureaucratic state reform models; it also has asserted a form of grassroots populism that is very consistent with the advancement of democratic projects, and it has done this at a time when democratic progressives have remained uninvolved in local school politics. Antistatism and antifederalism have been linked in American history to movements to maintain slavery, maintain separate but equal facilities for blacks and whites (including segregated schools), and (most recently) movements to pass local antigay ordinances. A democratic society must be committed to maintaining certain basic human rights throughout all communities and institutions in society; and this means that local control of the schools must always be tempered by broader social commitments that the state has a responsibility to both defend and advance. The state must assume an important role in guiding and overseeing public education in a democratic society, even if there must also be a good deal of local, grassroots involvement in constructing an educational program that is adapted to specific local conditions and circumstances.

But there is more to the fundamentalist Right's attack on OBE than the assertion of local control. In fact, the religious Right has not opposed top-down state reform movements of a certain type—such as the movement in the 1980s toward a state-mandated basic skills curriculum and high school proficiency testing. To understand why this is so, I need to say a bit more about the religious Right's participation in the neo-conservative power bloc that was dominant throughout the 1980s. Neo-conservatives sought to pull together several major social movements and constituencies into a hegemonic power bloc. First, and most significantly, neo-conservative discourse appealed to elements of the business community and the middle class interested in tax cuts, a reduced role for the state, and business models of running government. Second, it was designed to appeal to the so-called "Reagan Democrats"—primarily white, working-class males who were concerned about crime and opposed to affirmative action. Finally, it appealed to the growing new right-wing sentiment in the country associated with a revival of fundamentalist Christianity.

In mobilizing these diverse constituencies into a power bloc, neo-conservatives articulated an agenda for change that tapped into widely held sentiments in American culture. The neo-conservative reform agenda in education was organized around the slogan "back to basics," a slogan that was capable of taking on multiple meanings. For example, for many middle-class Americans it meant a return to the traditional values that supposedly had made American great—hard work, discipline, respect for authority, and so forth. The business community supported a "basic skills" orientation because it was concerned about the generally low functional literacy and computation skills of many high school graduates entering the semiskilled work force. For Reagan Democrats, back to basics and proficiency testing implied that inner-city, minority youth would have to earn their diplomas by adhering to the same standards as everyone else. It also was associated with "get-tough" approaches to discipline in inner-city schools and classroom. Finally, and aside from these other concerns, the fundamentalist Right saw in the back-to-basics and proficiency testing movement a means of returning public education to what it claimed was its original purpose—teaching the "three Rs": reading, writing, and computing skills. The argument is that public schools should stick to providing individuals with the literacy skills they need to function in society and leave all the rest, including values and attitudes, to the family and church. Of course, a basic skills curriculum may claim to teach the "three Rs," but in fact it comes with a whole set of values having to do with the virtues of following directions, conforming to prescribed work routines, and constructing correct answers. Nevertheless, they are values that most of those on the fundamentalist Right were not troubled by.

Such is not the case, however, with the values associated with the "new paradigm" reform movements in education. The fragile alliance between corporate elites and fundamentalist right-wing groups that was forged in the 1980s has begun to unravel in the 1990s as new paradigm approaches are becoming more influential in the business community and among policy makers in the state. Increasingly, teaching the "basics" is being expanded by corporate and state reform initiatives to include the explicit teaching of values, including learning how to work with others, as exemplified by OBE.

To this extent, the battle over OBE may be interpreted as the most recent manifestation of a protracted battle that has been waged by fundamentalists and cultural conservatives against progressive education, here used to refer to a general approach to education that emphasizes cooperation rather than individualism and that seeks to educate the "whole child" more than merely the intellect. As Joel Spring (1989, p. 7) remarks:

> The American public school since the beginning of the twentieth century . . . had organized around the principle that traditional free marketplace individualism was a thing of the past and that a modern urban industrial world depended not on economic individualism but on economic cooperation.

Immediately after World War II, as American culture began entering a period of cultural conservatism, fundamentalist and anticommunist groups on the political right in America led a well-organized campaign against progressivism in education. Most of their criticism was directed against a then-popular, mainstream form of progressivism called "life adjustment education" that emphasized the role of public schools in "adjusting" young people to modern family life and community life. Although mainstream progressivism in this form was hardly radical or subversive and was endorsed by most business leaders of the day, those on the right viewed it as a form of "brainwashing" of our children in the collectivist values of atheistic communism. The attack on OBE in the 1990s thus needs to be appreciated as part of a historical challenge to progressivism in education from the political and cultural right, although the terrain of that challenge has shifted somewhat in recent years.

Behind the attack on OBE is yet a deeper concern—one that has to do with the politics of sexual desire. Fundamentalist Christianity is associated with a highly repressive sexuality, one that limits sexual expression to heterosexual marriage for purposes of procreation (Carlson, 1991). Within this framework, certain sexual practices get labeled as immoral and certain individuals get represented as embodiments of the moral decay of modern society. In recent years, gays and lesbians have assumed an especially important role as the "other" whose stigmatization is used to affirm the moral correctness of traditional, sexually repressive constructions of identity (Carlson, 1997). Those on the religious Right fear, and somewhat justifiably, that states might use OBE to mandate outcomes in sexuality education that include a nonjudgmental presentation of information on contraceptives, abortions, and homosexuality, and that it also might mandate outcomes in multicultural education that include treating gays and lesbians as part of the new multicultural community. In fact, social movements on the democratic left (e.g., the civil rights movement, women's movement, gay/lesbian movement, pro-choice movement) have increasingly pressured the state to expand the role of public schools in sexuality education and in teaching respect for cultural diversity, including sexual diversity. As a consequence, many OBE documents at state and local levels have included some language on teaching sexuality education and on teaching respect for diverse lifestyles. Invariably, it is this language that provokes the most resistance among right-wing groups.

In Pennsylvania, for example, where fighting over OBE has been particularly intense, the state school board recently formulated an OBE plan that would require students to master 55 academic and nonacademic outcomes before they graduate ("Religious Right," 1993). While the new right-wing group, Citizens for Excellence in Education (CEE), opposed OBE in general in Pennsylvania, much of its energy was spent defeating a proposed section in the state OBE planning document titled "Appreciating and Understanding Others." This, it feared, would require that schools teach appreciation for "deviant lifestyles" such as homosexuality. In the face of mounting and entrenched new right-wing opposition, the section was ultimately dropped from the state's OBE plan. In many local school districts across the country, similar battles are being fought. So far, it is difficult to say who is winning this national battle being fought in local skirmishes; and state officials seem caught in a quagmire. If they cave in to pressure from the religious Right, they face alienating powerful progressive social movements and constituencies, yet the religious Right is proving to be a powerful force to be reckoned with as well as being arguably better organized and certainly more vocal.

CONCLUSION

I have, in this chapter, attempted to place OBE and the controversy surrounding it within the context of broader struggles occurring as we enter new and unsettling times. Public schools cannot help but be embroiled in these struggles, and efforts to remain neutral or to claim to speak for the "public" (as if it were some consensual, homogeneous whole) are becoming more difficult to manage. This is not, in itself, bad. As public schools become more embroiled in cultural struggle at both the state and local levels, it becomes more apparent that decisions about what to teach and how to teach are, in the end, always political questions that cannot be answered by professional "experts" alone or even primarily. Whose values are to direct curriculum decision making? Whose interests are to be served by various curriculum reform movements? And what power relations are being organized? These are the questions that need to guide our analysis of the battle between the supporters of OBE and the religious Right, as they need to guide our analysis of all curriculum reform movements. However, for democratic progressives, one other question will need to be raised along with these. Specifically, what lessons might be learned from the battle over OBE that might be useful in advancing democratic progressive agendas and values in education? For certainly neither the "new paradigm," corporate managerial discourse that lies behind OBE nor the antiprogressive, fundamentalist discourse of the religious Right can provide an adequate basis for forging a new democratic vision of public education.

One of the lessons democratic progressives might learn from the battle over OBE is that the new religious Right is most powerful and effective in mobilizing local support when school boards are most insulated from public input. The battle against OBE has been framed in terms of fighting the entrenched, bureaucratic state, professional educational establishment. In this context, democratic progressivism must not react by rushing to defend that establishment, as represented in this case by corporate- and bureaucratic state–supported OBE. It is more than a bit ironic that some progressive groups have sought to use OBE to mandate a progressive curriculum from the top down. If democratic progressivism is to remain true to its values and commitments, then it must support forms of curriculum decision making that emerge out of a broad, inclusive discourse on public school reform at local and state levels, in which diverse voices and interest groups get represented. While such a decision-making process would not guarantee that progressive approaches to education win out, it would help ensure that decisions are broadly supported once they are made and that all parties and interest groups have their concerns taken seriously. Furthermore, it is only through the renewal of such a broad, public discourse that we can be assured that a small but well-organized minority (as the religious Right is in most communities) does not dominate local educational discourse and "take over" local school boards because progressive voices have become too cynical to enter the political arena and engage in the struggle over the direction of public life.

This brings us to a second major lesson to be learned from the battle over OBE. The growing influence of the religious Right is partially a reflection of the disarray and fragmentation among democratic progressive forces at this historical juncture. Too often, democratic progressives have assumed a defensive posture, defending public schools and professional educators in the face of attacks from the religious Right. They have been less successful in defining and defending a vision of a "good society" that can serve as a basis for a proactive agenda of educational renewal. To adequately respond to the challenge of the religious Right will require the articulation of democratic moral claims having to do with promoting equity, building a caring community, and fighting oppression in all of its varied forms. It also will require a rearticulation of democratic rights, to include not only the rights of gays and lesbians to full membership in a multicultural society but also their right to be included in the curriculum as such. Finally, in responding to the challenge of the religious Right a new democratic progressive discourse may also need to acknowledge the rights of young people to an education that does not split spirituality and religion apart from the curriculum into a separate realm. Like the public/private split more generally, the attempt to separate public education from private lives is a vestige of modernism that we need to begin moving beyond. Among other things, this may imply allowing time in the school day for meditation or prayer along with organized study of spirituality and religion.

While the challenge posed by the religious Right is significant, it is important to remember that the most powerful threat to democratic conceptions of education may be from elite economic and bureaucratic state interests, who are driven by two primary metaphors: student as work and school as an efficiently run business. In some ways, democratic progressives and corporate elites seem to share similar perspectives. Both, after all, are likely to support cooperative education, portfolio assessment, site-based management, multiculturalism, and other "new paradigm" reforms. The challenge for democratic progressives, consequently, is to carve out a "third space" separate from corporate and bureaucratic state approaches to reform as well as those advanced by the fundamentalist Right. In the process, terms such as "cooperative education" and "multicultural education" will have to be rearticulated within a democratic rather than an economic discourse, one aimed at reconstructing democratic public life.

REFERENCES

Brockett, D. (1993, June 8). Outcome–based education faces strong opposition. *School Board News, 13,* pp. 1–2.

Carlson, D. (1991). Conflict and change in the discourse on sexuality education. *Educational Theory, 41*(4), 343–359.

Carlson, D. (1997). *Of gayness, multicultural education, and community.* In D. Carlson, *Making progress: Education and culture in new times* (pp. 99–118). New York: Teachers College Press.

Hall, S. (1990). The meaning of new times. In S. Hall & M. Jacques (Eds.), *New times: The changing face of politics in the 1990s* (pp. 116–134). New York: Verso.

Jones, J. (1993, April). Targets of the right. *American School Board Journal,* pp. 22–25.

Religious Right targets education. (1993, April). *American School Board Journal,* pp. 9–10.

Spady, W. (1992). *Outcome-based restructuring presentation.* Eagle, CO: High Success Network.

Spady, W., & Marx, G. (1984). *Excellence in our schools.* Arlington, VA: American Association of School Administrators and the Far West Laboratory.

Spring, J. (1989). *The sorting machine revisited.* New York: Longman.

CHAPTER 12

Outcome-Based Education: Can It Be Redeemed?

Charles L. Glenn

The controversy over outcome-based education (OBE), many observers fear, could bring to a screeching halt the school reform initiatives that seemed so promising a few years ago, initiatives stressing greater accountability and higher standards.

The controversy has caused divisions and bewilderment among political conservatives in particular. Those associated with business-initiated efforts to improve American schools have been among the leading supporters of outcome standards. As one told a reporter:

> Business leaders have been involved [in school reform] so long that many have grown tired of arguing over issues like the importance of raising teacher salaries. . . . Instead, they have turned to the results-oriented approach. . . . If we want results, standards are what we need. (Harp, 1994, p. 12)

Holding schools accountable for results seems so intuitively right that many find the controversy puzzling and only to be explained by conspiracy theories.

For the education Establishment, the explanation is obvious: the "Religious Right" is seeking to invade policy domains where educators should be free to exercise professional judgment without criticism by the laity—unless the latter are certified victims, a category that of course does not include parents animated by traditional religion. Fundamentalists seek to impose "a highly repressive sexuality" and oppose the curriculum that educators in their wisdom promote, according equal respect to every form of sexual expression, as an important aspect of the multicultural agenda.

To critics of OBE, the controversy is the predictable result of intrusions by an elite in sympathetic alliance with self-styled "progressive" pressure groups that seek to impose an unwelcome agenda of cultural change. These allies, it is charged, have used their influence in government to interfere in domains that have in the past been the exclusive responsibility of parents and those institutions of the civil society—locally controlled schools, churches, Scouts, youth sports leagues—to which they have entrusted a part of their responsibility for the education of their children.

Outcome-based education, of itself, requires no conspiracy theory for its justification. It is a straightforward concept, intended to achieve accountability for schooling by measuring its results in pupils' learning rather than by procedural controls. What could be more sensible? Public education systems, in this country and in other countries as well, have traditionally relied upon detailed prescription from above of what lower-level staff should do in all circumstances. Routines and required procedures, with periodic supervision, are an effective way to prevent corruption and abuse of the power that government places in the hands of those who deal in its name with the public, but they are a very ineffective way to manage what must be a large measure of discretion by those who provide human services. What works reasonably well (though not without public discontent) for issuing driver's licenses does not work at all well for educating children. As Max Weber put it, bureaucratic control is characterized by "the dominance of a spirit of formalistic impersonality, '*Sine ira et studio*,' without hatred or passion, and hence without affection or enthusiasm" (Weber, 1924/1964, p. 340). Affection and enthusiasm might be out of place at the Registry of Motor Vehicles, but they are essential ingredients of the sort of school to which most of us would want to entrust our children.

Supporters of OBE argue that it provides clear standards for accountability and gives a message of high expectations to teachers and (perhaps even more importantly) to students. Some responsible body identifies the skills and knowledge that students should have when they leave the system and that will be assessed through a variety of methods including tests, portfolios, and teacher observations. Schools are thus induced to change their curriculum, instruction, and internal assessment to ensure that their students can perform effectively on the external assessment. Advocates believe that OBE can promote an emphasis on higher-order skills, such as analysis, synthesis, and problem solving, and the integration of knowledge across subject areas.

This seems clearly preferable to measuring the quality of schools and school systems by how much money they spend or what courses they offer, or measuring the achievement of students by how many high school credits they earn. What could be more reasonable? And educational equity would be served as well, though identifying a "common core of learning" that every student should be expected to attain, some sooner and others later with more help. This common core would by no means represent the outside limit of what students should be encouraged to learn, but it would ensure that no student (extreme cases aside) would leave school without the knowledge and competence necessary to participate competently in the society, economy, and political system (Glenn, 1993b).

Performance standards for various areas of the curriculum are currently in some stage of development, with praise for those in mathematics but (significantly) criticism for those initially proposed for history. Why does history cause problems for the standard-setters? Because what is selected out of the almost infinite storehouse of the past, and how it is presented, requires making judgments about the *meaning* of history from the perspective of current issues and ways of understanding the world, about the uses of the past. Historians themselves are keenly aware of the significance of the framework that they—and their predecessors—adopt for their research and its presentation. How could that be less true for the teaching of history to schoolchildren? The history taught in schools must perforce be less nuanced, more selective; the qualifications and reservations appropriate to a scholarly account must to a large extent be lost in a presentation intended for children.

An even more serious problem has been caused by the inclusion, in some proposals for OBE, of goals that require the demonstration of the pupil's attitudes or character, rather than simply knowledge of the Bill of Rights or ability to do algebra. William Bennett (1993), a strong advocate of performance standards when secretary of education, said more recently:

> The real concern is when those in the education establishment use OBE to (1) do away with objective measurable criteria (like standardized tests); (2) do away with the traditional subject-based curriculum in favor of an emphasis on things like general skills, attitudes and behaviors; and (3) advance their own radical social agenda. Increasingly, OBE is applied to the realm of behavior and social attitudes—becoming, in effect, a Trojan Horse for social engineering, an elementary and secondary school version of the kind of "politically correct" thinking that has infected our colleges and universities. (p. 1)

Opponents of OBE are not opposed to high standards or to accountability for results, but they want to know who will set the standards and what they will seek to measure. They point to the work of William Spady, director of the High Success Network, an organization that provides services to school districts in designing "transformational outcome-based education" to change the attitudes and values of students in order, supposedly, to create a more just and tolerant generation than that of their parents (Manno,

1994). As Charles Sykes (1994) has put it, rather cattily, "Grades favor the smart and the studious. Spady wants to make up for the unfairness of it all" (p. 12).

Robert Simmonds of Citizens for Excellence in Education—an organization claiming to have helped thousands of culturally conservative activists to be elected to local school boards—charges that OBE is a conspiratorial effort of massive behavior modification and social engineering (Chion-Kenney, 1984). The criticism fairly applies only to those versions of OBE seeking to reshape attitudes and behaviors, which are of a piece with the longstanding impulse to reshape humanity through schooling (Glenn, 1988)—whether humanity wants to be reshaped or not! If the reshaping is intended to serve the present [exploitative] economic system, it is a Bad Thing; but it is a Very Good Thing if it serves those victimized by the system—not by making them more capable of prospering within it, but by changing everybody else so that it doesn't matter. Some make a distinction, for example, between use of cooperative learning techniques to produced future workers who are good "team players," which they disapprove of, and using the same techniques to produce "future citizens" for a democratic society. Parents ask the age-old question, "On whose authority do you do these things?"

OBE opponents are accused of a conspiracy to prevent critical thinking and "tolerance" among American schoolchildren—as though there were something about religious belief that prevented identifying problems and solving them creatively. The radical New Testament insistence on the unimportance of distinctions of barbarian or Scythian, Jew or Gentile, man or woman, slave or free, all summoned to lead lives pleasing to God, might seem a more promising basis for mutual respect than the currently fashionable presentation of every conceivable "alternative lifestyle" (except sexual abstinence) as equally "valid" and worthy of honor.

BATTLEGROUND STATES

Pennsylvania was the first battleground over OBE, and the idea may never recover. In March 1992 the board of education issued a list of more than 500 proposed outcomes in 51 categories, intended to replace course credits ("Carnegie units") as the basis for high school graduation. Many of the outcomes were unexceptional, but critics zeroed in on those that seemed to go beyond what could be measured or that government should seek to prescribe, such as that "all students understand and appreciate their worth as unique and capable individuals and exhibit self-esteem" and that students "should act through a desire to succeed rather than a fear of failure while recognizing that failure is part of everyone's experience" (Chion-Kenney,

1984, p. 1). Desirable as it might be for every student to have such attitudes, it is difficult to see how they could be made the basis for educational standards or measured in an objective and reliable way.

Controversy over the standards led Governor Casey to urge the board to drop those proposed outcomes that did not deal with academic competencies but required that students demonstrate personal qualities of attitude and character. The governor said that he did not oppose the standards but feared that the controversy would distract efforts from school reform; his request was ignored by the board (Rothman, 1993).

Pennsylvania in fact had a tradition of examining such aspects of learning, going back at least to 1967 when the Educational Quality Assessment program was established, "charged with developing assessments based on 10 very broadly stated goals" (Coldiron, 1993, p. 25). The assessments included hypothetical situations in response to which students were asked to select responses based either on peer pressure or on fear of punishment; convictions about what is right and what wrong were not among the multiple-choice options. A critic of this program wrote that "personal opinions are being assessed for 'correct' responses in a pluralistic society that supposedly treasures the concept of individual differences" (Eakman, 1993). A parent who objected to this form of assessment wrote that "the current push for educational reform has been a social experiment in Pennsylvania for over 23 years. We were the national pilot in testing and scoring attitudes, values, opinions, and beliefs, a process now called 'political correctness'" (Hoge, 1993).

The board may have expected general acquiescence in its new outcome-based high school graduation requirements, but an unexpectedly widespread opposition to OBE emerged, led by Peg Luksik, a former Catholic school teacher and mother of five. As a second-grade teacher, she said, "I listened to all of the stuff about self-esteem and counseling, but I wanted to make sure they could read. What good is it to make them feel good about not reading?" (quoted in Harp, 1993, p. 19).

This coalition of parents—by no means all of them members of conservative Christian churches—eventually derailed what they considered the more objectionable features of OBE as proposed in Pennsylvania. Students must now demonstrate mastery only in *academic* domains for high school graduation; school districts must provide opportunities to master softer goals like self-worth and tolerance, but these are not to be used for assessing students or schools.

Virginia also adopted outcome standards—labeled a "common core of learning"—in place of Carnegie units, only to back down in the face of widespread objections from parents; in September 1993, Governor Wilder ordered that the plans, which he said were "introduced with the best of intentions" but had become "tied to other fashionable approaches to curriculum reform," be abandoned (quoted in Manno, 1994, p. 6). The Virginia standards had been organized in terms of seven "life roles": fulfilled individual, supportive person, lifelong learner, expressive contributor, quality worker, informed citizen, and environmental steward. The last-named drew criticism because the required student outcomes reflected a politically loaded "eco-catastrophe" scenario.

CONCERNS ABOUT SCOPE AND VALUES

As we can see, the problem with OBE is not with the concept of a system of accountability for results but with the form it has taken in the hands of those planning for implementation. Chester Finn confesses, "For several years, I was among those promoting the [focus on outcomes], never imagining the twist it would take. *Mea culpa*" (quoted in Manno, 1994, p. 2). American Federation of Teachers president Albert Shanker (1993), another supporter of standards, wrote:

> They talk about world-class standards and the skills needed to compete in a global economy. But whereas the education standards in other industrialized countries call for things like solving algebraically and by graph simultaneous linear equations or analyzing the causes of the Cold War, OBE standards are vague and fluffy. . . . Vaguely worded outcomes like this will not send a message to students, teachers and parents about what is expected of youngsters. Nor will they help bridge the enormous gap between schools where students are expected to achieve—and do—and schools where anything goes. (p. 25)

Complaints that standards for OBE will be set too high or too low, rely too much or too little upon memorized knowledge or upon demonstrated skills, can surely be dealt with by judicious planning. Unfortunately, government officials often seem not to know when to stop when they are developing requirements. There is always another eventuality which they want to cover, or another worthy objective to include, and these tend to accumulate over time. Uniformity can seem, to those whose own work is governed by bureaucratic rationality, to be the only safeguard of quality. The "standards movement," intended to break the grip of bureaucratic controls of education, may serve, through overelaborate standards, only to strengthen it.

The mistake made by the Thatcher government in the United Kingdom, when what was intended to be a focused system of accountability in a few areas of the curriculum turned into a nightmare of complexity and overelaboration, was repeated in Pennsylvania, Virginia, and other states with respect to OBE. In each case, the devising of standards was turned over to groups of subject-matter experts, who put everything but the kitchen sink in their own sections without any regard for the overloading and incoherence of the whole.

Just as in the United Kingdom, there has subsequently been a drastic reduction in the scope and intrusiveness of national testing, so standards set in the United States, at any level, should be modest, demonstrably necessary, and measurable in reliable and comparable ways that do not intrude excessively upon time for instruction. The overelaborated form that some new systems of accountability have taken includes so many objectives, many too vague or sensitive to measure in a reliably comparable way, that it actually "undermines efforts to track and compare educational progress or failure" (Manno, 1994, p. 11).

A second concern about OBE may prove more difficult to allay: the fear that it will require schools to seek to reshape the values and attitudes of their pupils in response to an agenda set by the state. Proposals to do so are as old as our nation (Glenn, 1988) but have always been subverted by the stubborn tradition of local control and parent influence over the content of schooling. Critics of OBE insist that many of the legitimate goals of education should not be the concern of government, but only of parents and those to whom they entrust their children.

This is not to say that schools should limit their mission to value-neutral instruction. While much of the anti-OBE rhetoric has insisted that values are the exclusive concern of parents, in fact most want the school their children attend to make the development of character an important part of their mission. That does not mean that parents want *government* to dictate what forms that will take. Parents tend to make a distinction between their children's school, even though it may be government-operated, and government itself. They want to trust the school—it would be hard to send their children off each morning if they did not—but that trust does not generally extend to the educational system of which it is a part. "New social movements of identity and lifestyle" have found it all too easy to influence centralized decision making into adopting their agendas for education.

CHARTER SCHOOLS

Paradoxically, the ability of school staff to form coherent communities expressing a shared understanding of education for life is limited by efforts of government to require that they take on such agendas. It remains to be see whether education officials can resist the temptation to set standards in such a form that they inhibit the distinctiveness that is a natural result of collaboration to shape the life of an individual school. The rapidly spreading state provisions for "charter schools"—independent public schools—could provide the vehicle to create thousands of schools that are coherent yet publicly accountable, if government can resist the temptation to over-regulate. Clear but limited outcome standards are what is needed.

Support for charter schools reflects a growing awareness that conflict over the content of schooling is inevitable under a monopoly system. Your agenda seems virtuous to you, as mine seems virtuous to me, but education should not be imposed on my children in a form that undermines how I am seeking to raise them, just because you have been more successful in promoting your agenda. Majorities (much less influential minorities) do not rule, under our system, when fundamental rights are at stake; the Supreme Court has addressed this question eloquently in two prominent cases:

> The fundamental theory of liberty upon which all governments in this Union repose excludes any general power of the state to standardize its children. . . . The child is not the mere creature of the state; those who nurture him and direct his destiny have the right, coupled with the high duty, to recognize and prepare him for additional obligations. (*Pierce v. Society of the Sisters of the Holy Names of Jesus and Mary*, 268 U.S. 510 [June 1, 1923])

> Probably no deeper division of our people could proceed from any provocation than from finding it necessary to choose what doctrines and whose program public educational officials shall compel youth to unite in embracing. . . . If there is any fixed star in our constitutional constellation, it is that no official, high or petty, can prescribe what shall be orthodox in politics, nationalism, religion, or other matters of opinion. (*West Virginia State Board of Education v. Barnette*, 319 U.S. 624 [June 14, 1943])

Autonomy will not ensure that charter schools are able to educate in the fullest sense, unless they are animated by a coherent ethos. Such an ethos can be elaborated by those participating directly in the school, or it can be adapted from a tradition of schooling based on an understanding of the purposes of education and of human life. What it cannot be is dictated by government for every school.

Since such understandings are at least implicitly religious, those supporting charter schools seem likely to confront before long whether it is legitimate for them to be explicitly religious in ethos and thus in the distinctive character of their life and work. The question would not arise in most countries with comparable political and educational systems. In Australia, Canada, the United Kingdom, Germany, Sweden, and France, the right of schools with a distinctively religious character to public support—provided they meet quality standards—is well established (Glenn, 1989). In these cases, the basis of public funding for religiously based schools is the right of parents to make decisions about the education of their children, as expressed in the various international covenants defining human rights. Society's interest in more effective schools, schools based on a coherent and shared understanding of why and how to educate, may lead to the same conclusion.

Denying public support to a school because it expresses in the education it provides a clearly articulated ethos seems foolishly to punish what should be rewarded. Wishy-washy schools, morally incoherent schools, lowest-common-denominator schools enjoy the approval of public policy in the United States, while many schools of character do not, because that character is based upon a religious sense of life.

CONCLUSION

Ensuring that all members of the younger generation learn those things in school that will equip them for a useful and satisfying adulthood is a legitimate concern of public policy. The growing interest, here and abroad, in standards for content that must be covered and for knowledge and skills that pupils should acquire is entirely appropriate, and is likely to lead to more effective ways of determining whether schools are doing their job (Glenn, 1993a). But the recent debacles of educational assessment programs should serve as a warning to limit standards to academic areas for which there is broad support.

The challenge for educational policy is to design standards and systems for administering them in such a way that school communities will become more *free* at the same time that they become more *accountable*. An appropriately designed and implemented system of standards is entirely consistent with educational freedom, providing the assurance parents require that, whatever school they select for their child, the child will not be disadvantaged by failing to learn what is required for successful participation in the wider society. It is also an important condition for the exercise of freedom to operate a school that is out of the ordinary, provided that satisfactory outcomes are achieved. Standards are no more an enemy of freedom than the sonnet form is an enemy of poetical inspiration. This is what elsewhere I (Glenn, 1993a) have called

> the tension between the two major vectors of school reform in the nineties: on the one hand, an emphasis upon *high common standards* for the content and quality of education; on the other, an emphasis upon *school-level decision-making* and consequent diversity among schools. Finding ways to keep them in a dynamic and fruitful balance is a primary challenge for educational policy. (p. 336)

In a free and pluralistic society, on the other hand, imposing educational standards that take sides about issues on which we differ inevitably creates conflict; we become what the poet Yeats called "weasels fighting in a hole."

A healthy educational system needs air, and space, and structural arrangements that allow parents and teachers to agree on how children will be taught, on the basis of what understanding of the world and of the purposes of education they will be guided toward adulthood. Outcome-based education is consistent with such a free system only if it allows those decisions to be made school by school, by those who directly care for and care about the children, by their parents and their teachers. "New social movements of identity and lifestyle" enjoy many freedoms in our society, but among them should not be to come between parents and the education of their children.

REFERENCES

Bennett, W. J. (1993, May 27). Outcome-based education. *Empower America* [newsletter], pp. 1–2.

Chion-Kenney, L. (1984, September). Negotiating the challenge of outcome-based education. *The School Administrator.* Reprinted in Network News & Views, October 1994, pp. 10–14.

Coldiron, J. R. (1993, November 10). Letter to the Editor. *Education Week,* p. 25.

Eakman, B. K. (1993, October 20). It's about mental health, stupid. *Education Week,* pp. 40, 43.

Education Commission of the States. (1993). *"Outcomes-based" education.* Denver: Author.

Glenn, C. L. (1988). *The myth of the common school.* Amherst: University of Massachusetts Press.

Glenn, C. L. (1989). *Choice of schools in six nations.* Washington, DC: U.S. Department of Education.

Glenn, C. L. (1993a). *Common standards and educational diversity—How twenty-five nations strike a balance* (prepared for the Pew Forum on Education Reform). Boston: Boston University, Center on Families, Communities, Schools and Children's Learning.

Glenn, C. L. (1993b, February). *Standards and diversity in education.* Keynote address at the tenth anniversary symposium of the *Yale Journal on Regulation,* New Haven, CT.

Glenn, C. L. (1994). Common standards and educational diversity—how twenty-five nations strike a balance. In J. DeGroof (Ed.), *Subsidarity and education* (pp. 336–363). Leuven, Belgium: Acco.

Harp, L. (1993, September 22). Parent becomes mother of 'outcomes' revolt. *Education Week,* pp. 1, 19–20.

Harp, L. (1994, June 15). A G.O.P. divided: O.B.E. drives wedge in party. *Education Week*, p. 12.

Hoge, A. (1993, November 10). How do you measure that outcome? [Letter to the editor]. *Education Week*, p. 25.

Manno, B. V. (1994, June). *Outcome-based education: Miracle cure or plague?* [Briefing Paper 165]. Indianapolis, IN: Hudson Institute.

Rothman, R. (1993, January 20). Amid controversy, Pa. board adopts learner outcomes. *Education Week*, p. 12.

Shanker, A. (1993, October 11). Where we stand [paid advertisement]. *The New Republic*, p. 25.

Sykes, C. (1994, October). Dumbing down our kids. *Network News and Views*, pp. 9–18.

Weber, M. (1964). *The theory of social and economic organization* (T. Parsons, Trans.). New York: Free Press. (Original work published 1924)

A Matter of Fairness and Equity

Pigford: If objectives really allowed students to grow and to refine their skills in analysis, I would feel much better as a parent knowing what really is expected from my child. When we set expectations, however, we tend to focus on those that are easily measurable and thus settle on the most basic of skills and minimal competencies.

Burgess: In this state, we are told that "high standards" are being pushed—but for whom? Who are setting these standards and why? Do these standards suggest that we are truly interested in educating *all* of our children to their highest capacity or are we merely content to insure that business and industry have the people and skills they need to continue to amass huge profits while the workers eke out a living wage? I am not opposed to outcomes, however I may be opposed to OBE.

Sears: What does OBE mean to you?

Burgess: A poor, male black youth comes into my school who is swaying and bopping, but I have to convince him as principal, who also happens to be an African-American male, that if he wants to be "successful" in this society, such behavior is *not* acceptable. I have to send two messages. One, while there is nothing wrong with that behavior, he has to learn when it is acceptable and when it is not. Two, he is not going to "make it" unless he knows the middle-class, white code.

Pigford: Some matters as obvious as dress, behaviors, and hairstyles reflect class values that are culture-bound.

Burgess: The public school is a middle-class contraption. Students who are middle-class do the best in school. My son will do better in school

---

See the introduction for a description of the conversationalists.

Curriculum, Religion, and Public Education: Conversations for an Enlarging Public Square. Copyright © 1998 by Teachers College, Columbia University. All rights reserved. ISBN 0-8077-3706-2 (pbk.), ISBN 0-8077-3707-0 (cloth). Prior to photocopying items for classroom use, please contact the Copyright Clearance Center, Customer Service, 222 Rosewood Dr., Danvers, MA 01923, USA, tel. (508) 750-8400.

than some of my cousin's children because he has access to more resources.

Pritchett: We need academic outcomes. Certainly, these need to have parental input. At the state department we talk about "little OBE," and "capital OBE." No one argues against academic outcomes. But when you look at capital OBE, students are also held accountable for demonstrating a particular set of values. Now, like Glenn, I don't believe—even if we can agree on the set of values—that you can demonstrate, in a way to be held accountable as a condition for graduation, that you are "tolerant," for example.

Carper: I, too, am not comfortable with values being included in the outcomes for graduation. Another outcome may be that students, through the process of "self-discovery," will determine what "truths" will govern their lives. This makes many conservative Christians uncomfortable. The assumption that the only authentic values are those developed from one's own experiences clearly contradicts the concept of external moral authority as defined by Christianity, Judaism, and Islam.

Murphy: In many schools the value of the independent search for truth is neither expected nor taught. In this state, for example, it is difficult to engage in discussion with students about controversial issues such as creationism and homosexuality. There is little expectation for students to question, to criticize, or to engage in dialogue. One outcome that does *not* result is a generation of critical thinkers.

Pritchett: If today we can say "tolerance" is a value we wish students to be held accountable then, should the political landscape change, those in power may say that "intolerance" is the value.

Shearer: When did we ever reach the point that we felt that values had to be taught in a school? The school should have a system in which order, safety, and toleration are expected. But if a school is actually going to teach values such as "diversity"—not simply expect proper school *behaviors*—then we need to think about vouchers and educational options.

Murphy: As I read about OBE I kept thinking about the Order of the British Empire. The notion that teacher have to teach students skills or values rather than trusting in the process of their learning runs contrary to my idea of the purpose of education.

Shearer: As a parent and a citizen of the community, it is frustrating to discuss schools holding students accountable for values when the schools don't even have it together regarding expectations of proper student behavior or basic knowledge and skills. We can't even agree on the consequences of misbehavior or the value of accountability!

Murphy: But have you been in the schoolhouse recently? For instance, during the last few days my school suspended three of our middle school students—two for drinking alcohol before first period! There was swift and profound punishment.

Shearer: Well, that is not the perception of public schools.

Pigford: I understand the concern for school safety and that we punish students who do not act appropriately. My frustration, though, is that we do not do anything for these very students in the larger society. Much of what we have done as adults is what has caused the situations that we now wring our hands over. How often are we acting on those very Christian values that we espouse? What are the common values that we actually practice in our community, in our government, in our lives? Schools are a reflection of our community. They do not create these problems, but they have to deal with them. A simple answer is to throw a kid out of school. But that kid will be thrown somewhere. There is a reason why those kids are drinking before the first period, and the school didn't create that reason. In order to resolve these problems, it is going to require that we are sit down together.

Burgess: There has been an absence of dialogue. When I go to church, I go with people who tend to look like me and think like me. When I go home to my family, we all have the same name, we live under the same roof, and we have the same economic status. But when we enter the public school, everyone is together. While we have forced everyone into the public school, we have not prepared parents or students for dialogue when they do come together.

Murphy: Kids need to dialogue freely but they are too often not allowed to do that. Advocates of OBE are seeking formalisms and outcomes, but they are reluctant to foster open classroom dialogue.

Lindsey: When I was teaching in public schools, we practiced OBE before it existed. If we saw a child who was disrespectful, we worked with that student. But back then schools and teacher were themselves respected. Without that respect and trust, any educational reform effort will become controversial and likely fail.

Shearer: Most of the distrust among people centers around the uncertainty about whether their children will be able to read, write, and compete. Whether or not a child feels good about oneself is a factor of many circumstances *beyond* the schoolhouse. As a parent, what I want to know is when my children walk into that school will they be held accountable for their behavior, will the same academic standards will be applied to all, and will everyone have an equal opportunity to learn?

Pigford: How can they have an equal opportunity to learn if they come from unequal backgrounds?

Shearer: I don't know. But I do know that there is a strong feeling that we simply set the standards to the lowest common denominator so that no child is treated "unfairly." I am not questioning the sincerity of the teachers. Our disgust is that schools are no longer able to deliver on the real outcome: competing in a world system with adequate math, science, and communication skills. Whether or not they feel good about themselves is another matter.

Pigford: The two are not mutually exclusive. As a parent, I want my child to have a quality education. I want academic excellence, but not at the expense of my child being affirmed. If my child is in a situation where he is not being affirmed, I will probably act on that more quickly. Because I am middle-class, I have other options than relying on the school to insure academic progress.

Burgess: What about the children who come to my school from a poor background? Do I immediately begin to work on these children to mold them into the middle-class image?

Pigford: I wish I could tell you that all teachers are wonderful and they give all students access to all resources. Part of the problem is that just as we bring kids together without any understanding of each other, we put teachers in classrooms who have no understanding of kids with different backgrounds. Children have to deal with that reality day in and day out.

Burgess: I believe we have said to certain children that there is no hope. Yes, I would like for the child to feel good attending school, but at least I want them to have hope.

Shearer: I care if a child is affirmed; I also care about fairness.

Pigford: How do you define fair? Schools should be the same for all?

Shearer: I think so. Fairness is a value that is as important as a child's esteem.

Pigford: Treating students fairly does not mean treating them alike.

Burgess: When I stand up on Sunday morning to deliver a sermon, no one person is going to get what the other person receives.

Shearer: If children deserve to be educated, then disruption because of student misbehavior is *not* fair. If a child does not complete the work or fulfill the objectives of the grade, we should *not* record a passing grade or pass them along to another grade. It is a matter of fairness.

Murphy: Are you willing as a taxpayer to build the schools and hire the teachers necessary to educate those students who do not pass because they were abused by their father at the age of 5, or their mother is an alcoholic, or their brother is a cocaine addict?

Pigford: It amazes me, Bob, how teachers define disruption. You may have one teacher who, if a certain child looks the wrong way, calls that "disruption" rather than seeing it as a lack of cultural understanding between teacher and child.

Sears: One concern among some parents is the increased emphasis public school educators place on the affective at the expense of the cognitive. Thus we may pass along a eighth-grade student who has not done eighth-grade work because of the fear of psychological trauma, lowered self-esteem, or loss of hope.

Shearer: It is partly because the schools are so important that OBE has created such a controversy. It's our line in the sand. We simply can't let the schools cop-out and continue to slide by passing students from one grade to another in the name of self-esteem.

Pigford: That is an imposed organizational pattern. God did not ordain what an "eighth-grader" should look like or the requirements of eighth grade. We have created this system which places kids in a lockstep pattern. Maybe we should stop trying to put kids into patterns adults have created and try to come up with systems that are better suited for working with the children that we are educating today—many of whom do not have the same privileges that others have.

Lindsey: OBE emphasizes mastery, but I don't know how we do that if a child has to go from grade 1 to grade 2. We can't have a 12-year-old in grade 1 because he can't read.

Sears: Does OBE have the potential to do that?

Pigford: You are more much more likely to have a rigid structure where people have set specific expectations for all children.

Sears: Isn't that better than no expectations?

Pigford: I would like to see objectives for children. But let's not lock them into a grade pattern that specifies precisely what we expect them to know or the outcomes that they will demonstrate.

Sears: Well, let's talk about some specific outcomes. We seem to agree that students should read, write, and communicate. Well, read what? write what? communicate what?

Carper: Who makes the determination that this is what will be read or this is the outcome that will fulfill this reading skill?

Lindsey: The outcomes for each school may be different. Perhaps the school needs to be structured by the local community.

Murphy: Diversity disappears when you allow each community to define for themselves what will be read, written about, or communicated. As Carlson pointed out, leaving it to each community opens the possibility that Jim Crow can reemerge.

Carper: There is a fundamental tension between any systematic approach to matching instructional outcomes with assessment as a mandated state requirement in public schools. OBE might be successful in a school that reflected a distinct moral community but not in a diverse public school where you seek to foster those qualities. We simply will have different understandings of tolerance and respect. The fear of many persons is *whose* definitions of these qualities will be taught and assessed? Critics of OBE rebel against secularization, hierachization, and standardization of schooling. In a society that is moving more toward localism, voluntarism, and communities defined more by shared values than by geography, no wonder public schools that adopt OBE and that have lost their community base have become the focus of controversy.

Pritchett: Communities should design schools. But, should I be forced to move out of that community because of that design?

Sears: Let's assume for a moment that we are all involved in one community that, for good or ill, has chosen to use an OBE approach in education. In the academic area of history—which itself has received its share of controversy regarding proposed standards—what outcomes are important?

Pritchett: I would want my child to be exposed to a variety of viewpoints or perspectives on history and to be able to critically think through them.

Pigford: The issue for children to understand is "from whose perspective is this history being presented" and then to make some judgment.

Murphy: Whether we base our teaching of history on a Eurocentric perspective or an Afrocentric one, it can be dichotomous without dialogue. Students should understand the myriad ways in which humanity views itself.

Shearer: But we need to apply some historical tests to find the truth in history. Students ought to know how we got here in order to understand this culture. I don't think we necessarily have to know all there is to know about the role that Africa had to play in our community. This community is more clearly identified with the European culture and history. We can't just make ourselves feel good by putting "my heritage" in a balance that makes me feel comfortable. How *I feel* about it is almost irrelevant.

Burgess: So we would ignore the African experience?

Shearer: Let's study it historically, but it should *not* be the center of the history curriculum.

Murphy: Simply because we are the dominant culture right now, should this form the core of the curriculum? Students *should* see history from the perspective of the black slave who had his wife taken from him as well as from the view of the plantation owner or overseer.

Sears: What about the historian from Georgia whom Mr. Gingrich nominated to become the congressional archivist only to learn that she had insisted that the "Nazi point of view" be represented in a Holocaust display? Should all views, however untrue, however hurtful, be given curriculum space?

Shearer: It might be interesting or nice to know the Nazi mentality, but as far as educational outcomes I want students to know what actually happened: 6 million people were wiped out.

Murphy: It is critical that people understand what went through their minds.

Shearer: The school should concentrate on doing a *few* things well. The school should spend its time teaching children respect, obedience, tolerance, and submission along with being able to read and write. Schools and teachers should not be held accountable for doing something that they are incapable of doing.

Pigford: The key to turning around this society is not basic skills but our basic abilities to relate to one another.

Lindsey: I would be very naive to believe my kids will remember a lot about chemistry, U.S. history, or English. They will remember the qualities of that teacher who influenced them, they will remember how they felt when they entered that school, they will remember instances of caring and consideration. We may not have a good way of assessing this, but we are foolish not to realize that this is what our children learn and what we really want them to learn.

Suggested Additional Readings on Outcome-Based Education

Elaine Lindsey, with James T. Sears

Association for Supervision and Curriculum Development. Outcome-based education video series. Stock Number 614244. 703-549-9110.

Four tapes and a 232-page facilitator manual describe how Chicago and Phoenix are implementing OBE.

Barnes, S. (1993). *Creating the quality school for all students by implementing Outcome Based Education.* (ERIC Document Reproduction Service No. Ed 360 711)

Barnes examines the traditional educational paradigm and then, using Gestalt theory, contrasts it to the OBE paradigm and develops a seven-step staircase model.

Capper, C., & Jamison, M. (1992, April). *Outcomes based education reexamined: From structural functionalism to poststructuralism.* Paper presented at the annual meeting of the American Educational Research Association, San Francisco. (ERIC Document Reproduction Service No. Ed 346 555)

The authors use four paradigms to exemplify the tenets and origin of outcome-based education, particularly scrutinizing the claim that OBE reaches students who have typically been ill served by the traditional educational system.

Darling-Hammond, L. (1994). Performance-based assessment and educational equity. *Harvard Educational Review, 64*(1), 5–29.

Citing serious problems with norm-referenced tests, the proponents of OBE offer performance-based assessment as the preferred choice. Darling-Hammond argues that such performance-based assessments are not inherently equitable and that educators must be careful in employing such assessments.

Glatthorn, A. (1993). Outcome-based education. *Journal of Curriculum and Supervision, 8*(4), 354–364.

Based on the North Carolina experience, Glatthorn critiques OBE as a reform strategy.

Pliska, A., & McQuaide, J. (1993). *Pennsylvania's battle for educational reform* (Occasional Paper Series). Pittsburgh, PA: University of Pittsburgh, Department of Administrative and Policy Studies.

Describes struggles in Pennsylvania, where reformers changed graduation requirements from Carnegie units to 53 learner outcomes, provoking a public outcry.

Spady, W. (1994). Choosing outcomes of significance. *Educational Leadership, 51*(6), 18–23. (Entire Issue Devoted to OBE).

Spady uses a metaphor called Demonstration Mountain to show what are significant outcomes that should be demonstrated by students. He defines three zones, ending in "life-role functioning," and develops ten life roles that students should be able to demonstrate by the time they leave school.

Ysseldyke, J., & Thurlow, M. (1993). *Self-study guide to the development of educational outcomes and indicators.* Minneapolis, MN: National Center of Educational Outcomes. (ERIC Document Reproduction Service No. Ed 363 059)

Guide written to aid in the development of an outcomes-based assessment program using a four-step model.

PART VI

Science: Who and What Are We?

Since the *Origins of Species,* six generations have participated in the controversy regarding human origins. While historical fundamentalists, championed by William Jennings Bryan, staked out the claim that schools could enforce the prohibition against teaching evolution by natural selection (a judgment they won in the famous Scopes Trial), for the past generation the tables have been turned as Christian conservatives seek legal remedies from the enforced teaching of evolution.

But as the authors of these two chapters document, teaching biological science is more complex than choosing either a six-day creation lesson plan or a one emphasizing the primordial stew. Both authors express concern that too often science is taught dogmatically rather than critically. Brickhouse and Letts, though, advocate teaching about the controversy, stressing the "historicity of science," and advocating a science curriculum that examines social, political, and economic influences on the development of *all* scientific theories. Like Brickhouse and Letts, Johnson does not endorse the "creationist" view; however, neither does he find naturalism an acceptable alternative. Johnson explains the inherent flaws of naturalism in modern science which, by definition, negates any opportunity to theorize about or discuss other possibilities—most notably the hand of God in human affairs.

In this last community dialogue, participants again evidence a wide divergence of opinion, ranging from six-day creationism to naturalistic evolution. While the distinction between teaching science and teaching about science (i.e., creationism and other views) holds merit for some, for others it amounts to little more than "tossing us a bone." There is, however, agreement that many teachers charged with teaching science are ill equipped to go beyond lesson plans and textbook formulations even if we could agree that their student ought examine such knotty issues.

CHAPTER 13

The Problem of Dogmatism in Science Education

Nancy W. Brickhouse and William J. Letts IV

One of the central problems in science education today is that science is often taught dogmatically or, using Schwab's phrase, as a "rhetoric of conclusions" (1956/1978).[1] The science curriculum is typically primarily concerned with teaching students the theories and facts of science. Issues regarding the methodologies and social practices of science receive little attention. Not only is the science curriculum primarily concerned with theories of science, but there is considerable concern that we cover all the facts and theories of potential significance. This obsession with getting through all the major theories of science typically leads to the dogmatic teaching of science in a form that both oversimplifies and distorts the subject matter of science. Schwab (1956/1978) also argues that teaching only what the theory is about does not provide students with the scientific understandings they need as citizens. Only when students understand the complexity of scientific problems and what counts as defensible arguments in science are they able to understand changes in science and to develop the critical skills that are needed to prevent them from being duped by anyone with the label "expert."

It is ironic that although science is typically taught in a simplistic, dogmatic fashion, there are aspects of science of which students are quite skeptical. There is an outcry of concern regarding the credibility of science among nonscientists (Matthews, 1994). While school science continues to be regarded by students as important for getting into college and getting a good job (Costa, 1995), there are also many surveys documenting that some of the basic tenets of science are simply not believed by a significant number of people (Wynne, 1995). Perhaps scientists and science educators have unwittingly participated in the demise of the credibility of science by portraying science in school in ways that are both inaccurate and unbelievable. For example, science is portrayed in schools as though the theories of science have no historical fingerprints, have no remaining controversial aspects, contain no metaphysical assumptions, and are oblivious to the social institutions that constitute and surround them (Brickhouse, 1994).

We believe that it is important to portray science in the school curriculum in ways that acknowledge its dynamic nature, its relationship to broader cultural concerns, and the particular framework within which science operates (Brickhouse, Stanley, & Whitson, 1993; Stanley & Brickhouse, 1995). We believe this is important because it is honest and because it is potentially of tremendous educational value. Furthermore, the inability to recognize that science operates within a particular framework (not a universal one) can lead to a dangerous scientism that is intolerant of other ways of understanding the world (Stanley & Brickhouse, 1995).

We would like to illustrate how the theory of evolution by natural selection could be taught in a manner that avoids the dogmatism of traditional approaches and also has the potential of helping students understand important aspects of the nature of science. This is an approach we advocate for teaching *all* scientific theories, not just evolution by natural selection. Elsewhere we have written about a similar approach to teaching plate tectonic theory (Brickhouse, Letts, & Ramseur, 1996).

THE CASE OF EVOLUTION BY NATURAL SELECTION

The theory of evolution by natural selection, introduced to the public on a grand scale with the 1859 publication of *On the Origin of Species* by Charles Darwin, should be understood in terms of its development within a particular historical context. Although Darwin alone is often credited with devising and disseminating the theory of evolution by natural selection, in fact, the sources of the theory were many, and they were spread out over time. Without acceptance of an ancient earth, the political economics of Malthus, and the documentation of a very large number of living species, the theory of evolution by natural selection could never have been formulated (Futuyma, 1986; LeGrand, 1988; Ruse, 1995).

The history of evolutionary theory is rich with examples of how science has changed and how it has been influenced by the culture that surrounds it. Some of the earliest biological work in Western Europe was much like the early work in other sciences: Its purpose was primarily to describe nature in order to reveal the majesty of God. For example, Linnaeus' classification scheme was developed primarily for the purpose of glorifying God.

As the religious belief in a God who controls the everyday events of the world became less popular, science also changed. Gradually scientists began offering mechanistic explanations for natural phenomena rather than solely religious ones. Darwin (1859/1964) described his scientific work as laying out the physical laws God devised for the universe to operate (p. 489), though he was actually an agnostic when he wrote *On the Origin of Species*. To make the book more socially acceptable, he wrote it from the perspective of a deist.

Lamarck not only argued that different species originated from common ancestors but also postulated the origin of life from inanimate matter. Lamarck believed that evolution was guided by environmental factors (i.e., that organisms change their behavior in response to the environment and that the changes an organism makes within its lifetime are passed on to subsequent generations). Lamarck's theory was not accepted by scientists primarily because of critiques by prominent scientists such as Georges Cuvier, a creationist, who argued that the fossil record did not support a gradual series of ancestors and descendants.

Initially Darwin was not a believer in evolution. He believed in the special creation of species. However, when his belief in God was shaken, so was the foundation for this belief in special creation. When he visited the Galapagos Islands, he was struck by the fact that the organisms he observed on one island were so different from the organisms found on another and that the organisms on the island were so similar to organisms found on the adjacent mainland. This, along with analogical comparisons to artificial breeding, convinced Darwin of the fact of evolution (Singleton, 1982).

Darwin also wanted to describe a mechanism that could explain how the evolution of species occurred. Here, the political economics of Malthus played a key role in Darwin's thinking. Malthus believed that unchecked growth of human populations must eventually outstrip food supply and lead to an overt battle over scarce resources. Darwin viewed the competition between species as a similar struggle for survival in which only those species best suited for the environment survive. He wrote a paper outlining many of his ideas about natural selection and distributed it to close allies such as Charles Lyell. He was surprised in 1858 when he received a paper from Alfred Russell Wallace, who was also influenced by Malthus' political economics, describing many of the same principles of natural selection. Although there were differences in their views regarding sexual selection (Darwin believed the evidence from artificial selection supported his views of natural selection, whereas Wallace believed they provided evidence against natural selection), both papers were published in the *Proceedings of the Linnaean Society* in 1858 (Singleton, 1982).

Origin of Species, published the following year by Darwin, was a masterpiece of rhetoric and was effective in establishing a research program for biology that continues to be powerful today. It probably was not due to mere chance that evolution by natural selection became accepted near the end of the 18th century in England nor that somewhat different versions appeared in France and Germany (Ruse, 1995). The decline in providentialism, the secular opportunities created by the Scientific Revolution, and the belief in progress—that it is possible to improve human existence through effort and ability—created a culture that was interested in such ideas as how life has changed. Although few would argue that the claim that conceptions of progress played a significant role in the initial formulation of evolution by natural selection, contemporary neo-Darwinists such as Stephen Jay Gould believe that biological evolution is random—not directed. Therefore notions of progress are fundamentally misleading.

In fact, in the early years, when the theory of evolution by natural selection was being debated and the evidence for it was not nearly as strong as it is today, its main appeal was its corollary to progress (Ruse, 1995). The theory of natural selection is a reflection of the laissez-faire type of individualism that causes a struggle for existence that was prominent in Victorian England at this time (Bowler, 1989; Ruse, 1995). This focus on an individualistic, capitalistic model of evolution, with an emphasis on competition and "investments," was reflected in the cultural values of 19th-century England. Furthermore, Darwinism reflects Victorian precepts of morality, particularly with regard to the relationships between the sexes (Haraway, 1989; Hubbard, 1979). Drawing upon the stereotype of the active male and the passive female, observations of animals, bacteria, people, and so forth were described such that all passive behavior was labeled "feminine" whereas all active behavior was labeled "masculine."

Darwin's theory of natural selection has encountered numerous challenges and changed considerably. Initially, one of its most serious shortcomings, which Darwin himself recognized, was its inability to provide for a source of variation among organisms. Mendelian genetics, introduced in 1900, nearly dismantled evolution by natural selection by showing that new species could arise purely by mutation (Futuyma, 1986). It was not until the period from about 1936 to 1947 that the ideas of genetics and natural selection were synthesized into a theory of population genetics stating that populations contain genetic variation that arises by random mutation and recombination. These populations evolve by changes in gene frequency brought about primarily by natural selection. This gradually leads to reproductive isolation between the populations, and thus to new species.

Although natural selection is nearly universally accepted by scientists as a mechanism for evolution, Lamarckian ideas have not entirely disappeared (Futuyma, 1986). Additionally, there are still controversies among scientists regarding certain aspects of evolution by natural selection. For example, the theory of punctuated equilibrium as an explanation for a fossil record that rarely shows a smooth progression from one species to another (Ruse, 1995) is still a matter of some debate. There are also problems that natural selection cannot solve. For example, the causes of singular events such as the great diversity of flowering plants cannot be traced to a single cause, nor is population genetics able to predict the evolutionary pathway of a given population (Futuyma, 1986).

LESSONS TO BE LEARNED

Typically school science presents scientific theories dogmatically, with no discussion of what kinds of evidence are explained by the theory, with no historical or cultural context presented, and with no discussion regarding what problems the theory has faced or will face. We propose that if science is presented to students in the way we have just described (albeit in a very cursory and contestable form), they may develop a very different view of science—one that recognizes the dynamic framework in which science operates, the historicity of science, and the influence of the surrounding culture on science.

For example, scientists now assume that all natural events have natural causes, a belief commonly called "naturalism." Respected journals do not publish scientific articles that offer supernatural explanations or that make reference to God. (It is interesting to note that today it is only when writing for the public that scientists make reference to either belief or nonbelief in God.) The metaphysical assumption that natural events have natural causes is no longer even discussed by scientists. However, this assumption has not always been a part of the framework of science. Scientists such as James Hutton had to argue that it would be good for science if scientists relied only on natural causes for their explanations. There are other assumptions that are made as well: The growth of knowledge is good; explanations are important; explanations that explain a large range of data are better than more local ones. Although these assumptions are only rarely discussed today, they have all been the subject of debate at some point in the history of science. These are not testable assumptions. They have nevertheless become a part of contemporary scientific frameworks because they were deemed to be productive assumptions to make. (How far could science have proceeded if it were allowed to pose supernatural explanations?)

Lessons could be learned about how evidence functions in science. From these cases, one can see that evidence is crucial in science. Although there are probably many reasons Lamarck's ideas failed whereas Darwin's eventually succeeded (e.g., French Roman Catholic resistance, lack of a mechanism in the explanation), the evidence for evolution was stronger during the debate over natural selection than it was earlier. However, facts are never just facts; they always require interpretation. The same "facts" about artificial breeding that were taken by Darwin to be supportive of natural selection were taken by Wallace to contradict natural selection (Ruse, 1995).

The interaction between science and culture is very apparent in these cases. Religion, political theory, gender roles, and other belief systems have all influenced what is taken to be "real" and "true" in science. The shift from providentialism to deism had a profound effect on what scientists could study and what explanations they could develop. Malthus' political economics, which was in vogue at the time of the development of the theory of natural selection, influenced both Darwin and Wallace in the construction of that theory. Gender stereotypes were so pervasive in the culture that they also entered scientific descriptions.

Likewise, science has affected our beliefs in other domains. Some scientists, such as Gould (1991), have argued that applying scientific ideas to other domains of experience has led to mischief. For example, social Darwinists took the idea of "survival of the fittest," deemed to be the best description of what *is* in nature, and used it as a prescription for how human societies *ought* to be. This led to a naturalization of capitalist economics and emphasized its most immoral tendencies. Gould has also argued that science should not be applied to religious questions. He argues that while changes in life and the earth are within the purview of science, the question of the origin of life is the purview of theology (Gould, 1991). Science ought to stay out of that discussion. Natural selection does not address the question of the origin of life. However, there are scientists who have attempted to address questions regarding the origin of life, including Frank Tipler (1994), Carl Sagan (1980), Fred Hoyle and N. C. Wickramasinghe (1978), and Francis Crick (1981). However, these ideas are extremely controversial (Shapiro, 1986) and have little to do with evolution by natural selection.

Creationists often make no distinction between these various theories of origin. This is unfortunate because it is unfair to characterize all evolutionists as adhering to the blatant atheism of such scientists as Carl Sagan. Universal evolution, evolution by natural selection, and other theories regarding the origin of life have very different histories, explain different phenomena, and have different degrees of support among scientists. Science teachers must be responsible and educated enough to help students understand these differences.

Some people argue that the context of discovery (i.e., how scientists construct particular ideas) is not relevant to the final products of science. They would argue that the fact that Darwin was influenced by Malthus has nothing to do with the actual content of his theory of natural selection. Malthus may have helped him come up with the idea, but that has nothing to do with whether or not it is judged to be "true." Others argue that the context of discovery is important and should be studied because contextual features in the context of discovery make their way into the content of science (Duschl, 1990; Longino, 1990).

Our view is that students need to understand more about science than just the outcomes. Science educators should do more than teach students the "winning" theories. They should also help students understand how theories come to be accepted, how they change, what function they serve, and how they are situated within broad cultural contexts. Evolution should not be taught dogmatically—neither should plate tectonics or kinetic-molecular theory or relativity.

One final question remains. Should student beliefs about creationism be addressed in the science curriculum? Is the dictum stated in the California's *Science Frameworks* (California Department of Education, 1990) that any student who brings up the matter of creationism is to be referred to a family member or member of the clergy a reasonable policy? We think not. Although we do not believe that what people call "creationist science" is good science (nor do scientists), to place a gag order on teachers about the subject entirely seems counterproductive. Particularly in parts of the country where there are significant numbers of conservative religious people, ignoring students' views about creationism because they do not qualify as good science is insensitive at best. One of the most common criticisms students make of their science classes is that the knowledge they learn is irrelevant to them. They do not see how an understanding of kinetic-molecular theory is likely to make a difference to them in their lives outside the classroom. Perhaps allowing discussions about creationism in science classes might be an opportunity to address issues students care about. Many have reported that the evolution/creation debate is an issue that matters to students (e.g., Churchland cited in Callebaut, 1993, p. 195; Cobern, 1994; Noddings, 1993).

Some science educators have advocated that science teachers present the evidence for both evolution by natural selection and creationism, letting students decide which is better supported by evidence. We think this is wrong-headed for different reasons. First of all, it assumes that the controversy is actually about evidence. It is not. The vast majority of those who object to evolution by natural selection are primarily concerned about its religious implications. Secondly, it provides a misleading image of how one decides what gets to count as scientific knowledge. Evolution by natural selection is the currently accepted view of the scientific community—regardless of how the student vote turns out. Public opinion polls do not determine what gets to count as scientific knowledge either.

We believe a better solution is to have the students study the controversy itself. What is the controversy about? What are the positions of the various stakeholders? Are the only creationists who object to evolution by natural selection those who believe in a "literal" interpretation of the Bible? What are the other objections? What are their merits? What are the variety of positions held by evolutionists?

Examples can be given of evolutionists who quite clearly advocate atheism. Some evolutionists are quite satisfied that science and religion deal with different domains of human experience and do not attempt to meld them, whereas others believe science and religion serve the same purposes. Still others adhere to a middle ground—posing evolution by natural selection as simply the mechanism through which God works.[2] Just as it is wrong-headed to portray all creationists as having identical criticisms of evolution, it is a distortion to portray all evolutionists as having identical positions on religion and creationism.

Students could study the Balanced Treatment for Creation Science and Evolution Science Act that was introduced to the Arkansas legislature in 1981. After all, this debate was about *them*—what they and their teachers would be permitted to talk about. Who were the advocates of creation science and evolution science? What were their positions? What was at stake in this controversy? What is the status of creation science among scientists, and why do they always refer to their adversaries as "creationists" rather than as "creation scientists"? Why do creationists want the label "science"?

Why does evolution by natural selection seem to draw more criticism from the public than plate tectonics (or black holes, which are routinely described in science textbooks although there is relatively little evidence for them)? Is it the "naturalism" inherent in evolution? Naturalism is endemic to all contemporary scientific theories because science assumes that natural events have natural causes, not supernatural ones. Yet most critics do not suggest we throw out all of science.

In conclusion, we believe there are good alternatives to the teaching of science as dogma. In particular, situating science within its historical context may help students understand the complexity of how an idea gets to be accepted as scientific knowledge as well as the limitations and unavoidable biases of science. However, presenting evolution by natural selection as biased, limited, and problematic and the rest of science as the unquestionable truth would perhaps be the worst kind of distortion possible.[3] Plate tectonics and other theories ought also be presented in historical context. Teaching about the evolution controversy may also be highly educative. The challenge for teachers and students will be to work with questions for which there are no uniformly agreed-upon answers, yet also dealing with factual material where accuracy is important. There is also potential here for science teachers to address subject matter that students truly care about. We think we should embrace the opportunity.

NOTES

1. Special thanks to Rivers Singleton for reviewing this manuscript and providing his expertise on Darwin.
2. See Jackson, Doster, Meadows, & Wood (1995) for a study of how conservative Christian science teachers think about these issues.
3. One of us observed a middle school creationist teacher who attempted to avoid all content related to evolution. When it appeared in books and films, he consistently undermined the theory by arguing that there were some errors in what was presented. The rest of the curriculum was presented as dogma (Brickhouse, 1988).

REFERENCES

Bowler, P. (1989). *Evolution: The history of an idea*. Berkeley: University of California Press.

Brickhouse, N. W. (1988). *Teachers' beliefs about science and science teaching*. Unpublished doctoral dissertation, Purdue University, West Lafayette, IN.

Brickhouse, N. W. (1994). Bringing in the outsiders: Reshaping the sciences of the future. *Journal of Curriculum Studies, 26*, 401–416.

Brickhouse, N. W., Letts, W. J., & Ramseur, A. (1996, April). *The problem of dogmatism in science education*. Paper presented at the annual meeting of the National Association for Research in Science Teaching, St. Louis, MO.

Brickhouse, N. W., Stanley, W. B., & Whitson, J. A. (1993). Practical reasoning and science education. *Science & Education, 2*, 363–375.

California Department of Education. (1990). *Science framework for California public schools*. Sacramento: Author.

Callebaut, W. (1993). *Taking the naturalistic turn or how real philosophy of science is done*. Chicago: University of Chicago Press.

Cobern, W. W. (1994). Point: Belief, understanding, and the teaching of evolution. *Journal of Research in Science Teaching, 31*, 583–590.

Costa, V. B. (1995). When science is "another world": Relationships between worlds of family, friends, school, and science. *Science Education, 79*, 313–334.

Crick, F. (1981). *Life itself*. New York: Simon & Schuster.

Darwin, C. (1964). *On the origin of species, A facsimile of the first edition*. Cambridge, MA: Harvard University Press. (Original work published 1859)

Duschl, R. A.(1990). *Restructuring science education*. New York: Teachers College Press.

Futuyma, D. J. (1986). *Evolutionary biology* (2nd ed.). Sunderland, MA: Sinauer Associates.

Gould, S. J. (1991). *Bully for brontosaurus.* New York: Norton.

Haraway, D. (1989). *Primate visions.* New York: Routledge.

Hoyle, F., & Wickramasinghe, N. C. (1978). *Lifecloud, the origin of life in the universe.* New York: Harper & Row.

Hubbard, R. (1979). Have only men evolved? In R. Hubbard, M. S. Henifen, & B. Fried (Eds.), *Women look at biology looking at women: A collection of feminist critiques* (pp. 17–46). Boston: Hall.

Jackson, D. F., Doster, E. C., Meadows, L., & Wood, T. (1995). Hearts and minds in the science classroom: The education of a confirmed evolutionist. *Journal of Research in Science Teaching, 32,* 585–612.

LeGrand, H. E. (1988). *Drifting continents and shifting theories.* Cambridge, England: Cambridge University Press.

Longino, H. (1990). *Science as social knowledge.* Princeton, NJ: Princeton University Press.

Matthews, M. R. (1994). *Science teaching: The role of history and philosophy of science.* New York: Routledge.

Noddings, N. (1993). *Educating for intelligent belief or unbelief.* New York: Teachers College Press.

Ruse, M. (1995). *Evolutionary naturalism.* New York: Routledge.

Sagan, C. (1980). *Cosmos.* New York: Random House.

Schwab, J. J. (1978). Science and civil discourse: The uses of diversity. In I. Westbury & N. J. Wilkof (Eds.), *Science, curriculum, and liberal education* (pp. 133–148). Chicago: University of Chicago Press. (Original work published 1956)

Shapiro, R. (1986). *Origins: A skeptic's guide to the creation of life on earth.* New York: Bantam.

Singleton, R. (1982). Charles Darwin and the shaping of the modern mind. *San Jose Studies, 8,* 21–39.

Stanley, W. B., & Brickhouse, N. W. (1995). Multiculturalism, universalism and science education. *Science Education, 79,* 387–398.

Tipler, F. (1994). *The physics of immortality.* New York: Doubleday.

Wynne, B. (1995). Public understanding of science. In S. Jasanoff, G. Markle, J. Petersen, & T. Pinch (Eds.), *Handbook of science and technology studies* (pp. 361–388). Thousand Oaks, CA: Sage.

CHAPTER 14

The Two Controversies over Evolution

Phillip E. Johnson

There are two controversies over evolution and creation, not just one.

The first controversy is the one you read about in the newspapers and magazines, the one involving the Christian fundamentalists who insist that the universe is only a few thousand years old, that the fossil record is the result of the worldwide flood in the time of Noah, and that creation took place within a literal week of six 24-hour days, followed by a day of rest. This young-earth, Genesis-literalist position generally goes by the name "creation science." Science educators refuse to allow it any place in the curriculum on the grounds that science classes are no place to study the Bible or to indulge theories that are based on an inflexible adherence to the Genesis chronology.

The courts have backed the science educators, ruling that creation science is religion, not science. The Supreme Court has held in *Edwards v. Aguillard* (1987) that it is an unconstitutional "establishment of religion" for a state legislature to require creation science to be taught in the public schools as an alternative to evolution. School authorities have interpreted the judicial decisions as allowing (or even requiring) them to discipline individual teachers who want to present creation science as an alternative to evolution, and the courts that have ruled on the question have agreed with the administrators.[1]

The second controversy does not necessarily involve the Genesis account, or the age of the earth, or even any particular account of creation as an alternative to evolution. It involves a sense on the part of many persons that evolution is presented to the public in a dogmatic fashion, with highly questionable propositions stated as fact. Did life really emerge by some chemical process or leap of chance from a prebiotic soup of chemicals? Did it really require nothing more mysterious than random mutations and natural selection to produce human consciousness and intelligence? Is it a *fact* that unintelligent natural processes were capable of performing all the work of biological creation, so that no supernatural influence was required in the entire history of life? Or are all these things merely assumptions that biologists like to make, assumptions that might not be true at all?

NATURALISM

The second controversy is about the role of *naturalism* in science. Naturalism is the doctrine that nature is "all there is," or at least that nature is a closed system of material causes and effects that can never be influenced by a supernatural entity such as God. Naturalism is also frequently said to be the basis of science. If naturalism is true, then it follows as a matter of definition that human beings and all other living things had a natural origin, which means that they are the product of unintelligent material causes rather than of an intelligent supernatural being who created them for a purpose. God is out of the picture, except as a concept generated by the human imagination. Contemporary evolutionary science builds upon the logic of naturalism and claims to have confirmed it.

What philosophers call the "death of God" is simply the naturalistic understanding that human beings created God rather than the other way around. The death of God does not abolish religion or churches, because it is an observable fact that people have spiritual inclinations (presumably a by-product of naturalistic evolution). What it does do is to relegate religion to the realm of the subjective. Your religion is good if it works for you and doesn't cause you to become a bother to others. Truth has nothing to do with religion, because religious beliefs are held on the basis of faith, not reason. God is possibly a good thing as long as he stays in your own mind, where he belongs, and a very dangerous thing if you start to think that the imaginary "will of God" is binding on other people.

Naturalism dominates the intellectual world today largely because of the triumph of the Darwinian theory of evolution, which provides naturalism with its essential creation story. The most prominent evolutionary scientists make this point all the time. "Before Darwin," writes Stephen Jay Gould (1977, p. 267), "we thought that a benevolent God had created us." According to Richard Dawkins (1986, p. 6), "Darwin made it possible to be an intellectually fulfilled atheist." Douglas Futuyma's (1986) widely used college evolutionary biology textbook puts the essential philosophical issue in historical perspective:

By coupling undirected, purposeless variation to the blind, uncaring process of natural selection, Darwin made theological or spiritual explanations of the life processes superfluous. Together with Marx's materialistic theory of history and society and Freud's attribution of human behavior to influences over which we have little control, Darwin's theory of evolution was a crucial plank in the platform of mechanism and materialism—of much of science, in short—that has since been the stage of most Western thought. (p. 3)

Plainly, the platform of mechanism and materialism carries great religious significance. Promotion of this philosophy in the schools is properly a matter of concern to parents who believe that a benevolent God actually did create us (by one means or another) and that theological and spiritual explanations of the life processes therefore are *not* superfluous. The second evolution controversy is about whether such challenges to the naturalistic understanding of reality might conceivably have some merit.

PERSONAL AND PUBLIC OPINIONS

My own opinion is that the challenges have a lot of merit. The Darwinian theory is not true as a general explanation of life's history, and there is no unintelligent material mechanism that can produce living organisms from nonliving chemicals or complex plants and animals from bacteria or algae. I also think that naturalism itself is not true and that God actually has acted in the history of life.

My arguments on these subjects are set out in *Darwin on Trial, Reason in the Balance*, and *Defeating Darwinism—By Opening Minds* (Johnson, 1993, 1995, 1997). My purpose in this chapter is not to argue the substance of the scientific issues, however, but to discuss how educators ought to approach those controversial issues. Whether my views are right or wrong, they are certainly very far from unique. According to a 1991 Gallup poll, 47% of a national sample agreed with the following statement: "God created mankind in pretty much our present form sometime within the last 10,000 years." Another 40% think that "Man has developed over millions of years from less advanced forms of life, but God guided this process, including man's creation." Only 9% of the sample said that they believed in biological evolution as a purposeless process not guided by God ("The Creation," 1991).

The view of evolution held by the leading scientific authorities is the creed of the 9%. That evolutionary naturalism is a minority position among the public at large does not mean that it is incorrect, of course, but it does mean that public educators have a job to do. The science educators have made it clear enough that "evolution" denies the young-earth creationism of the Genesis literalists, but what about the large fraction of the public who think of evolution as a God-guided process?

Most of those people apparently are under the impression that they have reconciled religion and science by this formula, but they are mistaken. The scientific authorities do not view evolution as a God-guided process but as a completely naturalistic process. What the children of America are being taught in science classes is evolution as Gould, Dawkins, and Futuyma understand it, not the sentimental version of evolution that is preferred in most mainline churches. Darwinian evolution is a naturalistic process. God-guided evolution is better described as a soft form of creationism.

Science educators presently blur these issues by pretending that the only dissent from "evolution" comes from a particularly obstinate crowd of biblical literalists. A typical example of this "two-models" oversimplification comes from the book *Science Matters: Achieving Scientific Literacy*, by Robert M. Hazen and James Trefil (1991):

> Two strongly held views about the origin of our planet and its life are in severe disagreement. Biblical Creationists accept on faith the literal Old Testament account of creation. Their beliefs include (1) a young earth, perhaps less than 10,000 years old; (2) catastrophes, especially a worldwide flood, as the origin of the earth's present form, including mountains, canyons, oceans, and continents; and (3) miraculous creation of all living things, including humans, in essentially their modern forms. If you are a Creationist, the Bible—not nature—dictates what you believe. Creationists subordinate observational evidence to doctrine based on their interpretation of sacred texts. The tenets of biblical Creationism are not testable, nor are they subject to dramatic change based on new data. In other words, Creationism is a form of religion. (p. 243)

The only alternative to that religious (and hence unscientific) position is, as Hazen and Trefil say, in large bold type: "All forms of life evolved by natural selection" (p. 244). This caricature exemplifies what in logic is known as the fallacy of the excluded middle. For example, there are people who do not rely on a literal interpretation of Genesis, are undisturbed by the possibility that the earth may be billions of years old, but are not convinced that the evidence substantiates the claims that have been made for the creative power of natural selection. There are scientists who say that the neo-Darwinian theory explains only limited variation within the species and that some new mechanism awaits to be discovered which will explain major innovations such as the emergence of animals. Finally, 40% of Americans, who are not creationists in the usual sense, seem to think that God played some tangible role in an evolutionary process. Why are all these different positions about a complex subject defined out of existence?

The two-models caricature is useful to the naturalistic science educators, because it enables them to avoid some sticky issues. What they want to imply is that "evolution" does not really threaten "religion," because all the fundamentalists have to do to make peace with science is make a relatively minor adjustment—say, by interpreting the "days" of the Genesis creation week as periods of indefinite duration. This implication in turn justifies treating science and religion as separate subjects and classifying all dissent about evolution as religion. Evolution—*naturalistic* evolution—then stands alone as science, and no other position even needs to be discussed. This ploy was encapsulated in the official booklet of the National Academy of Sciences (1984) on science and creation:

> It is false . . . to think that the theory of evolution represents an irreconcilable conflict between religion and science. A great many religious leaders and scientists accept evolution on scientific grounds without relinquishing their belief in religious principles. As stated in a resolution by the Council of the National Academy of Sciences in 1981, however, "Religion and Science are separate and mutually exclusive realms of human thought whose presentation in the same context leads to misunderstanding of both scientific theory and religious belief." (pp. 5–6)

Such vague terminology is clearly designed to reassure rather than to inform. Does the statement mean that there is a conflict, if not an "irreconcilable" one? Exactly which "religious principles" are and are not consistent with the scientific understanding of evolution? Specifically, is there an inherent contradiction between belief in a supernatural creator, even one who chose to employ a gradual process over billions of years, and the kind of "evolution" the National Academy professes? If it is wrong to present science and religion in the same context, why do scientists—and not only evolutionary biologists but also famous physicists like Stephen Hawking, Steven Weinberg, and Paul Davies—spend so much time talking about God?

The December 28, 1992, cover of *Time* magazine asked the question: "What Does Science Tell Us About God?" (Wright, 1992). There was no protest from any official scientific organization, and the magazine had no difficulty finding prominent scientists willing to answer the question. This obsession with the God issue also characterizes the closing lines of the introduction by Carl Sagan to Stephen Hawking's (1988) *A Brief History of Time,* probably the best-selling science book of all time:

> The word God fills these pages. Hawking embarks on a quest to answer Einstein's famous question about whether God had any choice in creating the universe. Hawking is attempting, as he explicitly states, to understand the mind of God. And this makes all the more unexpected the conclusion of the effort, at least so

far: a universe with no edge in time, no beginning or end in time, and nothing for a Creator to do. (1988, p. x)

When the world's most prominent scientists write things like that, are the rest of us supposed to swallow uncritically the line that science and religion are separate subjects that must never be addressed in the same context?

THE TASK FOR SCIENCE EDUCATORS

Of course it is nonsense to say that theories about the origin of the universe, life, and human consciousness have nothing to do with religion or God. Either those theories are offered as filling out the details of God's action or—as is usually the case in contemporary science education—as alternatives to believing that God ever had anything to do with the business. If science educators were to adopt a policy of candor, and admit that the orthodox theory of evolution is the view of the 9% in the Gallup poll, they would face severe political and educational problems. The political problem is that the vast majority might be reluctant to support and fund a scientific program that is so explicitly antithetical to their own beliefs. The educational problem is that once the religious implications of evolution are out on the table, one can no longer claim that religion and science are separate subjects that have nothing to do with each other. It becomes hard to avoid allowing the people who think God may have had something to do with creation to state their objections to a scientific theory that claims otherwise.

An example of what this might mean in practice can be taken from another section of the National Academy's (1984) booklet on creationism, the section on "the origin of life." The section begins with the modest statement that "Scientific research on the origin of life is in an exploratory phase, and all its conclusions are tentative." It goes on to say, however, that "for scientists who are studying aspects of the origin of life, the question no longer seems to be whether life could have originated by chemical processes involving nonbiological components but rather, what pathway might have been followed" (p. 25). That sounds like a scientific statement about the origin of life, but to anyone with the least bent toward skepticism it is nothing of the kind. It is a statement about the mindset that causes some persons to devote their lives to attempting to establish the origin of life by chemical evolution. Of course they believe that the basic premise of the field they have entered is *true*; so do astrologers. Whether they have any solid experimental warrant for that belief is another question altogether.

There would be a lot to say on both sides of that question once it was raised; my point here is only to establish that the question is legitimate and, once raised, cannot be brushed off with a dogmatic statement about "what most scientists believe today." That is the reason that science curriculum designers are so determined to keep the question off the table—by labeling it as "religious" and thus disqualifying it before it has to be answered.

There is a substantial cost to a program that commits science educators to a program of avoiding issues and misleading the public about the true implications of science, however. One problem is that the policy tends to alienate many parents who want to be supportive of science and public education, but who sense that they are being played for fools. Martin Eger, Professor of Physics and Philosophy of Science at the City University of New York, expressed the frustration of those parents in responding to another scholar who had written that "creationism is framed within a viewpoint which is in opposition to science itself, not just to evolutionary theory." Eger (1988) responded:

> Perceptions of the situation have been distorted by an indiscriminate use of the term "creationists" for millions of very different sorts of people, of whom only a tiny fraction are the "creation scientists" or creation activists (as I prefer to call them) responsible for most of the news stories.
>
> Within that larger population of creationists, active if at all only on the local level, I found—contrary to media impressions—that the prevailing attitude is surprisingly respectful of science, despite the fact that it is also suspicious of science. In this there is no contradiction. As American political conservatives are suspicious of government, but consider it a good thing when kept in bounds, so creationist parents suspect that when it comes to evolution something is being pressed on them in the name of science that actually goes beyond science. . . . These people do not wish their own views to be in conflict with science.
>
> No doubt, as a maximum demand, most creation activists would like to see their beliefs studied in schools on equal footing. However, many parents would be content if, in their own district school, evolution were taught in what they regard as a "less dogmatic" manner. . . . Because creationism does come in many varieties, I would caution against the kind of language that needlessly places large populations "out of court"—including intelligent, educated men and women who are open to dialogue. The sorts of people I describe, not members of the creation institutes, are the ones who actually interact with schools. (pp. 364–365)

Eger put his finger on the crucial point. A public education system cannot endorse a religious position, but it also cannot afford to show contempt for the concerns of large populations that include intelligent, educated men and women who are open to dialogue. If such people are convinced that what is being taught in the science curriculum as "evolution" is based more on philosophy than empirical science, and is loaded with thinly disguised religious implications, then those issues need to be honestly addressed and not dismissed with a derisive label.

But can the schools address those questions without turning the classrooms into a religious battleground? My own experience as a guest teacher in evolution courses is mainly at the college level—the subjects I address being virtually barred by law in public high schools—but nothing in my experience leads me to think that controversies over evolution cannot be discussed with civility and solid educational benefit. Students love the subject and love to argue about it, but there is nothing unhealthy about that. The people who feel genuinely threatened, and tend sometimes to lose their nerve or their temper, are not the students but the evolution professionals, who have a very personal stake in maintaining their own authority. The claim that science classes cannot include a critical discussion of evolution is a form of special pleading that comes from dogmatists who want to present their own opinion on the subject without fear that it will be challenged.

One of the best reasons for addressing the evolution controversies frankly and fairly in the classroom is that such discussion can make the subject come alive. Where is the excitement in science if students are told that the basic questions have all been answered and only filling in the details remains to be done? What kind of teaching do we get when dissent over fundamental questions is suppressed, or treated only dismissively—often even in college classrooms? One consequence of present education policies is identified by Martin Eger (1988):

> Biology teachers are often *incompetent* to answer the classic challenges to evolution—never having faced those challenges themselves as did Darwin. In New York City for example, teachers are advised ahead of time to redirect such questions to the experts, questions that any bright teenager might ask. (pp. 303–304, emphasis in original)

The best reason for opening up the subject of evolution to critical scrutiny, then, is simply to encourage good teaching. If the case for the orthodox theory of evolution is as overwhelming as science educators claim it to be, and if teachers are properly trained to understand the questions that bright teenagers and college students might think to ask, then the cause of science has nothing to fear.

NOTE

1. See *Peloza v. Capistrano Unified School District* (1994) dismissing a lawsuit by a high school teacher who claimed that the school district was requiring him to teach "evolutionism" in violation of his rights under the religious freedom clauses of the Constitution.

REFERENCES

The creation: Religion's search for a common ground with science. (1991, December 23). *U.S. News & World Report*, pp. 56–64.

Dawkins, R. (1986). *The blind watchmaker*. New York: Norton.

Edwards v. Aguillard, 482 U.S. 578 (1987).

Eger, M. (1988). Reply to criticisms. *Zygon*, *(23)*, 303–365.

Futuyma, D. J. (1986). *Evolutionary biology* (2nd ed.). Sunderland, MA: Sinauer Associates.

Gould, S. J. (1977). *Ever since Darwin*. New York: Norton.

Hawking, S. (1988). *A brief history of time: From the Big Bang to black holes*. New York: Bantam.

Hazen, R. M., & Trefil, J. (1991). *Science matters: Achieving scientific literacy*. New York: Anchor.

Johnson, P. E. (1993). *Darwin on trial*. Washington, DC: Regnery Gateway.

Johnson, P. E. (1995). *Reason in the balance: The case for naturalism in science, law and education*. Downers Grove, IL: InterVarsity.

Johnson, P. E. (1997). *Defeating Darwinism—By opening minds*. Downers Grove, IL: InterVarsity.

National Academy of Sciences. (1984). *Science and creationism*. Washington, DC: National Academy Press.

Peloza v. Capistrano Unified School District, 37 F.3d 517 (9th Cir. 1994).

Wright, R. (1992, December 28). Science, God and man. *Time*, p. 38.

From Six Days to 4.6 Billion Years

Sears: Brickhouse and Letts assert "facts are not simply facts, they require interpretation."

Shearer: Well, that depends on your meaning of facts. We are not only talking about science but also, as they point out, history. Now historic fact will be proved in a process quite different from scientific fact. You prove science from a process of reproduction: reproducing it in a lab or a test tube. You prove history by authentication: evaluating the documents to determine whether they are authoritative. Our discussion of evolution should be based on both scientific and historic proofs.

Murphy: Fine, but don't call it teaching science. Call it a discussion of science and religion.

Shearer: I have a problem with the assumption that science is rational but those who advocate creationism are not. While I agree that it is not as scientifically sophisticated as the Darwinian approach, there is substantive historical documentation rooted in the Old Testament. Creationism is not irrational; it is based on both scientific and historic proofs.

Murphy: Science, as the Brickhouse and Letts chapter illustrates, is clearly a historical process developed out of culture, but it moves through a process of testing, evaluating, and criticizing. Therefore, over time, science is self-correcting. And, over time, it becomes transcultural. It's fine to say that "American Indians think this," or "biblical literalists believe this" but over time a lot of the assumptions held dear by many cultures or groups get winnowed out by the scientific process.

Carper: Science does tend to be self-correcting. But, as Johnson argues, isn't Darwinian science really naturalism disguised as science? If it is

See the introduction for a description of the conversationalists.

naturalism, you have bought into the positivistic notion of empirical verification. This principle asserts that if something can't be verified, it is not meaningful—which is, itself, not verifiable. The assumption that there could not have been any type of supernatural involvement—by definition, not proof—is excluded from the realm of "science." Religion is equated with myth, science with truth.

Pritchett: The scientific process is one where we continue to collect evidence or to replicate phenomena. However, that is only applicable with those phenomena that one can replicate or accumulate evidence. Along with Bob, I have to say that we can not replicate the creation of the world and, therefore, we must study evolution and creation science through a historical perspective. You have to look at the data that various persons bring to support a particular hypothesis about human origin.

Murphy: But there is tremendous evidence about evolution that has nothing to do with history; these data are in the geologic record and predate man.

Shearer: This gets at the heart of the issue. Creation *preceded* man.

Murphy: But man writes history.

Shearer: But he doesn't create history. History does not begin with man. The truth is that history began with God. Therefore, our process in understanding the creation of the world is not simply scientific but historic. We look at the Scriptures to understand these historic events, recognizing that we may not understand them quite as well as we would like.

Murphy: As a science teacher, what I see you proposing is the substitution of a mythical system—be it EuroAmerican, Middle Eastern, or Native American—in the place of scientific evidence. There is no scientific evidence for the creation myth of Genesis—it is clearly metaphorical writing.

Shearer: Perhaps no scientific evidence, but there is historical evidence.

Carper: If by evolution we are talking about it at the macro-level, cosmic evolution, that is one matter. However, if we are talking about evolution at the micro-level, evolution within species, that is quite another. If we are talking about creation of the world in the sense of the participation of an intelligent designer (deistic evolution), that is one matter. However, if we are talking about a literal six-day young earth (creation science), that is quite another.

Sears: Does anyone advocate teaching a six-day creation story in public schools?

Carper: Is the six day [version] construed to be an "epic" or a 24-hour day?

Pigford: It is not a big issue to me whether six days reflect six actual days or longer period of time.

Murphy: But is a big issue to scientists!

Pigford: I believe the world was created by God. Whether it took Him six days or not is irrelevant.

Murphy: But that view negates several dozen fields of science and many centuries of investigation and of empirical data.

Burgess: I believe in my heart in the six-day, literal creation.

Murphy: Would you call your belief science or religion? Would you *teach* it in public school?

Burgess: Religion. We should *discuss* this in the pubic schools, though perhaps from a less critical view than Brickhouse and Letts advocate.

Shearer: As a pastor I get a little concerned about the "literal six days." How can we define a "day"? If we define a day scientifically as the earth making a single rotation, then there is no literal six-day creation. You cannot get this out of Genesis, Chapter 1: "And God said Let there be lights in the firmament of the heaven to divide the day from the night; and let them be for signs, and for seasons, and for days and years. . . . And the evening and the morning were the fourth day." The literal day, therefore, was not even created until the "fourth day."

Murphy: But the literal six-day account is in the Bob Jones textbook and the Creation Institute materials.

Shearer: The Flat Earth Society was true to a lot of people, too!

Burgess: Well, I interpret the Bible quite differently. I don't have to debate that or prove that; I simply need to believe it.

Shearer: I believe in a "younger earth" than Jurassic Park but not as young as six days. I believe in a creator and a creative experience. These experts are going to keep taking it back to infinity.

Murphy: No, they stopped at 4.6 billion years.

Shearer: Well, that is begging the issue. I want us to teach that an intelligent creator began this process: "In the beginning, God created. . . ."

Murphy: But that is not subject to testing and is not within the realm of science.

Shearer: How about ontological proof? This proof is as rational as anything you have to offer students?

Murphy: The creation story in Genesis cannot be scientifically validated.

Shearer: The unmoved mover, the master watchmaker . . .

Sears: Well, neither of these two chapters advocate a young-earth, creation science perspective. Should either the literal six-day or the ten-millennia perspective be taught along with either a deistic or naturalistic "old-earth" [perspective] in the science classroom?

Murphy: Neither the young-earth point of view nor that of deism should be taught as science.

Pritchett: While I couldn't support the former, I see value in teaching both deism and naturalism in science classes along the lines of these two essays.

Murphy: Does deism really fall within the scientific framework?

Lindsey: I don't believe in the young-earth perspective. But I could be wrong.

Sears: Would you include that in the science curriculum of public schools?

Lindsey: Yes. There will be children who see that as truth.

Pritchett: We could certainly *discuss* that, but it shouldn't be *taught* as science.

Sears: Aretha, assume that you are a school superintendent. Gary, as a middle-school principal, relays to you a similar conversation he has had with students' parents and members of the community. He recommends that the young-earth theory be included in science. What is your position?

Pigford: I would say it would be fine to discuss it, but it shouldn't be taught as scientific fact.

Sears: Would you have the teachers at the school teach classic evolutionary theory as fact?

Pigford: Like Brickhouse and Letts, I would recommend presenting this topic as a controversy, presenting all the sides, and letting the students deal with the issues related to it.

Carper: A distinction between teaching science and teaching about science much along the lines of teaching religion and teaching about religion?

Sears: Sounds to me as though you are engaged in some political waffling. While Brickhouse and Letts advocate addressing the evolution controversy in discussions about science, this chapter does not support including it as one of the "sides" for examination in the teaching of science. I'm also surprised that some of you who most objected to a more relativist view or to having students look at all sides in other curriculum areas seem reasonably content with this position.

Pigford: What would you do?

Sears: Well, I would expect students to recognize that what we teach as "science" and the understanding of the world through the modernist lens is as mythological as those who choose to view it through the premodern lens of "religion." The difference, of course, is that science has a favored place at the curriculum table, religion does not.

Murphy: Said as a true nonscientist! The postmodern critique of science marginalizes all scientific work and our everyday experience.

Sears: What is science really?

Pritchett: Science is the quest to understand how the world works, but so is religion.

Murphy: Operationally, science is not religion. But when I teach science, I certainly allow talk about God in my class from my students. I grade papers where students write to me about their belief in the six-day creation. I don't call those "beliefs" science—they are the religious understandings of some students. If I am ever told that I must teach creationism, that will be fine. But no book is beyond scrutiny and if it is to be included as science, then, as a science text, the Genesis account must withstand the rigors of scientific critique.

Carper: Can the two science teachers give us your definitions of science?

Murphy: Science is a process through which we attempt to understand the physical world so that more of the unknown becomes known.

Lindsey: Science seeks to achieve this through replication that allows for prediction.

Carper: Do these definitions imply that the physical world we see about us can only be understood as the product of natural processes?

Murphy: No. But one's philosophical approach to science is personal and cannot be imposed upon students as "truth."

Carper: But when neo-Darwinian evolution is taught, students are getting facts along with some philosophical baggage. Namely, "We can understand speciation only by references to naturalistic processes. There can be no intelligent designer."

Murphy: In all my years of teaching, I've never met a science teacher who said that.

Carper: Well, it certainly is clear in the writings of scientists such as Carl Sagan and Richard Dawkins.

Murphy: Their naturalistic views are their own opinions. But science teachers are not teaching these views as science!

Burgess: In the schools with which I am familiar, most of the science teachers are also Sunday School teachers. They are professed and devout Christians. Even if they teach evolution, they certainly don't believe it.

Sears: When you teach science and the origins of the human species, do you include a deistic explanation—the intelligent designer?

Murphy: No. You cannot *teach* that and call it science. It is a *belief.* But we can *discuss* it.

Shearer: The problem is if you do it through discussion, you never accomplish what creationists call science. I think creationism needs to be taught in *both* science and history. I don't know many teachers who can do that. Parents want to teach it as part of science, not history. If you are not going to include an intelligent designer as a scientific possibility, then we are left with history or the philosophy of science. You are really just tossing us a bone.

Sears: When it gets down to Monday-morning science class, educators must move from a philosophy to pedagogy. So, what is the teacher to do? What will be in the curriculum framework? What will be written into the lesson-plan book?

Murphy: This week my students saw a film on how the earth formed. One 13-year-old student was very angry: "That's not true. God created the earth in six days." I said, "You're very passionate. What about the film angers you?" She replied, "Well, I just don't believe it." I said, "*Believe,* that is a word we are setting aside here in science class. No one really cares what we believe. Here we look at evidence." She couldn't set aside the word *believe,* and she couldn't see that maybe God created the earth but that He did it over time. Someone had already told her that these ideas were mutually exclusive.

Burgess: She couldn't hold onto her belief yet be able to discuss other theories?

Murphy: It was too frightening for her. Unless she changes in the next few months, she will join the 47% of Americans who won't look at the geological or biological evidence, who are scared of the evidence, and who will therefore be unlearned in science.

Lindsey: She has a right to believe if she respects and shows tolerance of those who view otherwise.

Murphy: But that's a social issue. I am talking about science: "Is the earth really old? Yes!" You can respect other views, but not all views can be [reconciled with] with scientific accuracy.

Pigford: Your ten pieces of evidence may not be equal to my one piece of evidence, but I have to make the judgment about the quality of those pieces.

Murphy: The scientific community makes that judgment. You are welcome to throw your evidence into the pot for peer review, however the quantity and quality of evidence for an "old earth" origin are overwhelming. My job as a teacher is to give evidence for theories and to teach students how then to find and judge evidence for themselves. How the scientific community looks at evidence must be studied by kids so they don't end up believing in "magical science."

Sears: What about the scientific community in the past that believed in a geocentric universe, in "bleeding" to combat illness, or in Euclidean geometry?

Murphy: Science has changed exponentially in this century! Eighty-five percent of all scientists who ever lived are alive today and the process of information gathering and scientific criticism are far beyond retreating into a Ptolemaic vision of the universe.

Pritchett: What is "magical science."

Murphy: What I hear Henry Morris of the Institute for Creation Research as well as some kids saying is that the earth is 10,000 years old, that dinosaurs and man lived together, and if I fail to believe this, I reject Jesus. Magical science bends and throws out the rules of science to justify philosophical and religious positions.

Lindsey: I don't think Morris would ever say that if you don't believe in the 10,000-year-old earth that you will lose your faith.

Murphy: Well, the evangelical ministers I have interviewed said precisely that.

Lindsey: I listened to those taped interviews. I don't feel they said that. That is what *you* heard them say. They were saying that the Bible is God's word and if they do not believe in the Bible, they lose their faith. Now, you can believe the Bible is God's word, but how you interpret that Bible becomes a different issue. Morris uses the begats in the Bible to arrive at 10,000 years. But most of the preachers in this town would not say that every single statement in the Bible is interpreted in precisely this way and if you don't interpret it in this way, you reject Jesus.

Pritchett: In the South Carolina curriculum science framework for ninth through twelfth grade, it states, "Students will explain various hypotheses for the formation of the universe and the evidence to support them."

Lindsey: As a former science teacher, it makes as much sense to discuss the possibility of an intelligent creator as it does to discuss random chance. Both are based on presuppositions, not replicable facts. Now, as you move to processes in science, you have to seek verifiable evidence, but at that point we are not discussing origins.

Carper: The distinction here is between the "what" and the "why." Plate tectonics is not controversial; that is the *what*. When you get into natural selection plus mutation plus time, you get into the *why*. In the science classroom, the ultimate question is not how long or how but are we are a product of an intelligent designer? This is, of course, a philosophical issue. I do *not* want students to leave the classroom mistaking naturalism for science.

Pritchett: I agree that the "why" is the ultimate question. However, I do not want the school to be a proponent of a particular theory. When we are talking about what to teach in the public schools, I *do* care whether this discussion is in science or philosophy.

Carper: Education is inherently a value-laden enterprise and we, frankly, differ in our understanding of the nature of the cosmos. A state institution should not teach anything as orthodoxy.

Pritchett: The science curriculum framework leaves room for each community to have this discussion and to decide how they want it to be taught.

Murphy: Forty-seven percent of Americans believe in the literal six-day creation and 40% believe that God was the unmoved mover. If I am a science teacher and half of my students' parents—or in rural, isolated communities, perhaps most of these parents—believe in the Genesis creation story, I have a real problem with their making science curriculum decisions.

Lindsey: Knowing that 47% of the public believe this and then for children to go and read the elementary textbook for science confuses them. How can one read the Silver Burdett or the Macmillan textbooks for third grade, where the formation of life as "primordial soup" is portrayed as undisputed fact? In Helen Curtis's biology textbook she tears you down if you even consider an intelligent designer. How can you teach like that? How can you live like that? Why has the public not sought to change that?

Burgess: Simply because it is not being taught as evolution in the class-rooms. No science teacher I know is teaching that the universe began by chance; they simply convey the isolated facts about fossils and so forth. If we ever taught naturalistic evolution, there would be an uprising in my community.

Sears: That is a good example, Gary, of both the gap between the curriculum as text-bound and teacher-based as well as the absence of critical thinking in science that concern both Brickhouse and Letts and Johnson. Let me ask Pam a question in her capacity as a state department of education official: If these parents decided to include the literal six-day creation as one of the hypotheses for the formation of the universe, would that be acceptable?

Pritchett: Yes.

Murphy: Without critiquing the source document?

Pigford: We would teach about it and discuss it while pointing out to the students that if we were to apply scientific principles to this hypothesis, it would not pass the test of science.

Murphy: Okay, if I am going to use the Genesis creation myth in my science class as the basis for another hypotheses, why would I be so ethnocentric as to say that it is this ancient Middle Eastern culture that I will relay to you as true as opposed to the Navajo or Ibo cultures, which have their own creation myths? Don't just sit the Bible down as a talis-man that comes from heaven and speaks scientific "truth," and not include all other religious myth systems.

Carper: But that is what it proclaims to be!

Shearer: It is not a matter of taking a vote to determine the truth. The scientist doesn't care about a vote, but neither does God. Truth is truth.

Pigford: In this state, do science teachers actually engage in this level of discussion? Who is making these curriculum decisions?

Murphy: Some South Carolina school principals have told science teachers to "shut up." Every year I hear from some earth science teachers, "I don't touch evolution because I don't want the hassle." That comes from fear, misunderstanding of the issues, and lack of content knowledge. So without firing a shot, the creationists have amended, in some instance, otherwise good science teaching.

Carper: On the other hand, science teachers who even attempt to address creationism in states like California are routinely called on the carpet. Even those teachers at the college level who suggest the possibility of an intelligent designer find themselves in difficulty.

Burgess: As principal, I do not see this level of discussion among teachers. In the classroom, material is presented and kids absorb it. There is no discussion. Controversy is not allowed in public schools. I am amazed that we are having this discussion here. I certainly don't see it happening within our curriculum framework or our community.

Lindsey: Although teachers may not do this, I have found textbooks almost always give you the feeling that if you don't believe the primal soup of evolution, you are a troglodyte. This is where the parents get so frustrated, particularly if you have a novice teacher at the elementary level who really is not comfortable with science. These teachers simply take what the textbook gives them, which suggests only one view for origins.

Pritchett: Many teachers do not have the thoroughness of knowledge that Carolyn or you have to engage students in these more complex issues.

Pigford: I, too, want multiple approaches presented to students that still allow for the child and parent to make their own decisions. But we often don't have teachers out there who can accomplish this.

Murphy: That says something about our teacher education institutions. We have to improve education at my level and at yours. We must get people to understand science in a three-dimensional way—that it has theory and history and doesn't consist of just facts.

Pigford: We are not going to create these teachers in our colleges; these thinking skills have to be developed early. We too often train elementary students to be compliant, passive receivers of knowledge. In order to have a classroom where students engage in these controversial discussions, you must have a teacher about whom the community feels comfortable.

Pritchett: We have a generation of teachers that have been trained to teach by the textbook, use a cookie-cutter curriculum guide approach, and be evaluated by APT. Why should we expect anything other than what you have described?

Pigford: But, you know, we can talk about "teacher empowerment." But there are a lot of teachers who don't want to be empowered. With empowerment comes responsibility.

Burgess: I don't think we want them to think.

Murphy: As a principal, can you change that?

Burgess: I'm not sure I want to change it!

Sears: While both of the chapters advocate engaging in critical thinking and the controversies of human origins, it sounds as though when "the rubber hits the road" all of this becomes irrelevant in the day-to-day science classroom: Students are compliant; teachers are ill-prepared; school administrators are cautious; the community is polarized.

Burgess: That's how I see it. How can we engage in a controversial discussion in science when we can't even get into the true history of this state in *social* science? The community cannot deal with it, and so the students will not deal with it. We have not structured the school in a fashion to encourage students to debate issues in a safe environment where they can voice their opinions without feeling threatened or feeling the need to respond physically because another's opinion is in opposition to their position.

Pigford: We haven't encouraged this among our teachers and within our community. Until we, as adults, engage in this level of debate, we shouldn't expect to find it in our public schools. If we want students to consider controversial issues in the school, then we need to begin with adults.

Suggested Additional Readings on Science

Elaine Lindsey, with James T. Sears

Barlow, C. (Ed.). (1994). *Evolution extended.* Cambridge, MA: MIT Press.
   A series of essays, written from both the creationist and the evolutionist position, examine the role of evolutionary debates and the meaning of life.
Ellaissi, B., & Allen, M. (1991). A dialogue of ideas: Science, religion, and morality in public schools. *The High School Journal, 75*(1), 1–6.
   A simulated dialogue between an evolutionist and a creationist.
Johnson, P. (1991). *Darwin on trial.* Downers Grove, IL: InterVarsity.
   Evolutionary theory as proposed by Darwin, according to Johnson, lacks confirmatory evidence and was accepted prematurely with meager evidence to support it.
Marsden, G. (1991). Why creation science? In *Understanding fundamentalism and evangelicalism* (pp. 153–181). Grand Rapids, MI: Eerdmans.
   Until recently, Christians made accommodations for a middle view. Marsden explores why the polarization between creationist and evolutionist views developed and their popularity.
Mills, G. C. (1995). Theistic evolution. *Christian Scholars Review, 24,* 444–458.
   There are two common theories of creation: special creation (fully formed organisms created) and theistic evolution (original molecules and atoms created). As a geneticist, Mills postulates a third theory, a continual creation of DNA, that could be taught in the public schools as an alternative to naturalistic evolution.
Provenzo, E. (1990). Creationism and the schools. In *Religious fundamentalism and American education* (pp. 51–64). Albany: State University of New York Press.
   Provides historical and legal insight into the evolution controversy in the public schools.
Toumey, C. (1994). *God's own scientist: Creationist in a secular world.* New Brunswick, NJ: Rutgers University Press.
   An ethnographic study of creationists, emphasizing that their belief in creation is foundational to their understanding of morality and social issues.

Webb, G. (1994). *The evolution controversy in America*. Lexington, KY: University Press of Kentucky.

> A historical look at why the evolutionary controversy has continued in the United States, tracing the debates from the time of Darwin's work. Emphasis is placed on the role of education to open the eyes of the public to what is believed in science.

PART VII

A Concluding Conversation Among Education Scholars

This dialogue is among several leading educational scholars who, like you, have read these chapters and conversations. Participants are

Richard Baer, author of *Toward a Critical Politics of Teacher Thinking*
Paul S. Brantley, editor of the *Journal of Research on Christian Education*
Peter McLaren, author of *Life in Schools*
Alan Peshkin, author of *God's Choice*
Eugene Provenzo, author of *Religious Fundamentalism and American Education*
Paul C. Vitz, author of *Psychology as Religion*

Each articulating one of the four traditions of thought (evangelical conservatism, orthodox culturalism, secular progressivism, and critical postmodernism), these educators address several broad questions: Is there evidence of common ground among persons with differing religious and ideological positions? Is the search for overlapping or social consensus a realistic goal within our communities? Can educators facilitate these dialogic encounters?

This dialogue is notable not only for its occasional pungency but for unexpected areas of agreement. While many of us commonly think in terms of left/right ideological binaries, the areas of common agreement between critical postmodernists and evangelical conservatives, or disagreements between progressive and postmodernist thinkers, illustrate the complexities of these issues and suggest bridges of understanding that may not readily be apparent to the casual observer of school–church community relations.

Vitz: One strand that went through *Curriculum, Religion, and Public Education* was that if we could only get together and start talking issues over, we would find bases for common agreement. Unfortunately, at present, I don't think if we get together and talk that most people will reach agreement. In fact, they may reach greater disagreement due to their recognition of the different assumptions from which they are operating.

Provenzo: Indeed, I, too, firmly came to the conviction in reading these materials that the extent to which we engage in genuine dialogue and engage in understanding one another's points of views is sadly limited and circumscribed.

McLaren: Understanding another's point of view often does lead to greater disagreement. The point is that all groups must be given access to the political public sphere so that they are able to articulate their perspective and engage in a conscientious deliberation.

Peshkin: I did not read in the words of the conversationalists or authors of those on the [religious] Right's willingness to suspend *their* views. Marshall and Kincheloe assert a "zone of uncertainty" in which "all positions are worthy of analyses and contextualization"; fundamentalist Christians do not believe this! They would say: "How dare you engage us in alternatives on matters to which our absolutes apply? On such matters, we know what the answers are. How can you confuse our children?" So the issue is not *when* they enter the "zone of uncertainty," but *if* they could even think to enter it on actual matters of any importance.

Baer: I believe there is absolute truth and what we might call objective values. At the same time, I recognize that none of us possess knock-out arguments that will immediately compel every good and reasonable person to accept our positions or be guilty of irrationality.

McLaren: I do not believe objectivity translates into absolute truth. As the German philosopher Jürgen Habermas observed, we need to be careful when we equate truth with rational acceptability. Objectivity is a well-founded illusion.

Brantley: Fundamentalists aren't the only ones who hold tenaciously to firmly held beliefs. Scholars of every stripe—right and left—hold a diversity of core assumptions about what is real, true, and good. The point is that people can differ on basic assumptions and yet find abundant opportunities for common ground when they engage in dialogue with civility and mutual respect.

McLaren: The most significant issue for me that emerges from *Curriculum, Religion, and Public Education* is the emphasis on the necessity of dialogue. I favor such an emphasis. But not on dialogue in the romantic sense of some wonderful and complete intuitive immediacy, mutual correspondence with another person's subjectivity, or union of intersubjective perspectives, as Schleiermacher might have it (I'm thinking of his critical rationalist approach in *Discourses on Religion*), but rather in the critical hermeneutic sense advocated by thinkers like Ireland's Richard Kearney and Italy's Gianni Vattimo. Following in the footsteps of Heidegger, Gadamar, Ricoeur, and Levinas, Kearney endorses the idea that meaning is never reducible to the immediacy of speaking subjects or intersubjectivity.

Our subjectivities are always already populated by other people's meanings. Our ideas always *exceed* what we intend them to mean, especially when they are expressed in written texts. Our discourses serve in some fashion as palimpsests that carry the historical traces of different language users. All interpretation is parasitic upon some type of shared discursive material. As educators our task is to decide what texts to share and *how* to share them.

Sears: What is your point, Peter?

McLaren: My point is that whatever these texts are—religious texts and doctrines, for instance—we have to interpret them by making a sustained detour through critical theory, through ideology critique, through a negative dialectics. If we can follow Richard Kearney's advice and manage to arrive at a dialectical compatibility between phenomenological hermeneutics and critical theory, then we could really lay the basis for an exciting dialogue on religious understanding and interpretation. Vattimo encourages us to think of truth not as the reflection of an object by a subject committed to self-transparency but as interpretation. Truth is *belonging* and not reflection. What possible worlds might we open up in our interpretations of religious texts? What possible interpretive horizons can we create through dialogue? What truths can we create?

Peshkin: However, if the foundation of your belief is absolute truth and if that truth is based directly on the Word of God, then there is no room for interpretation or compromise except in those shadow areas that are not of any particular importance and where the Bible does not speak on that point. Now, if I had heard in my careful reading of this book *one* word from Lindsey or Carper that sounded like they could *ever* meet the conditions of the "zone of uncertainty," then you would have good grounds for optimism. What Jim missed is that by continuing the conversation they have the promise of changing *him*. When you add proselytizing as an imperative of God, then you are *always* a target.

McLaren: According biblical passages a sacerdotal status is a problem. Transcendentalizing historically and geopolitically specific meaning is the way in which fundamentalists reproduce the circular thinking that is the very condition of faith. That's why the Word of God has to be performed. Performing faith through proselytizing is a constitutive act that creates the condition that enable fundamentalists to justify their interpretation of Scripture and their positions on civic and religious issues.

Baer: Well, both politically and theologically I oppose any attempts to Christianize government schools. For me as a Christian, it is never legitimate to use the power of Caesar to further the claims of Jesus Christ. I only wish that secularists were as scrupulous about not forcing their moral views—their moral relativism and hedonism—on public school students, especially in light of the fact that many attend public schools only because they have no other realistic choices. If dialogue is to be carried on in good faith, it must include discussion of school choice. Liberals have been anything but open-minded on this issue.

Provenzo: There certainly has been a failure to establish a series of middle positions. I think the idea of bringing all groups together in the process of dialogue and, from the dialogic process, arriving at some sort of consensus is worthwhile. American democracy is a series of compromises, just as the meaning of the Constitution is subject to judicial interpretation. What we have done, though, is that we have made issues in education and culture into absolutes rather than compromises. That is a terrible loss.

Baer: Compromise is essential in the political realm. But when Strike tries to apply his concept of overlapping consensus through public reasoning to education—a concept that may well have some validity in the political sphere—it just doesn't make any sense. How can education be limited to the narrow concept of justice as fairness—in the way John Rawls uses the term politically? How can you decide curriculum or matters concerning the philosophy of education on the basis of public reason? The answer is simple: You can't!

Vitz: I don't think that is possible given the facts of political life. The nature of communication to a wider audience demands simplification; dichotomizing of issues is a common way this simplification takes place. Nuanced and carefully weighed arguments, such as found in the science section here, are impossible in the public square.

Provenzo: Clearly, if you don't have much background and your world is largely mediated though television, where everything is simplisticly set up, being forced to engage in really tough questions—How does someone else's view differ from mine and how might it be valid? How might my point of view be only a partial explanation of the world?—is a really exhausting process. Most people prefer not to be challenged.

Baer: Jim, the call you and others make for a certain kind of dialogue seems problematic to me. It's like saying to the Japanese Americans who were placed in detention camps during World War II: You don't have any choice about being here but we'd sure like for you to learn how to talk nicely to each other and to your guards. Most of the authors in this volume simply overlook the fact that the curriculum of the government public school is determined by the education establishment functioning as a kind of cultural elite, not by parents or by students. It is a winner-take-all system based on financial and ideological coercion. As Stephen Arons writes in *Compelling Belief*: "We have created a system of school finance that provides free choice for the rich and compulsory socialization for everyone else" (p. 211). How can a system that routinely violates the consciences of millions of parents and children really be conducive to open dialogue?

Provenzo: You know, I was at a meeting several years ago with key educational leaders, including labor heads and university leaders in Tallahassee, Florida. I put forward the proposition that the fundamentalists—who clearly range in their spectrum of beliefs—had a valid set of concerns that needed to be listened to and addressed. I was heartily attacked. They could not understand how someone as supposedly "well educated and thoughtful" as myself could even consider that these "unacceptable" people could have a valid point of view.

Peshkin: Fundamentalists are the Vince Lombardis of doctrine; they do not leave an honorable place for me in their lives. That antagonized me when I did my study, *God's Choice,* and it scares the hell out of me today. And yet they are genuine, honest, sincere, respectful, and decent people. On the one hand, on many issues, I see them as the enemy. On the other, they cannot and do not deserve to be dismissed. So, as an educator and a citizen, I have terrible dilemma; *Curriculum, Religion, and Public Education* addresses that dilemma but does not come close to settling it.

Provenzo: The whole issue I find so engaging here is establishing a dialogue and establishing a shifting, complex, and meaningful "middle ground." We need to go back and do careful readings of people like Sebastian de Castillo, the Renaissance scholar who as much as anyone is responsible for establishing the concept of tolerance. Tolerance is a relatively modern concept, existing only for the past 400 or 500 years— and certainly imperfectly.

Peshkin: I was waiting for the hint of tolerance such as: "We do have our absolutes, but I am comfortable in thinking those absolutes only apply to me and my children; you and your children are really okay." If I heard that, I would be celebrating today.

Baer: Alan, you put forward a very strange argument. You worry about people doing exactly what *your* camp is doing. It's not Christian conservatives who force their beliefs and values on a captive student audience in our government schools but rather the secular educational establishment. That's why when People for the American Way complains about censorship in public schools, they seem so hypocritical, their complaints so bizarre. Like clockwork, every September they whine about fundamentalist parents who object to particular books and films their children encounter in public schools. But PAW totally overlooks the fact that it is not the parents or the children but agents of the state who choose all of these books and films in the first place. The PAW's tactics are like saying to citizens compelled to eat in state-run dining halls: "Whatever you do, don't be so ungrateful and disloyal as to complain about the menu."

McLaren: It's not as simple as that. It seems to me you are reifying the state into a monolithic Orwellian dictator. That's a terribly undialectical view. There is a difference between working within a state system and statism. I think the struggle is really between achieving a state dedicated to achieving democracy and one so gripped by the imperatives of monopoly capitalism that it loses its axiological foundations of protecting people and capitulates to the logic of privatization. Let me speak both politically and theologically for a moment. I don't think any discussion of schooling, values, or religion really can begin to develop without first engaging a critique of capitalism.

I need to emphasize with all due respect that capitalism represents the ironclad refuge of *hoi ex eritheias*—the men of discord who trust in injustice and who enslave the world and who subvert the biblical hope that the just will reign on the earth. I agree with Jose Porfirio Miranda that Marx coincides with the Bible in his articulation of an *eschaton,* which, to my mind, certainly represents the outcome of true dialectical thought. Capitalism detemporalizes history and purges it of its axiological imperatives and hence abandons the real subject of history, which is—as Miranda and other theologians have noted—the conscience of humankind. Hegel discovered that history is constituted by meaning. What meaning are we prepared to give it? The reality of sin—expressed through capitalism and otherwise—is not inherent to our human nature; rather it is caused through human work and interhuman injustice. Revolutionary praxis becomes the means to remake history. It is such a practice that we need to take seriously if we wish to challenge in our schools the individualism of our culture and the social practices that sustain it.

Vitz: It is individualism, not capitalism, that is the culprit, Peter. The notion that "I shall be as God" has a longer and deeper history than capitalism. As almost every social commentator has pointed out, individualism has gripped our nation more and more and the concept of community less and less. This has even had an impact on the conservative Christian Right, who are much less tolerant now of the community's needs than they might have been 30 or 40 years ago. Ironically, the emphasis on individualism, diversity, and self-empowerment has led the religious Right to attempt to empower itself, which is just what every other group has been doing, creating the problem that this book seeks to address.

McLaren: I am not saying capitalism predates *individuality*—but it does provide the context for a particular formation of *individualism*. Individualism is not free of history and the forces of production. Desires are reified insofar as they are expressed through the objectivity of the commodity price system. We invest in the body of Capital as we do in the divine power of Christ, since our essence as commodities both transcends and incarnates itself in the interest-bearing power of capital. This is the meaning of transubstantiation, of capitalism as metaphysics.

Brantley: But are there not a number of values that all reasonable cultures hold in common? In the *Abolition of Man*, C. S. Lewis chronicled scores of core values common to ancient and modern civilizations both East and West. For starters, public education—indeed all education—can do a much better job of addressing these commonalties. Of course, certain core beliefs held by a pluralistic public of necessity will be ontologically incongruous. Some countries make real efforts to accommodate diverse opinion. A heterogeneous student body meets most of the time as a unit, but when certain beliefs are incompatible, opportunity is provided for each stream to meet separately and learn more about its own belief system. Not a solution, but maybe a reasonable accommodation.

Vitz: I still think there is a chance to emphasize the role of schooling in teaching virtue and character that all cultures admire. If we can find virtues that we can agree on—honesty, courage, altruism, perseverance, optimism—and accentuate positive values that we do have in common, then some of the "heat" might lessen.

Provenzo: I think we've made a serious mistake in asking questions like, "What values do we teach?" There is the assumption that there are a set of objective, fundamental values like "courage." I think what values are taught becomes highly personalized and specific to one's "tribal" group. Because of the complexity of these social groups, the idea of establishing a common set of values is virtually impossible. But, if we get into concrete examples of what this value is, there are very different models: the courage to remain silent; the courage to endure; the courage to act. Each of these is different in terms of the context in which it is exercised. So, just as there are many truths, values are very redefinable and amorphous.

Vitz: But most moral questions are not intellectual dilemmas. Character is a performing art; it is not mainly cognitive. Aristotle said that until you had been well trained in the virtues, you didn't get theory. This is true in all of the performing arts. Even in football, you learn how to block and tackle before you read books on football strategy. In general, it is a problem of learning how to practice virtue, not cognitively understand it. The problem is to reward students in the school environment for following these values and to reward teachers for fostering them. Here, most people can find agreement across cultures—unless you want to begin debating the nuances of these values. Around the world people do agree that certain values are "good," for example, altruism, courage, honesty.

McLaren: What we mistake here is that capitalism criminalizes moral impulses, hiding the human faces crying out as we wait euphorically for the deregulation of the marketplace to allow the best in people to be expressed. The bureaucratic spirit of corporations and the displacement of morality by business should not deter us from taking responsibility for our moral judgments.

Baer: Why are people so bashful about teaching their children what they think is true? That is what education *should* do. It's not good education to expose a young child to a multitude of alternatives. We must rather initiate a child into a consistent way of looking at the world. The problem is that in government schools there is no way to do this without offending the religion clause of the First Amendment. This is because whenever public schools address the Big Questions—Who am I? How should I live? What is the good life all about?—they are within the realm of religion broadly interpreted. Émile Durkheim clearly understood this when he argued that it is largely irrelevant whether the basic stories, myths, symbols, and understandings of a society are supernatural or secular. Whenever the Big Questions are addressed—something impossible to avoid in education—we are within the realm of religion, at least in a functional sense. As for our children failing to understand that they live in a pluralistic society, I'm not too worried. How can they possibly avoid coming to that realization?

Brantley: We are certainly living in an increasingly pluralistic age. Public education has an obligation to accommodate a spectrum of ideologies— which for some are at variance with a neatly codified body of ethics, virtues, or values they wish to engender in their children.

McLaren: One way of achieving this spectrum is through critical theory. Let's bring the discussion back to religion for a moment. We can only accommodate a spectrum of ideologies if we have a means of evaluating them. I think we need to follow the liberation theologians in calling for a critique of religion, or a critique of the function of traditional religion. I think public schools are the place for this type of critique. Such a critique would address both the metaphysical and ineffable regime of the spirit and the implacable logic of capital in its quest not for addressing the needs of the poor but the appropriation of surplus value.

Liberation theology speaks to the power of the poor as the poor have erupted in history. We need to reread the history of ideology from the perspective of the poor. Our faith needs to reveal itself in solidarity with the poor. It is here that religion as it is taught in schools needs to engage with a critical multiculturalism as well as political economy.

Baer: Well, I, too, am concerned about the poor. But there is no religiously neutral answer about how they might be liberated. Christians have far more faith in the liberating power of the gospel than in the power of economics, but don't hold your breath waiting for this position to be articulated in our schools. So far, my experience of multiculturalism in public education suggests that only politically correct diversity will find its way into the curriculum. You cannot understand our society even remotely if you don't understand something about the Enlightenment and English liberalism as well as Christianity. But you can understand our culture very well without understanding these tiny minority cultures.

Brantley: I'm not sure what is meant by "tiny minority cultures." I do know that many students and teachers alike can profit by a broadening awareness of other peoples, other views, other paradigms. At least public education could make students aware of alternatives, allowing them freedom to pursue a line of investigation that may not necessarily square up with official wisdom, whatever *that* is. We do want students to be thinkers rather than mindless reflectors of the thoughts of others.

Sears: Well, might we come to terms if not find consensus on specific curricular areas such as the teaching of evolution or sexuality?

Vitz: One position was not mentioned at all in this book: that sex education shouldn't be in the schools, period. Should the schools take over the function of the family when the family fails? People have responsibilities that the state cannot just take over from them. The nature of letting people be responsible, in part, for their lives is to allow them to be irresponsible.

Baer: Johnson's and Brickhouse and Letts's views seem naive to me. For example, who will lead the discussions they refer to? Many, perhaps most, teachers know very little about the issues mentioned; they are not well enough grounded in philosophy, religion, and ethics to do a competent job as discussion leaders. Most people would be nervous about fundamentalist Christians in public schools leading serious discussions with their children on religion, just as, in Jim's case, most South Carolina citizens objected to his leading serious discussions about the role of evangelical and Christian fundamentalists in education.

Provenzo: We need to talk about a series of points of view regarding evolution. The great tragedy of education is that so few issues are contextualized. How did the idea of evolution evolve? What were the competing philosophies? Whose views are represented today and whose views are excluded? Why? To engage people in a critical discourse, I think, ultimately allows people to come to terms with those things we value. We don't spend much time asking questions that go beyond our limited perspectives and ways of knowing.

Brantley: I think if we searched a bit, we could find significant points of overlap between the essays of Johnson and of Brickhouse and Letts, for example. When we get rid of some of the broadsides and labels, and tease out the particulars, some common values do emerge. This is not to minimize basic differences among the populace, however.

Provenzo: Part of the problem is that "progressive science" and the progressive liberal tradition do not perceive their own biases or their own specific way of viewing the world. The scientific arrogance of philosophies such as empiricism are clearly at work in our culture; they need to be recognized and explicated.

Peshkin: You can't talk about science as if it is a closed system, with science yielding "truth" with a capital T. There are important things to be learned about being reserved, cautious, and uncertain that should be incorporated into the classrooms. There are counterparts also in English, history, and so forth.

Baer: Here, I agree. The Enlightenment view that secular reason is rational and scientific in a way that religious reason is not is dead in the water today. All human research programs and knowledge enterprises entail initial worldview commitments, which, although they may not be unreasonable, are not compellingly rational in such a way that every reasonable person will immediately accept them. That is why I find it unacceptable for educators today to refer to religious reason and religious schools as "sectarian," while at the same time describing secular reason and secular schools as "nonsectarian." Such bigoted language, which even the U.S. Supreme Court cannot resist using, is totally out of place today.

Sears: One of the outcomes that struck me as a participant in the community dialogues was that most conversationalists, ranging from the Reverend Shearer to the Reverend Burgess, voiced distrust with the public schools—albeit for very different reasons. Now, it is one matter to agree on our critical analysis of public education, but quite another to determine what one does with that analysis.

McLaren: You are correct, Jim.

Provenzo: In my comparison between revisionist educational historians and radical educational historians coming out of the late 1960s, I found that the arguments they were making with respect to the interference of the state with the personal rights of education regarding the raising of our children and the regulation of knowledge read remarkably similar to those being made by fundamentalist writers like Rushas Rushdooney, who wrote *The Messianic Character of American Education.* What that suggests to me is that while these two groups are so polarized and fall on such opposite ends of the ideological spectrum, they are pointing at the same phenomenon as a problem, which suggests to me the assumptions of modernism that so dominate the university and the elementary and secondary school curriculum are suspect. Yet it is almost heretical to speak about alternatives. The awareness of the hegemony of the scientific set of values and approaches in terms of organizing the curriculum carry not only into the teaching of biology and physics but also into how we define culture and whose values will be emphasized. There is little understanding that these strongly held values shape and limit the nature of discourse, or that other discourses are possible.

Baer: Yes, some of the left's critique makes sense to me. My own position—which draws heavily on the work of Skillen, McCarthy, Glenn, and others—is that we must now proceed to disestablish our system of government schools and universities. There simply are no good moral or constitutional reasons why they should have monopoly access to tax monies, while independent schools, both religious and secular, are excluded from sharing in public funds.

Provenzo: At some point Sears talks about crossing borders. In terms of training teachers and the content of the curriculum, teacher educators should be looking at making people into travelers: individuals who can cross cultural borders, perhaps not become permanent residents, but who can come to understand the differences across different tribes. Training people as cultural voyagers engaged in the process of border-crossing is absolutely essential and a serious failure of our educational system for a series of very complex reasons.

McLaren: I applaud attempts to help students cross borders, but not all students are able to cross the same borders in equal measure. My Chicano/a students tell me: "We didn't cross the border, the border crossed us." It's one matter for whites to cross borders; it's quite another for students of color to cross those same cultural, legal, and linguistic borders *within* our white, patriarchal, capitalist society.

Vitz: Most teachers would resent that, they would be unprepared to do it, and historically our schools have *never* done that. It would be very hard on schools and the community for the school to get rid of its boundaries. This tends to undermine the function of any organization in which boundaries serve useful purposes. In the case of schools, it would underscore the notion that they are separate from the community; teachers closed their classroom doors and you trusted them. If we engage in more discussion, are we going to trust each other more?

Peshkin: What has been very positive in reading these articles and dialogues, coupled with my own research some years ago, is to understand who "they" are. We need to be respectful for what it is that animates their lives. We cannot denigrate; they cannot dismiss. They must understand how to respect people who don't agree with them, because when they don't, they perpetuate the worst of what I see that they make possible: the total disregard for difference.

Provenzo: I feel very strongly that a role for teachers in a postmodern school is the notion of the "teacher as organizer of dialogue." Teachers must teach others how to engage in such discussions, and this should be a critical role for schools.

McLaren: You talk about dialogue. Well, let me say this. The real interlocutors of critical pedagogy constitute the absent voice of history, the voice of the displaced, the marginalized, the most despised and exploited of humankind, the nameless ones, the *olvidados*. Educators have a responsibility for the just upbuilding of the world through a critico-practical reason, one that stresses a politico-eschatological and criticoliberative memory. Such practices of critical theory should be taught in our colleges of education.

Baer: It sounds like you have the true gospel for everyone. Should Christians also be permitted to proclaim their gospel in our public schools?

Brantley: One of the essayists pointed out that educators are quite ill equipped to foster dialogue within the school. Perhaps they have shied away, too, because of the potential for misunderstanding and political discord.

Baer: Take, for example, the community dialogue about whether values are subjective or objective. Perhaps 90% of the public school teachers I encounter are not capable of discussing this issue with even a moderate degree of sophistication. Most of them claim to be relativists, even though they can offer no good reasons for their position. Do I want them leading discussions on ethics with my children? Of course not! My Christian faith and my morality constitute an integrated whole, and I do not want teachers as agents of the state meddling in my children's lives with regard to such sensitive issues.

Provenzo: An educational system that genuinely engaged in the process of dialogue would do something very threatening to existing political power. It would ask fundamental questions: Why does one district have more resources than another? Who gets ahead in this society? In doing so, it would reveal the structural and social equities within this culture.

McLaren: I have no problem with speaking more specifically about challenging existing political power. We need as educators to respond to the demands of the historical times in which we live! This "social gospel" means, does it not, that we are called upon to transform ourselves and the world around us? Does this imperative not enjoin us to struggle against the perfidy of monopoly capitalism and the social sins and disvalues of political and economic repression, racism, sexism, militarism, homophobia, and the destruction of our environment?

Here I urge educators to acquaint themselves with the African American theologian James H. Cone, who argues that whites cannot say anything relevant to the self-determination of the black community until they destroy their whiteness and create themselves anew in a black being. An educational system genuinely engaged in the process of dialogue would have the courage to purge itself of its whiteness. The only way to achieve this is to engage the voices of our Latino/a, African American, Asian brothers and sisters.

Baer: Why should I purge myself of my whiteness any more than blacks should purge themselves of their blackness? Whites who agree to such nonsense are still trying to work through hidden guilt feelings—but in a depressingly unproductive manner.

Brantley: Let's purge ourselves at a deeper level than skin color. We would do well to purge ourselves of any ideology that is arrogant and disrespectful. Again, such commonalties as civility, empathy, fairness, consideration for others (e.g., the "golden rule") might serve as a good platform for mediating our differences and for transforming the world based upon love.

Peshkin: School leaders must be good mediators. Jim was playing a mediation role in those dinner conversations, which is very important and very hard to play. These skills are necessary for educators to carry on their work in these complex times. Teachers, too, must ask themselves, "To what extent is it possible for me to honor what concerned parents are asking of me? What is going on in their lives?" As an educator, it is appropriate to listen, not to dismiss. Listening may not lead to any solution, but part of the frustration expressed in some of the conversations is that the Christian position is not even taken into account.

Provenzo: If we had a dialogic process of education, we would be discussing fundamental issues that would be very upsetting for a lot of people and *really* change the balance of power in society. We need to begin to think of our institutions like families. Families can provide us the best things in our lives *and* the worst things. We must demand that our institutions, including public education, do the right thing.

Baer: I don't want the schools to respect everyone's beliefs. I think some beliefs are reprehensible: the caste system as part and parcel of Hinduism; Christianity's support of slavery; various perverse forms of homosexual (as well as heterosexual) behavior. I want my children to learn to respect the rights of all individuals. But I don't want them even to be exposed to certain despicable beliefs and practices.

McLaren: To "respect" does not mean to "approve," it means to recognize that some beliefs are "different" and need to be engaged and evaluated culturally and historically—not dismissed perfunctorily without good, solid ethical justification.

Baer: But who can rightly claim a neutral or objective standpoint from which to perform such evaluation? In a society that holds to the First Amendment, we must conclude that teachers as agents of the state are acting illegitimately whenever they presume to play such a role.

Peshkin: Parents should be as meaningfully involved as anyone in education, but if the fundamentalist notion of what education should be prevails, then you will have teachers serving ends that are antithetical to education in any sense that I can take education. Educators currently are not prepared to face such complexities.

Baer: Teachers are professionals, and thus I'm not in favor of parents micro-managing the school curriculum. Let the parents choose the school—whether a government public school or an independent public school—and thus by extension the teachers. With school choice, parents will trust the teachers, thus permitting them to be the professionals they are.

Vitz: There are times when I think that the future is the 18th and 19th centuries. Private education will come back, home education will return, and tutors will reappear. Modernism—especially the modern state—will decompose. Macro-systems and their ideological support will be seen as antihuman, as oppressive.

Provenzo: I have a terrible problem with all of that. I've been reading recently some of the people applying ecological theory to education, such as C. A. Bowers and David Orr. They have some very profound insights for us. Essentially, they remind us that education is part of a larger ecological and social system and that we need to understand the organism as a whole. We have been ignoring that, and I think that the idea of privatizing and segmenting off the education system represents a movement away from looking at the ecology of the total system.

Peshkin: I began the reading of *Curriculum, Religion, and Public Education* with Jim's sense of hope joined to my understanding of the fundamentalist Christian school. However, the form of Christianity that I learned about in my study—the basis for hundreds and hundreds of schools across the country—has led me to conclude that such people could *never* be happy in public schools unless they controlled them. I am glad that there are schools for them because their strong and unyielding sense of what they think ought to transpire in schools make them implacable in the kind of democratic forums you and others advocate.

Baer: But government public schools have always had more to do with control than with dialogue or "democratic forums." You seem to ignore both the history and structure of the common school. Charles Glenn forcefully makes the point that Horace Mann was at least as interested in social control as in basic instruction. His model for the common school came from Prussia and from postrevolutionary France. The common school has always been experienced as culturally oppressive by one minority or another. In the 19th century the Protestant-Unitarian elite oppressed Catholics, Jews, humanists, and others. Today a secular elite oppresses millions of Americans who take their religious beliefs seriously. Blacks have never made out too well. We simply cannot overlook the basic fact that millions of Americans today experience government schools as violating their consciences. They permit their children to attend these schools only because they have no power economically to do otherwise.

Brantley: Although I am a Christian educator, I believe public education plays a critical role in an increasingly diverse America. Notwithstanding our pluralistic culture, the fact remains that we all have to live together in this place we call home. Public education can be a unifying agency that takes full advantage of points of agreement—the social "glue" if you will—to keep us all intact and coherent. Private schools remain an option for those who desire more focused preparation than can be accommodated by public education, which, of necessity, must be responsive to the entire populace.

Baer: Well, those who favored a religious establishment at the time of our founding made similar arguments. Without an established church, they argued, we will fragment as a society. But, historically, that didn't happen. When children grow up with a deep understanding of their heritage as Christians, Jews, Muslims, or humanists, we will have a strong and vital society—much more so than when children grow up with the blandness of lowest-common-denominator public education.

Vitz: Albert Shanker is fearful of vouchers because he believes they will polarize and essentially get rid of the common ground in the country. There might be ways to overcome this by taking a look at the Catholic schools in American history, which have not been especially divisive in preparing Americans. One of the reasons for this is that there have been other features that have integrated them into the society. If we had a lot of voucher schools and if we had some common exams, or shared competitive leagues and had other common frameworks within which they competed with each other, we would avoid this divisiveness.

Peshkin: At the end of *God's Choice*, I state that in 18 months of close contact with the school, I never heard one word of support for pluralism in America. They never ever acknowledged that the reason there can be Christian schools like theirs is because we live in a pluralist society. Their entire rationale is antagonistic to pluralism because it supports diversity. I am comfortable with people having options to public schools if they have the resources, the initiative, and the leadership. They are free even to create schools that are antagonistic to the fundamental principles of American democracy. But it would be crazy as hell to provide public support for these schools!

Baer: Just like many Christians think it's crazy (not to mention unconstitutional) to spend tax dollars to promote anti-Christian, secular humanist beliefs and values in government public schools. Moreover, there is no empirical evidence that students coming out of independent religious schools are more intolerant or less open to others than are children educated by the state.

Provenzo: When I was in college and graduate school, I spent quite a bit of time living in Florence, Italy, where I saw neighborhoods where the poor, middle class, and wealthy lived together. It wasn't that there weren't differences in terms of economics, education, ability, status, and education; but there was a much more unified culture. These Florentines were engaged and involved with one another—sometimes painfully. People from perhaps different "tribes" must live in proximity to each other and engage in dialogue in order to survive. The whole privatization movement contributes toward the tribalization of the culture. With it is a loss of a sense of broader community. Ironically, new technologies such as the Internet may contribute to this isolation by allowing "tribes" or special-interest groups to congregate in cyberspace or online. There they can isolate themselves with others who hold the same values, never moving beyond the confines of their own belief systems and communities.

Brantley: Given the fractured nature of our society, I am not sure that we will ever come to common ground that would accommodate everyone. For this reason, private education fulfills a distinctive, important, and complementary role. However, we all—public and private—can afford to be a lot more civil toward others. Civility and respect for the rights and responsibilities of others might be a wonderful way to begin our search for common ground.

Vitz: We had a common culture because of the happenstance of history, but now that is collapsing. Yet those who argue about the beauties of diversity don't yet realize that that argument will soon have very unpleasant social consequences. My belief is that once we begin to experience those Yugoslavian consequences, we will realize how imperative it is that we find a common basis for government. I can see Americans who are now so enamored by diversity changing their mind when they realize that diversity is just another name for a bunch of neighbors who are going to kill you. How do we find the common ground before we have to pay too much of a price?

McLaren: The issue is not *finding* a common culture but rather creating a common ground of struggle. There is a powerful difference between the two. Let me say this: Unity is not born of common culture, but rather of collective endeavor. A collectivity is all the more powerful because of its differences and the creative tension produced by them. We live at a time of fertile ideas, at a time when we can imagine new social arrangements that will take us through the new millennium. We need not judge these new social arrangements by their "sameness" but by their commitment to justice and an ethics of hope. To what degree do they speak to the nameless, the forgotten, the excluded? Hope and freedom do not spring from agreement and consensus; they emerge from struggle.

Index

About the Editor and the Contributors

James T. Sears, *Editor,* is Professor of Curriculum Studies and Higher Education at the University of South Carolina. A Fulbright Senior Research Scholar on sexuality and culture, he is the author or editor of eight books, including *Growing Up Gay in the South, Sexuality and the Curriculum, Lonely Hunters,* and *Overcoming Heterosexism and Homophobia.* He is co-editor of the international journal *Teaching Education* and serves on a variety of editorial boards, including the *Review of Educational Research, International Journal of Qualitative Studies in Education,* and the *Journal of Homosexuality.* He resides near Charleston, SC, and in cyberspace at www.JTSEARS.com.

Richard Baer teaches in the Department of Natural Resources, Cornell University, and is the author of *Toward a Critical Politics of Teacher Thinking.*

Paul S. Brantley is Professor of Education at Andrews University and founding editor of the *Journal of Research on Christian Education.*

Nancy W. Brickhouse is Associate Professor of Science Education in the Department of Educational Development at the University of Delaware. She specializes in work on teaching and learning about the nature of science, in particular with regard to issues of feminism and multiculturalism.

Gary Burgess is a graduate of Wofford College (then an all-male school). He completed graduate work at Converse College and currently serves as principal of a middle school in Duncan, South Carolina. He is also an ordained minister and pastor of the Universal Body of Christ Non-Denominational Church in Inman, South Carolina.

Dennis Carlson is associate professor of Educational Leadership and Director of the Center for Education and Cultural Studies at Miami University in Oxford, Ohio, specializing in educational reform and urban schools. His most recent book is *Making Progress: Education and Culture in New Times.*

James C. Carper is Associate Professor of Educational Foundations at the University of South Carolina, where he specializes in history of American education. His books include *Religious Colleges and Universities in America* and *Religious Schooling in America*. He recently served as educational advisor to Governor David Beasley.

Charles W. Dunn is Professor of Political Science at Clemson University, South Carolina, and Chair of the J. William Fulbright Foreign Scholarship Board. He is the author or editor of ten books, including *American Political Theology*, *Religion in American Politics*, and *American Conservatism*.

Charles Glenn is Professor of Educational Policy at Boston University, and previously for 21 years was the Massachusetts official responsible for civil rights and urban education. His most recent books are *Educational Freedom in Eastern Europe* (1995) and *Educating Immigrant Children: Schools and Language Minorities in 12 Nations* (1996).

Maxine E. Greene is Professor Emeritus of Educational Philosophy at Teachers College, Columbia University. She is past president of the American Educational Research Association and author of numerous books, including: *Dialectic of Freedom*, *Public School and the Private Vision*, and *Landscapes of Learning*.

Richard Hohn is associate professor in the Department of Physical Education at the University of South Carolina. He is co-editor of *Health and Fitness Through Physical Education*.

Phillip E. Johnson is Professor of Law at the University of California–Berkeley and author of numerous books, including *Darwin on Trial* and *Reason in the Balance*.

Joe Kincheloe is Professor of Curriculum Studies at Penn State University and the author of a variety of books, including *Toward a Critical Politics of Teacher Thinking*.

William J. Letts IV is a doctoral student in science education at the University of Delaware. He specializes on teaching about the nature of science and on equity in science education.

Elaine Lindsey grew up in China, where both her parents were missionaries. She graduated from Houghton College, where she majored in chemistry and zoology. She is the academic director of Ben Lippen School, a Christian K–12 academy in South Carolina.

J. Dan Marshall is Associate Professor in Curriculum Studies at Penn State University, specializing in textbooks and educational reform. He is co-author of *When Best Doesn't Equal Good* and co-editor of the *Teaching Education* journal.

George Marsden is professor and religious historian at Notre Dame University in Notre Dame, Indiana, and the author of *Understanding Fundamentalism and Evangelicalism.*

Martin E. Marty is the Fairfax M. Cone Distinguished Service Professor at the Divinity School of the University of Chicago. He is the author of more than 20 books, including *The Righteous Empire* and the multivolume edited set *Fundamentalism,* and Senior Editor of *Christian Century.*

Michael W. McConnell is the William B. Graham Professor of Law at the University of Chicago, specializing in constitutional law, and a senior fellow at the John M. Olin Center. He is the author of *Senate, Courts and the Constitution* and a member of the Christian Legal Society.

Peter L. McLaren, Professor of Education and Cultural Studies at UCLA, is the author of numerous books, including *Life in Schools, Schools as a Ritual Performance and Critical Pedagogy,* and *Predatory Culture.*

Carolyn Murphy is an earth science teacher at a South Carolina public middle school. Her doctoral dissertation focused on conceptions of science and religion held by Christian middle adolescents. She is the author of *Carolina Rocks! The Geology of South Carolina.*

Richard John Neuhaus, of the Religion and Public Life Institute in New York City, is the editor of *First Things* and author of several books, including *The Naked Public Square, Democracy and the Renewal of Public Education,* and *Piety and Politics.* He holds honorary degrees from several universities.

Nel Noddings is Lee Jacks Professor of Child Education at Stanford University and Professor of Philosophy and Education at Teachers College, Columbia University. She is the author of nine books, among them *Educating for Intelligent Belief and Unbelief.*

Alan Peshkin is Professor of Education at the University of Illinois–Urbana and author of *God's Choice.*

Aretha Pigford is professor in the Department of Educational Leadership and Policies at the University of South Carolina. She has served as a high school teacher, principal, assistant dean, and, most recently, associate superintendent.

Pamela Pritchett is Senior Executive Assistant in the Division of Education Initiatives at the State Department of Education in South Carolina. Her primary responsibilities include Curriculum Frameworks and Standards, Instructional Materials and Technology, Assessment, and the State's Systemic Initiative efforts.

Eugene Provenzo, Professor of Social and Cultural Foundations of Education at the University of Miami, is the author of *Religious Fundamentalism and American Education.*

George A. Rekers is Professor of Neuropsychiatry and Behavioral Science and Research Director for the Child and Adolescent Psychiatry Outpatient Service at the University of South Carolina School of Medicine. He is the editor of the *Handbook of Child and Adolescent Sexual Problems.*

William Schubert is Professor of Education at the University of Illinois–Chicago. His books include *Curriculum: Perspectives, Paradigms and Possibilities* and *Reflections from the Heart of Educational Inquiry.*

Gilbert T. Sewall is Director of the American Textbook Council and author of *Religion in the Classroom: What the Textbooks Tell Us.*

Robert Shearer is pastor of Harbison Baptist Church, a charismatic church which he established in 1985. He earned his B.A. from Kalamazoo College, his M.Div. from Southern Baptist College, and his law degree from the University of South Carolina.

Kenneth A. Strike is Professor of Education at Cornell University and the author of *Ethics for Professionals in Education.*

John Vaughn is pastor of the Faith Baptist Church in Greenville, South Carolina. He completed his undergraduate and graduate work at Bob Jones University, receiving an honorary D.Div. degree from the university in 1989. He is past president of the South Carolina Association of Christian Schools.

Paul C. Vitz is a member of the Department of Psychology, New York University, and author of *Censorship: Evidence of Bias in Our Children's Textbooks* and *Psychology as Religion: The Cult of Self-Worship.*